SPEAKING
FOR MYSELF

The Personal Reflections of Vernon R. Alden

To Terry
with warmest best wishes and
appreciation of your friendship
Vernon Alden

SPEAKING FOR MYSELF

The Personal Reflections of Vernon R. Alden

UNIVERSITY PRESIDENT
CORPORATE DIRECTOR
INTERNATIONAL ENTREPRENEUR

Foreword by Robert Glidden

OHIO UNIVERSITY LIBRARIES

ATHENS, OHIO

Frontispiece: photograph of Vern Alden by Yousuf Karsh

Library of Congress Cataloging-in-Publication Data

Alden, Vernon, R.

    Speaking for myself : the personal reflections of Vernon R. Alden, university president, corporate director, international entrepreneur / foreword by Robert Glidden.

      p. cm.

    Includes index.

    ISBN 0-9650743-2-3 (cloth : alk. paper). — ISBN 0-9650743-3-1 (paper : alk. paper)

    1. Alden, Vernon R. 2. Ohio University—Presidents—Biography. 3. College Presidents—Ohio—Athens—Biography. 4. Educators—United States—Biography. 5. Directors of corporations—United States—Biography. 6. Businessmen—United States—Biography. 7. Boston (Mass.)—Biography. 8. Athens (Ohio)—Biography. I. Title.

CT275.146413 1997

378'.0092—dc21

[B]   97-36704

                                             CIP

CONTENTS

FOREWORD

VERNON R. ALDEN, a multifaceted person and scholar, left an enduring legacy at Ohio University. When he came to Athens and the university in 1961, he brought energy and vitality, a commitment to excellence, and a penchant for action that he still exhibits today, thirty-six years later. As president he aspired to build a university of national prominence, and he pursued those aspirations with a passion. As he explains it, "Arriving in Athens, I found a university much better than the rest of the world perceived it to be, but in some ways not as good as several people on campus thought." Within these parameters, Vern Alden helped to forge the institution that many of us know today—a beautiful, cosmopolitan campus born out of his international influence, his sense of style, and his ability to get things done. You will recognize many people in his memoir, some of whom work for or are still associated with Ohio University today. "I needed action-oriented young people in my administration because we were in a hurry to bring about change," he writes. Yet Vern Alden always had time to listen, working sixteen-hour days to meet with students, faculty, and residents and appreciating their needs and concerns.

During his presidency, Vern's competitive streak and sense of fairness led him to initiate the effort for a more equitable distribution of state appropriations among Ohio's state-assisted universities. His vision for the future led him to spearhead the development of southeastern Ohio, including the moving of the flood-prone Hocking River and construction of the Appalachian network of highways, providing a safer and more accessible environment in Athens today. His interest in the faculty and staff as the key resources of the university brought about better salaries, sabbatical leaves, tuition remission for the families of all university employees, and the creation of the Faculty Senate. Vern Alden, known for his keen imagination, envisioned all units of the university—including students, faculty, trustees, alumni, and administration—working together "like fingers of a hand." If all worked together, he writes, "much could be accomplished."

Vern Alden is not only a man of vision but also of enormous charm, a fact that is apparent in the reading of these memoirs. He loves people, is a great competitor, and has a good sense of humor. One of the most enchanting anecdotes in this volume concerns how he and his wife Marion, driving a dusty road on the Caribbean island of Antigua, picked up two young hitchhikers. He introduced himself as Vernon Alden. One of the hitchhikers was dumbstruck by coincidence, telling Vern, "We're going to a university with a library by that name!" Those lucky students returned to their alma mater with deeper appreciation of Vern's contributions. Indeed, we all are grateful that his sense of the aesthetic and of history prevailed when he insisted that new residence halls maintain a common theme of traditional, Georgian-style architecture, making Ohio University one of the most beautiful college campuses in America today.

This is the Vern Alden legacy that I know best because of my association with Ohio University. But of course there is another huge and influential side of this man—membership on some thirty-two corporate or non-profit boards of directors, including long and distinguished service on such boards as McGraw-Hill, Mead, Digital Equipment, Colgate-Palmolive, and the Boston Company; the Boston Symphony Orchestra, the Boston Museum of Science, and as chairman of the Massachusetts Council of Arts and Humanities for twelve years and the Japan Society of Boston, which he served as chairman and president for fifteen years; his alma mater, Brown University, and visiting committees at Harvard, MIT, and the Fletcher School of Law and Diplomacy. "Without writing a several-hundred-page volume," Vern confides, "it would be impossible to describe all of the fascinating, enlightening, and humorous experiences I have enjoyed on various boards." As you can see, productivity was never a problem with Vern, chiefly because he associates it with learning.

Vern Alden's breadth of interests is amazing, especially with regard to service. As he puts it, "Friends can identify other shortcomings of mine, but my greatest weakness is the inability to say 'no' when approached for a good cause." That sense of duty has not gone unnoticed. Because of his knowledge and love for Japanese culture and people, he has been honored by the Emperor of Japan with the highest tribute accorded foreigners by that country, the Order of the Rising Sun. He is the recipient of fourteen honorary degrees. He has balanced his efforts and accomplishments between public life and private business, and he has had an enormous impact on the people who have been fortunate enough to work with him. Throughout his life he has devoted untold energy to the development of young leaders, and perhaps one of the most impressive results of his leadership is that, during his Ohio University years alone, fourteen of those whom he mentored became presidents of other colleges or universities.

You will enjoy reading Vern Alden's thoughts and recollections. Prepare to do so with a smile, appreciating Vern's enormous accomplishment and penetrating personality. In fact, the twinkle in Vern's eye will spark another in your own as you relive these experiences with him and reflect on Ohio University.

Robert Glidden
President, Ohio University
May 1997

PREFACE

SINCE 1950, almost half a century has passed: I have spent more than one-half of those years in the academic world and two decades in business activities. During the 1950s I served as a faculty member and administrator at the Harvard Graduate School of Business Administration; in the 1960s I was president of Ohio University; in the 1970s I was chairman of the Boston Company, a diversified investment and trust company; and during the 1980s my major commitment was to international activity and corporate board memberships, activities that have continued into the 1990s. In every decade I have had the unique opportunity to be involved simultaneously in academic affairs, business, international activity, and the arts. I have had the privilege of meeting and working with many interesting people, some of them well known. Their influence upon me is described in the following pages.

My greatest satisfaction has come from working with young people, helping them to recognize their talents and possibilities, and assisting them with counseling and supportive letters of recommendation. I have watched with pride and satisfaction as many of them have achieved significant success in the arts, business, education, and government.

My story will begin with the invitation to consider the presidency of Ohio University.

ACKNOWLEDGMENTS

In crafting these memoirs I am grateful to many friends for their encouragement and assistance. Salinda Arthur, assistant dean of Ohio University Libraries, has been outstandingly helpful in the editorial process and overseeing the many details involved in publication. Douglas McCabe provided valuable editorial comment; William Kimok, useful research. Karol Halbirt patiently typed the many drafts en route to the final manuscript.

I wish to thank Dennis Marshall as editor, Allen Greenberg as indexer, George Bain, department head of Alden Library's Archives and Special Collections, and other members of the Library's oral history committee for their evaluations and recommendations. My thanks also to Dean Hwa-Wei Lee of Ohio University Libraries, David Prince, director of Electronic Media Services, and members of the Ohio University Press: David Sanders, director; Gillian Berchowitz, senior editor; Nancy Basmajian, project editor; and Chiquita Babb, text and cover designer.

For their valuable comments and suggestions, I am grateful to my brother Burton Alden and to Lynn Shostack, Thomas Courtney, Edward Rudman, James Whalen, and John Burns.

For the continuing help from my administrative assistant Willma Nash, I am indeed indebted. My wonderful wife, Marion, has patiently observed my scribbling away on airplanes and at almost every place where there was a chair and a desk, and has offered critical comments and constructive suggestions.

SPEAKING
FOR MYSELF

The Personal Reflections of Vernon R. Alden

CHAPTER 1

From Harvard to Ohio

THE TELEPHONE RANG at my desk in the dean's office at the Harvard Business School in October 1960. The voice at the end of the line belonged to John Baker, a longtime friend who at one time held a job similar to mine at Harvard.

"Vern," he said, "I just turned sixty-five, and I told the Ohio University trustees last May that I would retire as president next July. Furthermore, I have suggested your name to the board as a possible candidate to succeed me. What do you say?" After telling John how honored I was to be recommended by him, I told him that I couldn't possibly leave my position as associate dean and gave him some of the reasons why:

In many ways I felt I had one of the most satisfying of all jobs. My day-to-day responsibilities were challenging and rewarding. Each summer I had an opportunity to teach in a Harvard-sponsored advanced management program in either Japan, Hawaii, or Mexico.

With sponsorship from the Carnegie Corporation of New York, I had written more than 150 case problems involving academic administration and taught in programs for college and university presidents, deans, and trustees. Serving as a consultant to the Young Presidents' Organization, I had initiated a University for Presidents—so-called— to which I invited faculty members from various disciplines to teach in one-week seminars at exotic places in Puerto Rico, Arizona, Florida, and even Europe and East Asia. I was serving as a director of four interesting local companies: Digital Equipment Corporation, the Ludlow Corporation, Textron Electronics, and the Boston Safe Deposit and Trust Company. And, as important as everything else, Marion and I enjoyed the Boston Symphony Orchestra, the Museum of Fine Arts, the lectures at Harvard, the ambiance of Boston and the little schoolhouse that our children, Rob and Anne, attended at the end of our street in Wellesley Hills. To top it all off, we were able to spend our vacation times at a home in Bermuda, which we owned with the dean.

In my early years in the dean's office at the Harvard Business School, I helped to create a unique financial-aid program. Rather than being a combination of student loans and outright scholarships, the program consisted of loans and advances in aid. The latter carried a moral obligation for repayment when the recipient was able to do so.

Because the program was different from the conventional financial-aid package, administrative colleagues and I traveled around the United States over a period of two years visiting more than three hundred colleges and universities and meeting with outstanding students. Our message was, "If you qualify for admission, the lack of financial resources will not prevent you from attending the Harvard Business School. Through loans and advances, we will provide you with the funds needed."

Over the years, the advance-in-aid concept has been astonishingly successful. We had truly "cast our bread upon water," because successful alumni returned their obligations manyfold. Today the Harvard Business School is the most highly endowed graduate school in the world. In 1996, the Twenty-fifth Reunion Class contributed $13 million to the school as its class gift.

As I rose through the ranks of the administration, I became the associate dean of the school. My training in the MBA program, combined with my English Literature major at Brown and my teaching experience, prepared me well for academic administration. In my visits to colleges and universities, I established friendships with many presidents who expressed concern that they were not fully prepared for the complexity of their position and the public exposure facing an academic leader. Most presidents had risen through faculty ranks, perhaps had been a dean or provost, but rarely had acquired experience in financial administration, fund raising, and crisis management.

It occurred to me that our mini advanced-management programs at Harvard might be appropriate for newly appointed college and university presidents. With Professor Robert Merry, I wrote several "case problems" describing academic issues that a president might face and approached the Carnegie Corporation of New York for funding. They liked what they saw, and with their support we created the Institute for College and University Administrators.

Our first summer sessions for thirty-six newly minted presidents and their spouses included case-method discussions and speeches by seasoned academic leaders. The program far exceeded our most optimistic expectations. As we continued to offer the summer sessions, presidents suggested that we launch similar programs for deans, provosts, and even trustees. More than thirty-five hundred individuals attended the institute programs over a ten-year period.

My involvement as the administrative head and teacher in the institute sessions gave me visibility in the academic world I had not anticipated. Search committees at Sarah Lawrence, Carleton College, and the University of Hawaii invited me to consider presidencies. I declined each of those opportunities for the same reasons I had given John Baker.

But John Baker was persistent. Early in 1961 he telephoned again to report that members of the Ohio Search Committee, led by trustee

Gordon Bush, were planning to visit Boston. They treated me to dinner at the Locke-Ober Restaurant, which had been a favorite dining spot for Franklin Roosevelt and John Kennedy. I listened to their enthusiastic description of the opportunity at Ohio University, but I wasn't moved to change my plans.

Then John Baker involved Donald David, former dean of the Harvard Business School, in their efforts. Along with Henry Wriston, former president of Brown University, Don David was a paradigm as an academic administrator and had been my mentor for many years. David's advice was: "You and Marion should at least go out to Athens to look at the university. You owe it to the Ohio trustees and to yourselves."

On July 1 we were met at the Columbus airport by insurance executive and trustee Fred Johnson, then flew to Athens on the university plane. From the moment we met him, Fred described his vision for Ohio University. Located in the beautiful Appalachian foothills, the campus, with its Georgian-style architecture, looked very much like an Ivy League university. For many years after the coal-mining industry had left southeastern Ohio, the area had languished in poverty and underdevelopment, and Fred Johnson believed that the university could take the lead in attracting high-technology investment, much as Harvard and MIT did along Route 128 in Boston. He spent the weekend trying to convince Marion and me that we should accept this challenge.

As we left for Boston, I began—for the first time—to think seriously about the opportunity to lead a university still not as well-known nationally as it deserved. I was aware that the student population of the United States in the 1960s would be doubling and that most of those students would be attending public universities. I thought about the challenge of combining the best qualities of a private college with the strengths of a public university to create a truly distinctive institution. Change could come about quickly in a rapidly-growing organization. I promised Fred Johnson that we would give his invitation serious thought.

Ohio University trustee John Galbreath telephoned two weeks later. I recognized Galbreath's name as the famous Columbus real-estate developer who owned the Pittsburgh Pirates (later he was to be owner of two Kentucky Derby winners). He invited me to the baseball All-Star game in Boston on July 31. We watched the National and American League players battle it out through the fifth inning, when rain ended what, as it happens, was the only tied game in the history of the All-Star series. John's approach was a very soft sell: he hardly mentioned Ohio University during the game, but as we were leaving in the rain, he patted me on the shoulder and said, "You're our man, Vern."

On August 4, 1961, Marion and I left for Japan. Since we had flown to Japan in 1960 from Hawaii, teaching in Harvard's Advanced Management Program there, we decided to fly this time via Europe—Paris, Rome, Istanbul, Calcutta, Bangkok, and Hong Kong, celebrating our tenth wedding anniversary at the Hotel Peninsula in Hong Kong. In Japan, as we have so many times since, we enjoyed our days with friends and on teaching assignments in Osaka and Nikko.

Within a day after we returned to Boston, early in September, Ohio trustee Ed Kennedy was on the telephone inviting me to his New Jersey home on September 13. Ed met me at the Newark airport and told me that John Baker and the Ohio trustees were awaiting our arrival in New Vernon. No sooner had we left the airport than Ed's car began bumping along on a flat tire. I jumped out and changed the tire as quickly as I could and we stopped again only to let me wash my hands at a service station.

When we arrived at Ed Kennedy's home, there they were: President Baker, several members of the board, and Professor Amos Anderson, the faculty representative on the selection committee. Conversation went on and on as various people present asked me about Japan, the world economy, and other topics. After a while, trustee Gordon Bush harrumphed and impatiently said, "Let's cut out this chitchat. We're here to officially offer Vernon the presidency of Ohio University." People clapped, and I was embarrassed to reply, "I have thought seriously about Ohio University, but I cannot say 'yes' just now because I must consult with two or three people who mean a great deal to me, including my boss, Dean Stanley Teele, at the Harvard Business School."

I had not realized that just behind the living room door Ruth Kennedy was standing with a tray of champagne glasses ready to provide the celebration toasts. If I have ever felt like a skunk at a picnic, it was then. I did promise the trustees that I would give them an answer within three weeks. On October 5 I confirmed that I would indeed accept their invitation to become Ohio's fifteenth president. One of the more inspiring reactions to this announcement came from a college president who had attended one of our institute sessions at Harvard. He sent me a telegram saying, "Physician, heal thyself!"

I did not waste much time getting ready for my new responsibilities. In late October I spent several days on campus and returned again with Marion in mid-December for the faculty Christmas party and meetings with faculty members, student leaders, administrators, and nonacademic employees. With each passing day, I became more and more enthusiastic about Ohio University and convinced that I had made the right decision.

On January 2, 1962, I left Marion and the children in Boston to finish midyear school terms and flew to Pittsburgh to meet the university plane. That trip was the beginning of seven and one-half wonderful and satisfying years as president of Ohio University. Already I was writing notes to myself tying Ohio University's beginnings to Boston. One of the reasons I was attracted to Ohio was its rich early history.

Most Ohio University alumni are familiar with the story of General Rufus Putnam, Rev. Manasseh Cutler, and members of the Ohio Company who met in the Bunch of Grapes Tavern in Boston in 1786. Three years earlier, Putnam had written to George Washington requesting land in the new Northwest Territory, which included what later became the states of Ohio, Indiana, Michigan, Illinois, Wisconsin, and part of Minnesota—land to which veterans of the Revolutionary War were entitled. Thomas Jefferson was named chairman of a committee to draw up plans for the Western country. The resulting

Ordinance of 1785 provided land warrants requiring a portion of each section to be set aside for schools. Within the Ohio Company purchase, two whole townships were given over to a university.

Few people are aware of the influence of Ivy League colleges and universities on Ohio University. Manasseh Cutler, a graduate of Yale, sought the advice of both President Joseph Willard of Harvard and President Ezra Stiles of Yale in planning the proposed school. Stiles and Cutler influenced the Northwest Ordinance and its salient statement that appears on the front gate of the Ohio campus: "Religion, morality and knowledge being necessary to good government and the happiness of mankind, schools and other means of education shall forever be encouraged."

On February 18, 1804, the General Assembly of the new State of Ohio passed an act establishing The Ohio University (*The* has since been dropped from the name). School opened in 1808 with one building, one professor, and three students. The first president was the Rev. Jacob Lindley, a graduate of Harvard. The trustees of the university patterned their charter after Yale's and adopted regulations borrowed from Princeton. Ohio's third president, Robert Wilson, received his doctor of divinity degree from Princeton. In 1828, during Wilson's tenure, John Newton Templeton graduated—the first black student at Ohio University. Oberlin claims to be the first college in the United States to admit African Americans, but their first black student entered eleven years after Templeton enrolled at Ohio. Oberlin was founded in 1835.

I was hoping that there might be some connection between Ohio and my alma mater, Brown. I asked Brown's president, Barnaby Keeney, to do a little research. Sure enough, a member of Brown's first graduating class in 1769, James Mitchell Varnum, was a member of the Continental Congress and an officer in the Ohio Company that founded Ohio University. A century later, in 1896, Ohio University hired its first football coach, Sam McMillen, who came from Dartmouth. At that time Ohio's school colors were light blue but changed to Dartmouth green and white. At the turn of the century, a contest was held to select an official school song. It was won by

Kenneth Clark, who wrote "Alma Mater, Ohio." Clark was a graduate of Princeton.

In 1908, the Ohio University president, Alston Ellis, took a swing through the East to visit Massachusetts and call upon the president of Harvard. The only information recorded about the trip was that Ellis was much impressed with the gray squirrels that romped around Harvard Yard. Upon his return to Athens, he asked the trustees to approve a committee to bring a family of Harvard squirrels to the College Green. (They surely proliferated, and I suspect that today some Athenians would happily send them back to Cambridge.)

ARRIVING IN ATHENS I found a university much better than the rest of the world perceived it to be, but in some ways not as good as several people on campus thought it was. I was distressed, as well, that there were members of the community with insufficient pride in Ohio University and lacking in concern to make it better.

I felt the need to energize the place—to lift the level of aspiration. We needed to become better known for what we were and build upon the legacy that my esteemed predecessor John Baker left. I am sure that in my early years at Ohio I overused the words *excellence, greatness,* and *distinction,* but a brilliant Ohio fellow's aide, Lynn Shostack, queried: "What would you have accomplished if you had used such inspiring words as *goodness, modest achievement, the advantages of being average,* or *It's all been done before.*"

In the early 1960s, there was a climate of optimism in the United States. In his 1961 Inaugural Address, the young President Kennedy spoke of an exciting new era and challenged his countrymen to aspire to a new level of accomplishment. The concept of the New Frontier—of vistas created by new perspectives—echoed throughout the country and the world. Several months later he outlined the goal of landing a man on the moon before the end of the decade.

Communities, as well as individuals, have occasional peak experiences—periods of time when, for whatever reasons, optimism and a sense of accomplishment pervade the atmosphere. I believe that this feeling of excitement, for beckoning and attainable horizons, was to characterize Ohio University in the 1960s.

Whenever I felt that we were not living up to the challenges presented to us, I thought of the words of Pericles, who, in ancient Greece, spoke of another small but glorious town: "Day by day, fix your eyes upon the greatness of Athens, until you become filled with the love of her, and when you are touched by the spectacle of her glory, reflect that this majesty has been acquired by men who knew their duty and had the courage to do it."

CHAPTER 2

Change Is Now a Way of Life

TWO EVENINGS AFTER I had settled into my new quarters, I spoke at a large dinner meeting in the university's Baker Center. Halfway through my address, a note was slipped onto the lectern: "A female student has been shot on campus."

I quickly finished my remarks and hurried over to the campus infirmary. "What kind of place have I moved to?" I wondered as I prepared myself for a situation I had never before encountered. Fortunately, the young lady was not seriously wounded by the .22 caliber bullet fired by her disgruntled boyfriend. I rose early the next morning to meet with her parents. They had driven overnight to be with her.

The injury turned out to be a superficial flesh wound. The young woman was released from the infirmary within a matter of hours, and our efficient student-personnel organization took appropriate action with respect to the young man involved. Nevertheless, for me it was a surprise introduction to the kind of unpredictable event that can take place on a large, coeducational campus.

During the first week on campus I was encouraged by several heartening observations: faculty members were sincerely interested in teaching undergraduates; the students seemed wholesome and unspoiled; the campus and its Georgian-style buildings were strikingly beautiful; there seemed to be a healthy balance between the athletic and academic programs; and the university had an international outreach through its USAID-sponsored program in Nigeria. Of course, there was also the glorious history of the university dating back to the Continental Congress.

But there were disappointments, too, making me aware that the challenges ahead were larger than I had anticipated: I was troubled by the inequitable support among the state's universities—Ohio State receiving a disproportionate share of the funding. The highway access to Athens was distressingly poor, and Route 33, the main route to the university, entered the most depressed section of the town. The first road sign one encountered proclaimed: "Jesus Saves." A prankster had erected another sign: "But Satan Invests." I was soon made aware of the flooding problem: the Hocking River poured its waters onto the campus every spring, cutting off Athens from the rest of the world. Then there was the noisy railroad line that cut through the center of the campus. Dormitory facilities were inadequate for even the eight thousand students then on campus, and there was the prospect of doubled enrollment within five years. A campus our size desperately needed a new library, science facilities, classrooms, and recreational buildings to meet a projected on-campus population of eighteen thousand.

Before moving to Ohio, I thought it might be necessary to bring with me from Harvard my able assistant, Willma (Billie) Nash. In fact I invited her to Athens for two days to convince her to move from Harvard. But she declined—albeit reluctantly—because of her father's ill health at the time. Luckily, I inherited Marie White from John Baker and found her to be an extraordinarily talented assistant—

intelligent, discreet, and capable of handling anyone, from the most sophisticated visitor to the most rude student. During her thirty-five years at the university, she served five presidents. She was recognized with the alumni Medal of Merit in 1996.

Happily enough, Billie Nash joined me again in 1981 when I was working on behalf of the Massachusetts Business Development Council. She continues to serve as my associate today.

Before my family joined me in Athens, I worked about sixteen hours per day, meeting with students, faculty, and townspeople, searching for ideas on a variety of subjects. The first formal faculty meeting was held in early February, just a month after I arrived. Rather than deliver a speech, I put forth a series of questions, asking faculty members to join me in resolving these issues:

> Do we have now at the university some of the environmental forces that encourage great teaching and productive scholarship?

> Is our present administrative organization—which was established for a student body of 4,500 to 5,000 students—appropriate for a student body of 9,000, 12,000, 15,000 . . . ?

> If the State of Ohio is not prepared adequately to finance a doubled student enrollment, can we admit students on a selective basis rather than "first come, first served?" Is our present balance between in-state and out-of-state students appropriate?

> What should be the relationship between graduate and undergraduate programs? The balance between them? In how many fields should we offer Ph.D. work?

> Is our present mix of schools and colleges appropriate? Should every new field be undertaken? In reexamining our schools and course offerings, should some be forced out?

> What should be our policy of involvement in international organizations? On continuing education programs? Are there other ways in which we can be of service to students, the state, and the nation? Shall we experiment with new teaching techniques—teaching machines, closed circuit TV, and so forth?

What should be the role and character of our branches? Expand the number and the size of individual branches? Should they remain two-year programs? Will they become four-year satellites? Will they eventually be spun off?

Should we develop relationships with small private colleges, offering master's degrees relating to undergraduate majors in a shorter period of time?

Can we be more effective in influencing student attitudes and values? Can we do more to raise their sights, their aspirations?

And, finally, is our present semester system appropriate today? Should we consider a move to a new academic calendar—the quarter system, for example?

Interestingly, my first formal speech on campus was entitled, "Change Is Now a Way of Life."

Clearly, all of these issues could not be tackled at once, but I was determined that major changes would take place. I began with moves that were not profound but symbolic. Cutler Hall, the lovely historic campus centerpiece built in 1816, was festooned with telephone and electrical wires that gave the appearance of a giant spider web. Within weeks all lines were buried, and we began the process of establishing Cutler Hall as a national historic landmark. In 1966, Secretary of the Interior Stewart Udall officially registered it. Bulletin boards that sprinkled the campus and whose messages trashed the otherwise beautiful lawns were taken down overnight, and no one raised a voice of complaint. The university catalog and promotional materials were shockingly poor and screamed out a message of mediocrity; one by one they took on a professional, sophisticated look, molded by the artistic talent of Don Stout and the creative writing of Anne Fitzgibbon.

The university was often referred to as *OU,* and although even my wife thought it was silly, I began a relentless effort to identify our beloved Ohio University as *Ohio*—naming our state, as was done by prestigious institutions in Michigan, Illinois, Indiana, Wisconsin, and California. We were chartered as "The Ohio University," but over the years Ohio A&M—later to become Ohio State University—stole our name. Ohio State even tried to change its name: in 1914 and again in 1917, a bill was introduced in the Ohio Senate proposing that the institution in Columbus be renamed "The University of Ohio," to correspond with the names of other major state universities; the proposal died in committee and was forgotten with the onset of World War I. When *OU* was uttered in my presence, I am sure I became a pain in the neck by asking, "Do you mean Oklahoma, Oregon, Occidental, or Oshkosh?" I added that prestigious universities such as Harvard were not called *HU*; Michigan was not *MU*; Stanford was not *SU;* and least of all was Princeton known as *PU.* The athletic teams got the message, and all uniforms carried the name Ohio prominently. But trying to convert alumni, faculty, and students was like pushing on a string.

I soon discovered what it was like to be a president when every word uttered had to be carefully considered for fear of the consequences. I innocently asked Dean Rush Elliott, "What kind of exams do we give in the College of Arts and Sciences—essay exams, multiple choice quizzes, or what?" Within a week, my desk was piled high with copies of examinations, as the department chairman and individual faculty members responded to Dean Elliott's order.

One day I received a carefully crafted, twenty-five page analysis of a Harvard Business School case, written by a young instructor who had perhaps spent two whole days on the task. Puzzled by this volunteer offering, I tracked down the culprits. Two senior professor-wags in the Department of History had told the neophyte that the "president urgently needs this analysis."

As we began the urgent effort to build the vitally needed new dormitories, I used as our model the Harvard "house system." We would build additional "campus greens"—the South Green, the West Green—in which individual dormitories would be part of a distinctive community. We would not build monolithic, impersonal, multistory dormitories so prevalent on other public university campuses.

Building the almost 90 million dollars' worth of new dormitories, laboratories, and classroom buildings, we used materials that would enhance and blend with the Georgian style of architecture that had so impressed me when I first arrived on campus. My predecessor John Baker often refers to this as one of my major accomplishments. And well he might. We were under constant pressure to adopt a more contemporary style. At one point, the trustees and I received a petition signed by 3,700 "concerned individuals."

In addition to the serious changes taking effect, my first few months at the university were not without amusing incidents. Speaking to the Ohio Alumni Club in Youngstown, I was introduced by one of the university's former star football players. Relishing his position as master of ceremonies, he launched into an expansive introduction: "We are delighted to have Dr. and Mrs. Alden with us this evening. Dr. Alden has spent the past several years working at Harvard, so I know he'll upgrade our academic standards. Mrs. Alden, an artist and interior designer, will be very helpful to our College of Fine Arts. But what really impresses me about Dr. Alden is his interest in athletics. I understand that he visits the Bobcat locker room after every basketball game, and he is helping Bill Hess in recruiting football talent. Ladies and gentlemen, it's a great pleasure to introduce our new president, who is a warm athletic supporter." The audience was convulsed with laughter, while the perplexed MC wondered what he had said to bring on such a response.

Another incident involved Anne, our daughter. Upon their arrival in Athens, our children—Rob, Anne, and Jim—were enrolled in the university-run Putnam School. With an extraordinary teacher-student ratio, helped by student interns, Putnam far exceeded our expectations as an excellent elementary school. One day Marion received a call from Anne's teacher: "Mrs. Alden," she said, "perhaps you should have a word with Anne. She continues to boast about her father being president of the university. I'm afraid it could alienate her classmates." A week of so later, two of Athens's distinguished elder ladies, white gloves and all, saw Anne playing in the yard in front of our home. "Young lady," they asked, "aren't you the daughter of the new president of Ohio University?" "No," said Anne innocently, "my Mom says I'm really not."

In the late afternoons—at least three or four times a week—I tried to squeeze in some exercise. Frequently, I would telephone several young administrators and invite them to join me in Grover Center for a pickup game of basketball. One afternoon I was the first to arrive on the court, dressed in shorts and a T-shirt, dribbling a basketball. A loud voice roared from the end of the building, "Hey! Get out of here. The courts are closed." I was about to leave when one of my teammates arrived and explained to the embarrassed supervisor that everything would be OK.

MOMENTUM ACCELERATES

On May 18, 1962, I was formally sworn into office by Governor Michael DiSalle. Several hundred delegates representing other universities, from the oldest, Harvard, to the most recently established, gathered on the College Green. James Perkins, of the Carnegie Corporation of New York, gave the main address, followed by informal remarks by former Dean Donald David of the Harvard Business School.

In my inaugural address, I traced the early history of Ohio University, beginning with the meeting of founders Manasseh Cutler and Rufus Putnam in the Bunch of Grapes Tavern in Boston. I brashly referred to the lack of financial support that the state universities in Ohio were receiving, comparing our situation with the California system with its reputation for quality, the result of generous and continuing support by the State of California. I recommended that we establish four immediate goals for Ohio University:

> *The creation of an Honors College*—staffed by many of the university's most outstanding faculty members, who would identify, recruit, stimulate, and inspire gifted students

The planning and construction of a substantial new library—
desperately needed for undergraduate and graduate programs
of study

The development of additional doctoral programs—vitally needed
in the recruitment of young scholars and mature faculty members and in the enrichment of undergraduate fields of study

*The establishment of a program to revitalize that most precious re-
source, the faculty*—through research activity, sabbatical leaves,
exchange professorships, and opportunities to teach in our
rapidly expanding overseas program

The university desperately needed additional dormitories, classrooms, laboratories, faculty offices, and recreational facilities, but I
mentioned only the library in my inaugural address. In the late 1950s
the Ohio legislature had been slow to recognize their obligation to
provide for a doubling of student enrollment in the 1960s. Demog-
raphers had predicted the coming tide of students, but Ohio—as I
pointed out in my address—ranked forty-eighth among the states in
public financial support. The old Chubb Library had served the
needs of a smaller faculty and a student body of three-to-four thousand, but could not possibly contain the volumes, the data-process-
ing equipment, and the national and international resources of a
modern teaching and research university. Thereafter, every year I
pleaded with legislators for capital funds for a new library. Appropriations met our building needs in chemistry, mathematics, biol-
ogy, physics, journalism, and television, but funding for a modern
library kept dropping off the legislators' list.

Although by 1966 we had created the Honors College, had added
several doctoral programs, and had established the faculty revitaliza-
tion programs—sabbatical leaves, overseas teaching assignments and
research opportunities—promised in my address, we had not accomplished the other "immediate goal, a substantial new library."
My concerns vanished when, that same year, we received the necessary funds to plan and build the library.

In 1969 the trustees surprised me by naming our new library the

Vernon Roger Alden Library. No honor could have pleased me more. Today, the Alden Library houses more than two million volumes, growing by fifty thousand new volumes each year, and is a member of the prestigious Association for Research Libraries, ranking it as one of the top 120 research libraries in the United States and Canada. To celebrate one of my wife's "significant" birthdays, I provided funds to establish the Marion Alden Southeast Asia Collection. Alden Library's Southeast Asia Collection is widely recognized today as one of the outstanding research collections on Southeast Asia in the world.

The trustees approved the awarding of honorary degrees to four individuals who had played an important role in my life—the fourth being a surprise. The first, James Perkins, vice president of the Carnegie Corporation, had enabled us to establish at Harvard the Institute for College and University Administrators, which I administered and in which I taught before moving to Ohio. Perkins later became the president of Cornell University.

The second, Donald David, was the dean of the Harvard Business School when I entered as a student in 1948. In his welcoming remarks to the new class, he challenged us to "reach for the stars. You may never get there, but you may be able to guide your course by them." In 1951 he invited me back to Harvard from Northwestern to establish and administer the unique financial-aid program described in chapter 1.

The third, General Georges Doriot, had been in charge of the U.S. Army Supply Corps during World War II. He was the most popular and revered professor at the Harvard Business School. Serving as president of the American Research and Development Company, he founded several successful high-technology companies, most notably the Digital Equipment Corporation. In 1959 he invited me to join the board of directors of Digital, which, at the time of writing (1997), I have served for thirty-eight years. Both Donald David and Georges Doriot were valued mentors to me throughout their lifetimes.

The fourth, as I said above, was a surprise. The Ohio board members demonstrated their thoughtfulness and generosity by awarding a doctor of divinity degree to my father. His influence on my life was profound. During his lifetime he persuaded more young people to pursue careers in the ministry, in missionary work or in academia, than any person I know. From the earliest days of my life, I never wanted to disappoint him, and this was reflected in my school work.

Typical of most clergymen, my father had only a very modest salary, but his goal was to provide the finest educational opportunity possible for his four children. When I was a junior in high school in Illinois, he made it clear that he wished for me an Ivy League education; but that seemed financially impossible. He wangled an invitation to a Congregational church in Providence, Rhode Island, and in my senior year at Classical High School, he accompanied me to the Admission Office at Brown. I was able to attend Brown thanks to a full scholarship and by living at home. Pearl Harbor was attacked four months after I entered Brown, and soon I moved onto the campus as member of the Navy V-12 program. Throughout the time I was in the North Pacific, in Japanese Language School, or on the aircraft carrier USS *Saratoga*, my father wrote to me every day. I treasure his memory and his profound influence upon my life.

My parents were determined that each of their four children would have a college education. My sister, Janet, is a graduate of Bryant College. Janet went on to become the administrative assistant to Henry M. Wriston, president of Brown University. My brother Don is a graduate of Brown University, the Rhode Island School of Design, and the Chicago Art Institute. He has had a distinguished career as art director for several advertising agencies and the *Providence Journal-Bulletin*. Burt was graduated from Northwestern University and Harvard Business School. He has served as a senior executive, consultant, and board member for a number of corporations.

My mother was a saint. While my father was busy building churches, traveling, counseling young people, and visiting the sick and the bereaved, she raised the four children in our family. My father's salary was never more than $3,000 per year, so she did all of the laundry, cleaning, sewing, and entertaining. She provided strong support to my father. I remember during the darkest days of the Great Depression out-of-work itinerants would appear at our back door looking for a meal, which she always provided. She was a beautiful person with an unbelievable memory for names and events. I was indeed blessed to have had such outstanding parents.

My father's first church was in a tiny town in Minnesota—Dassel —home to fewer than 2,500 citizens and commuting farmers. My mother, who was born in Rockford, Illinois, did not trust the local hospital in nearby Cokato when I was about to enter the world, so she traveled to Chicago for my birth.

When I was five, we moved to Moline, Illinois, population 32,604, where we spent the next twelve years. I grew up at a time when ice took the shape of sawdust-covered blocks delivered in horse-drawn wagons. Frozen foods, television, contact lenses, jet airplanes, computers, dishwashers, and credit cards did not exist. Our activities were simple then: walking downtown to the dime store to watch a Japanese salesman perform tricks with a yo-yo, or daring to place on the railroad tracks pennies that were flattened by the Golden Gate Limited roaring through town.

Minister's children are expected to be paradigms of good behavior. When they are not, they become the talk of busybodies in the congregation. My sister, my brothers, and I behaved ourselves fairly well and rarely gave our parents cause for concern. On one occasion, however, my mother received a telephone call from a woman in the parish alerting her to the activities of seven-year-old Vernon and five-year-old Janet. We had gathered bouquets of flowers that my mother had thrown out in the trash and were going door to door of neighborhood homes attempting to sell them.

On Saturdays my brother Don—the third of my parents' four children—and I raced to the corner store to buy five-cent packs of baseball cards, sold the gum at our sidewalk stand, and hustled off with the cash receipts to buy more cards. My collection of baseball stars of the 1920s and 1930s grew to more than nine hundred, only to be lost when my mother gave them to another lad when I left for U.S.

Navy service. Alas, if I owned them today, I could endow several scholarships at Ohio and Brown. I also had a sizeable collection of "first day covers," envelopes carrying postage stamps on the first day of issue. They, too, would be valuable today, and I accused my youngest brother, Burt, of selling them when I was away in the navy.

Almost all of our relatives on both sides of the family lived in Chicago. At least once a year the Alden family would pile into our old Nash and drive the narrow, two-lane highway to Chicago, 175 miles or so away. One of my uncles, Eric Wallgren, was a senior executive in the company that manufactured the Radio Flyer wagons. The 1932 World's Fair—which Chicagoans named the Century of Progress—featured a giant replica of a Radio Flyer wagon with a model of my cousin, Fred Johnson, as the driver. Though only nine years old at that time, I still recall the sights and scents of the fair, especially the strong smell of unfiltered tobacco in the Camel cigarette exhibition hall.

Newspapers in the early 1930s carried stories of bank robbers who prowled the Midwest—Roger Touhy, "Pretty Boy" Floyd, and the most notorious of all, John Dillinger. Each was labeled by the FBI at one time or another as Public Enemy Number One. John Dillinger was captured in 1933 but was rescued by members of his gang. After robbing banks in several states, he was again captured in Arizona and returned to jail in Indiana. Within a few months he managed a re-markable escape and became the target of a massive manhunt by the FBI. On July 22, 1934, he was lured to the Biograph Theater in mid-town Chicago by a mysterious woman, described in the press as "The Lady in Red." Dillinger was gunned down by FBI agents as he left the theater. My parents and I happened to be in Chicago at the time. Along with hundreds of other curiosity seekers, we drove by the Biograph Theater the day after the shooting. We observed people trying to dig bullets out of a telephone pole, and we were told that other souvenir hunters had dipped handkerchiefs in Dillinger's blood on the sidewalk. Needless to say, this event has loomed in my memory ever since.

Many years later Marion and I met one of the FBI agents who had participated in the ambush of Dillinger. He was by then an assistant to J. C. Penney, the legendary founder of the chain of stores bearing his name. While working at the Harvard Business School, we occasionally entertained J. C. Penney—and his assistant—in our Wellesley Hills home. We, of course, enjoyed Penney's tales of the early years of the stores, but I was especially captivated by the description of John Dillinger's last hours, told colorfully by the assistant.

On other visits to Chicago, I stayed with my cousin, Fred Johnson. In the same apartment building lived Stanley Hack, the third baseman of the Chicago Cubs—my boyhood baseball hero. What a thrill it was to play catch with Stan Hack! If you liked baseball as much as I did, there was no greater dream than having the Cubs come to your hometown for a game. When they made a stopover in Moline between spring training at Catalina Island and opening day in Chicago, I rushed to the train station at five in the morning to greet my heroes. Hours went by before the late-sleeping Cubs emerged from the train, but I collected autographs from all of them. The biggest thrill was still in store, however: my friend Stan Hack arranged with manager Charlie Grimm for me to be batboy in the exhibition game with the Cubs' farm team, the Moline Plows.

Baseball was an obsession with me. Little League did not exist in the 1930s. We played our brand of baseball without the guidance of adult managers or the coaching of hovering parents. All summer we played pickup games, interrupted only by ice-cream breaks—quarts available for a dime. In the early evening, I practiced fielding grounders for hours by throwing the ball against our front steps. With adolescent vanity I was confident that major league baseball was my calling. I could visualize my name in the Chicago Cubs' starting lineup and could hear WGN announcer Bob Elson describing my sparkling play in Wrigley Field, "the home of the Cubs."

At World Series time we trotted down to the *Moline Daily Dispatch* to watch the series played out on a huge, magnetized metal board depicting a baseball diamond. From behind the board, an operator, listening to a teletype machine, manipulated a metal ball from pitcher to home plate and then to other reaches of the diamond if the batter connected with the pitch. Little figures represented men on base, and a scoreboard indicated balls, strikes, outs, the inning, and the score. Fans gathered on the street roared after every play. We were surely part of the larger World Series crowd.

I was good enough as a baseball player to earn a starting slot as third baseman on the Junior American Legion squad. I had a great year in 1938, capped by my being chosen to play in the season-ending all-star game. However, my father was pastor of an evangelical church, and I could not play baseball on Sundays: I had to remove myself from the all-star lineup. Providence intervened when rain postponed the game to Monday evening and I was tapped to start in center field. I had three sharp singles in four appearances at the plate. I should have had at least a double in my final turn at bat, but the opposing third baseman made a spectacular diving catch of my slashing line drive.

At Moline High School, I concentrated on my studies, aiming to please my father by being valedictorian of the class. I held two jobs—high school sports reporter for the *Moline Daily Dispatch,* for which I was paid five cents for every column inch, and sales clerk at Temple's sporting goods store. I worked every afternoon after school and all day Saturday for the grand sum of four dollars a week. Once when I was sweeping up the store, I found a quarter and immediately turned it over to the assistant manager. He would leave me in charge of the store whenever he left early to play golf. I was somewhat disillusioned, however, when I saw him scoop up a handful of golf balls, a pair of sweat socks, and a golf glove—without paying.

Church was the center of our lives. Sundays included Sunday School, church, choir practice, and evening service. Wednesday evenings found us in church again for the mandatory prayer meeting. Sunday afternoons I usually sat close to the radio listening to the play-by-play broadcasts of the Chicago Cubs. As a family we also listened to Sammy Kaye's *Sunday Serenade.* Many years later my sister,

Janet, was invited to lead his band upon his appearance at a concert in Providence. When I became president of Ohio University, I was delighted to discover that Sammy was an alumnus, and we became good friends.

Each of the Alden children was required to sit in the front row in church. When, as tiny tots, we occasionally misbehaved, my father reprimanded us from the pulpit. Although it sometimes embarrasses Marion, I have never outgrown my desire to sit in the front row. I like to observe the speaker closely and learn whatever I can from him or her. In the past two or three years, it has become more necessary because of my slight hearing loss.

From my earliest years, I was required to speak from the platform —in Sunday School or in church services. I am grateful that my father gave me this opportunity. Our son, David, was required to give a public speech once a week in elementary school at Dexter, and he has developed into an excellent public speaker. Every youngster should have this opportunity early in life. Expressing oneself articulately and confidently is a valuable asset.

At the beginning of my junior year in high school, we moved to Providence, Rhode Island. The trustees of my father's new church were gathered at the parsonage when we arrived. My brothers, Don and Burt, and I always carried our baseball gloves, ball, and bat in the car trunk. We started a pickup game in the street while the trustees were showing our new house to our parents. Within a few minutes, a line drive shattered the glass of the front window, causing the trustees to wonder what kind of family they had invited to Providence.

Classical High School in Providence, with a well-set lineup already in place, did not need my services on the baseball team, but I did score points as a half-miler on the track team, editor of the school paper, and *cum laude* student—enough to win a full scholarship to Brown in September 1941. Dreams of professional baseball receded, and I concentrated on my studies, achieving Phi Beta Kappa and honors in English literature. My father and I were both pleased.

During that time I also turned in baseball heroes for a new set of role models. I admired the Brown president, Henry Wriston, a towering leader in the academic world who also lent his advice to the U.S. State Department and a couple of major corporations. I sat in the front row at compulsory weekly chapel listening with rapt attention as he lectured us with unmitigated certainty. As I watched him stride confidently across campus, I thought to myself, "What a lovely life!"

Engrossed as I was in English literature, and listening often to the recorded poetry of T. S. Eliot and Robert Frost in the John Hay Library, the lure of baseball was nevertheless always present. Brown's baseball coach was a former New York Yankee, Eddie Eayrs, a tobacco-chewing cross between Don Zimmer and Tommy Lasorda. By the time the spring baseball season rolled around, the Japanese had attacked Pearl Harbor, and those of us who remained in college were wearing V-12 or Naval ROTC uniforms. Our schedule included other Ivy League schools, plus Holy Cross, Rhode Island University, and an assortment of military service teams.

I rode the bench for most of the first season because Coach Eayrs had never heard of me. Well into the season we faced the Boston Coast Guard squad, who had Cleveland Indians star Jim Hegan as catcher, Pete Appleton of the White Sox pitching, and St. Louis Cardinals star Johnny Hopp in center field. In the ninth inning, with a Brown runner on third, Coach Eayrs looked for a pinch hitter to bat for our pitcher. I was summoned from the end of the bench and, much to the surprise of the entire ball club, especially Coach Eayrs, I rapped into deep center field a towering drive that the fleet Johnny Hopp caught over his shoulder. Our runner scored the winning run from third, and I basked in my new-found celebrity in the postgame showers.

From that game on, I secured the slot at second base, starting against Harvard in our next outing in Cambridge. As lead-off batter, I ripped a long drive into deep center field for a stand-up triple. The next time at bat I popped a lazy double along the right field line. In my third and fourth times at bat, I drew walks. In the ninth inning, I was eager to round out the day with another base hit, so with the count three and one, I bit on a bad pitch and missed. The crafty Warren Berg, who later pitched for the Red Sox, struck me out while I held my bat on my shoulder. Despite my six putouts, one assist, a triple, and a double, Coach Eayrs blistered me on the train back to Providence for swinging on a three-and-one count. Nevertheless, I secured my position as a regular until being assigned to midshipmen's school at Columbia University in 1943. On the day I broke into the lineup as a starter against Harvard, my brother Don, pitching for Classical High School, struck out fourteen batters while pitching a two-hit ball game. After army service he pitched for Brown and had the distinction of twice striking out Yale first baseman George Bush.

Except for baseball and track, I did not have time for other extracurricular activities. I worked in a screw-machine factory part-time while in school and full-time during summer and spring vacations, frequently opting for the night shift so that I could earn more money. In many ways I am grateful that I had to work my way through college, because I learned much about the world of work at an early age.

Fulfilling my responsibilities aboard a small ship in the wild waters of the North Pacific off the Aleutian Island chain, learning the Japanese language from Japanese-American citizens who had been uprooted from California to Colorado, and serving aboard an aircraft carrier all played a part in preparing me for leadership positions I would assume while relatively young.

When the war ended, my aircraft carrier, the USS *Saratoga*, was one of several old naval vessels sent to Bikini Island to be sacrificed in the atomic bomb test. I had volunteered to stay with the ship for the test, but when I discovered that I would have to extend my navy career for two more years, I chose to return to Brown University to complete my undergraduate degree. President Henry Wriston invited me to work part-time in his office and in the Admissions Office while completing my studies in English literature.

Beginning in mid-1946, I worked full time at Brown. President Wriston asked James Cunningham and me to assume responsibility for the Veterans College that he created to accommodate the flood of veterans entering college under the GI Bill. Many who applied had spotty or incomplete high school records and would normally not be admitted to a college with the standards of Brown. But Wriston, a risk-taker and academic pioneer, was confident that the war experience would have given the applicants maturity and a sense of purpose. He was right. Most of the young men did well in the Veterans College and qualified for transfer into the established academic program.

Working with Henry Wriston reinforced my desire to pursue a career in academic administration. To do so I felt I would need an advanced degree. By 1948 I was so far removed from my undergraduate major that I concluded I would almost have to start over in an English literature Ph.D. program. I opted to apply for admission to the Law and the Graduate Business Schools at Harvard. Having been accepted by both places, I chose to go to the business school for the simple reason that I preferred not to read the tedious legalese material I had struggled with on the law school aptitude test. The experience of discussing real-life administrative problems through the case method of study was appealing and turned out to be a significant next step in preparing me for my future responsibilities.

CHAPTER 3

Student Affairs: Politics, Free Speech, and Sports

WHEN I ARRIVED in Ohio, Democrat Michael V. DiSalle was in his last year as governor. John Baker took me to Columbus to introduce me to the governor, and we spent several pleasant moments discussing mutual friends. As noted earlier, Governor DiSalle administered the oath of office when I was officially installed as president of the university at the inaugural exercises in May.

While in Columbus, John Baker took me to meet the auditor of state, James Rhodes, suggesting to me that Rhodes, a Republican, would undoubtedly be the new governor following elections in the fall. My initial meeting with Rhodes was not auspicious. What I did not know was that John Baker and Jim Rhodes were not on the best of terms. Apparently, my debut as Baker's successor was not greeted with much warmth.

John Kennedy had been inaugurated as president of the United States the year before I arrived in Athens. I was told that Rhodes wondered why I had left Boston to move to Ohio. He believed—

inaccurately—that the Kennedys had arranged for me to be a political factor in Ohio. A rumor circulated in Columbus—again without truth—that I had authorized the university's vice president, Martin Hecht, to deliver a trunkload of liquor to the wedding reception of Governor DiSalle's daughter. It didn't help that *Life, Time,* the *Wall Street Journal,* and several Ohio papers carried major stories about our successes at Ohio University. Governor Rhodes began to believe —again without any real evidence—that I was waiting in the wings to challenge him at the next election. Much to my embarrassment, the *Cincinnati Post-Times* headlined an article in April 1966: Ohio U. Head May Run for Governor . . . on the Democratic Ticket. The story was picked up by newspapers all over Ohio and I felt it necessary to issue a denial: "The rumor is completely unfounded. I have no political ambition, and my only interest is the continued development of Ohio University."

Jim Rhodes was a skillful campaigner; his earthy, country-boy style went over well with Ohioans. One evening we were together in Portsmouth, Ohio, for the dedication of a new building on our branch campus there. Both of us were scheduled to speak, but before we were introduced almost every local dignitary spoke—the mayor, the chairman of the city council, the state representative, the labor union leader, and others. By the time the governor was called upon, it was almost midnight. His entire speech was as follows:

> Some years ago we had a corn borer problem in Ohio. State troopers were instructed to stop every farm vehicle for inspection. One day a farmer was driving his wagon with his son sitting in the rear, legs hanging over the back of the wagon. A state trooper stopped them: "What do you have there, sir?"
>
> "A load of manure, and my son, John." A few minutes down the road they were stopped again—same question, same answer: "a load of manure and my son, John."
>
> When about to be stopped a third time, the young boy sat up and shouted to his father: "Next time, would you mind introducing me first?"

With that the governor sat down.

I have other memories that include the governor. On the day President Kennedy was assassinated, I was in Governor Rhodes' office when a secretary burst in to announce that the president had been shot. When Ohio University's football team was invited to play in the 1968 Tangerine Bowl, the governor and his son joined my son Jim and me for the game. Despite frequent meetings, however, the governor and I never really became close friends. Perhaps he continued to view me with suspicion.

In 1964 President Johnson appointed me chairman of the Appalachian Regional Commission. When legislation was being proposed to assist the poverty-stricken region, the president needed the endorsements of Republican governors to ensure partisan support for the bill. Rhodes refused, claiming the legislation was a boondoggle despite the fact that southeastern Ohio would benefit from development funds included in the proposal.

The chairman of our board of trustees, Fred Johnson, and I invited on short notice area business leaders, mayors, and labor union leaders to meet with us at the university. We persuaded Governor Rhodes to join us. When the more than four hundred area leaders expressed almost unanimous support for the Appalachian development legislation, the governor asked me to join him in telephoning President Johnson. The president was en route to Texas in Air Force One and unreachable by telephone, but the governor told Jack Valenti, the chief of staff, to inform the president of his support for the bill.

Funds generated by the Appalachian development legislation were enormously helpful to the university and much of southeastern Ohio. From my first days in Athens, I had been concerned about the isolation of our community—the poor highway access, the small university airport, and the flooding problem that closed the university for three or four days every spring.

The Appalachian Highway, which was built in 1969, provided four-lane access to Cincinnati and Eastern cities, and Route 33 was improved from Columbus, creating magnificent new approaches and views of the university. With funding and a land trade, we built the new and safer university airport, capable of handling executive jet planes. With the help of the Corps of Engineers and Southeastern Ohio business and political leaders, the Hocking River was moved, solving the flooding problem and enhancing the scenic beauty of Ohio University.

Governor Rhodes and I frequently discussed the possibility of developing Athens County as a premier recreation center complete with golf courses, a business conference center, and sites for industrial development. Those plans never materialized during my tenure as president, but I remain hopeful that some day the beautiful southeastern Ohio area can be a vital economic force, sparked by university involvement.

Such a spark first came in May 1964 when President Johnson visited the campus to announce his vision of the Great Society. The governor and Mrs. Rhodes joined the university trustees and members of our administrative team in welcoming the president, his daughter, Lynda Bird, Franklin Roosevelt Jr., and several members of the Johnson administration. The governor accompanied the president and me in an open-top car to the main Campus Green. Although President Johnson and Governor Rhodes appeared to enjoy their visit together, I subsequently learned that Rhodes was not happy that I had invited the Democratic president to our campus in a campaign year. I then began writing to former President Eisenhower at his farm in Gettysburg, asking him to speak and accept an honorary degree. After three rejections, my fourth appeal resulted in a warm response from Eisenhower; he would visit the campus. I invited Governor Rhodes to join us but he declined indicating that he would be seeing the former president in Cleveland two nights later. I suspect that he was shocked when he discovered that Eisenhower appeared in Cleveland not in person but on video screen.

Less than four months after I had assumed my new responsibilities, I was projected into a controversy that drew statewide attention. Ohio State University had denied three left-leaning speakers the right to appear on campus, invoking what came to be known as the

"OSU gag rule." Thousands of Ohio State students responded with mass marches and sit-ins. The OSU chapter of the American Association of University Professors (AAUP) passed a resolution requesting an investigation by national headquarters. Nevertheless, in support of the OSU administration's position, that university's faculty voted 1,036 to 509 in favor of the gag rule.

I was approached by a group of Ohio University students asking me to make a public declaration of my stance on the issue of free speech. I promised to work on a statement and announce it in a campus speech. Three days before my scheduled talk, the students returned to tell me that there was sufficient interest to necessitate moving my presentation to the large Memorial Auditorium. As I stood backstage with statement in hand, I was prepared to greet several thousand students. I was astonished to find, as I walked to the podium, only three sparsely filled rows. In spite of my deflation I delivered my speech, which became a major university policy and is included in the faculty handbook even today. The key paragraphs were:

> A University cannot proclaim its belief in the concept of freedom of expression and then deny individuals with whom it disagrees a chance to express their views. The genius of free men has made our society the greatest known to recorded history. The right of free speech has been an essential part of this greatness.

> We cannot for a moment in our educational institutions give students cause to believe that we fear exposure to alien ideas. Any individual with the deep and abiding faith in freedom is not afraid to test his ideas and beliefs against others.

> At Ohio University we believe that freedom of inquiry and discussion is essential to a student's educational development. We recognize the right of our students to engage in free discussion, to hear speakers of their choice and to speak and write without fear of administrative action.

Although my statement did not endear me to Ohio State partisans, most of the major metropolitan newspapers supported my position. The *Toledo Blade* observed: "The difference between these two Ohio campuses, only 75 miles apart, on speaker policies is significant. . . . Ohio University would seem to be fulfilling the true function of a university the more completely."

The battle of ideals was far from over. A scant seven months later, a bill was introduced into the Ohio legislature (House Bill 800) that made it mandatory for boards of trustees of Ohio's public universities to ban controversial speakers. I traveled to Columbus to oppose the bill and was supported again by Ohio's major newspapers—most notably the *Akron Beacon Journal*. I also sought the help of Stanley Mechem, president pro tempore of the state senate. Stanley owned a shoe store on Court Street, the main downtown street, and I made it a point to visit him in the basement of his store from time to time. He was a likable person with great common sense. He chewed tobacco and would spit into an old, sawdust-filled shoe box while we talked about southeastern Ohio, the university, and Columbus politics.

In discussing the speaker-ban bill, I stressed that we needed to expose students to a broad range of ideas, including controversial ones, to show them the weaknesses of certain ideologies and allow them to strengthen their own beliefs: "Look," I said, "I abhor Communism and Nazism just as much as you do, but in an educational institution you have to educate people as to what these ideologies are. I think you can do more to persuade people about the evils of those systems if they see a living example of them. We will never be able to recruit great faculty members and students to Ohio University if we have a speaker gag rule."

Senator Mechem agreed to try to amend the bill in the Senate. Unfortunately, the day the bill went before the house a group of vociferous students from various Ohio campuses gathered outside the state house and harassed legislators on their way to session. The effect was disastrous: the gag rule was passed by the House.

Several years later, on a trip to the University of North Carolina, I slipped into a free-speech rally there and was amazed to hear a former student of Ohio State University describe how she and other students had "killed" House Bill 800 in Ohio by demonstrating at the statehouse and "convincing" the legislature of its error. In reality, the opposite had occurred. The House of Representatives, at least slightly aggravated by the harassment, voted overwhelmingly "for" the gag rule. The next day I called upon Senator Mechem, again asking his aid in amending the bill in the Senate. Mechem pointed out that unless I could keep the students away, he did not stand a chance of amending the legislation. Nevertheless, he continued to press his colleagues with the argument that the issue concerning campus speakers was not whether or not Communist or extreme right-wing speakers were allowed on campus; the issue was *who* would make this decision. To my great satisfaction, the bill was indeed amended in committee and gave individual boards of trustees the right to formulate their own policy for each state university.

SHORTLY AFTER WE arrived in Athens, we made plans to join a church. While living in Wellesley Hills, we were members of the Covenant Congregational Church. Marion had been brought up as a Methodist, and for both of us the quality of the minister and the depth of his sermons were more important than the type of Protestant denomination. So we visited many of the churches in Athens over a period of several Sundays. Word got back to us that "the Aldens are 'shopping around' for a church."

Soon we joined the Presbyterian church, where the Reverend Lew Kemmerle gave carefully prepared, intellectually stimulating sermons. Rev. Kemmerle proved to be more liberal than many of his parishioners desired. He had gone South with many other clergy, students, and concerned Northern citizens to help blacks register to vote. He had been arrested while there, but returned knowing he had done the right thing. At an annual meeting, the congregation voted not to give him a salary increase, despite speeches of support by several faculty members in the congregation. After a long evening of debate that seemed to be going nowhere, I was moved to rise and suggest that Marion and I would contribute an amount of money in addition to our annual pledge, "provided that it would be used as a salary increase for Rev. Kemmerle." The congregation voted to accept the money, but I am not certain that our gesture endeared us to many local citizens. In any event, we believed that our action in defense of Lew Kemmerle's stance on significant social issues was as necessary as our commitment to freedom of speech on campus.

My "free speech" policy was finally tested in March 1965. Bush Hall men's dormitory inaugurated a controversial speakers' series and invited George Lincoln Rockwell, then head of the American Nazi Party. When announcement of the Rockwell invitation was made, I found myself under attack from many of the same people who had applauded and defended my 1963 statement advocating freedom of speech and my battle against the legislative gag rule. A committee of Jewish faculty members, deploring the activities of the Nazi Party in Germany, demanded that I "uninvite" Rockwell. The American Legion post in Athens passed a unanimous resolution condemning Ohio University and embarked on a statewide campaign to block the visit. A storm of letters, both signed and unsigned, was sent to our trustees, the governor, and even J. Edgar Hoover. A group of vigilantes in town threatened to "tar and feather" Rockwell if he dared enter the community.

Meanwhile, rioting had erupted at Ohio State University over its gag rule and its refusal to allow Marxist Herbert Aptheker to speak on campus. He was also barred from North Carolina by a similar rule that prohibited both Communists and evokers of the Fifth Amendment.

I refused to back down in the face of outside pressures and threats. Instead, I urged the dean's office to use the occasion to publicize the virtues of democracy and point out the true nature of Rockwell's ideology. Films showing Nazi atrocities were shown on campus and lectures were given prior to Rockwell's visit. We arranged for maximum security in the auditorium, not because of apprehension over student conduct but in view of threats from several community members to form a vigilante group.

The actual visit proved to be personally satisfying. In the crowded auditorium, students greeted the Nazi's rhetoric calmly and quietly. Many of them wore white shirts in protest of Rockwell's brown one. The following day, the Columbus newspapers ran side-by-side pictures: one showed Ohio University students peacefully listening to Rockwell; the other showed thousands of OSU students demonstrating on the main campus oval in protest of the gag rule. Letters of commendation came from the trustees and a formal statement of appreciation was issued to the student body.

Yet the mayor of Athens sent me a letter insisting that the town had to have a voice henceforth in speaker selection, calling the invitation to Rockwell "an ill-advised and irresponsible act."

RECRUITING AND MOTIVATING STUDENTS

Although Ohio University enrolled many students whose homes were outside of Ohio, and a fairly impressive number of foreign students, they represented a small proportion of our total student body. To be a truly national and international institution, the university needed to launch a nationwide school-visitation program. Having worked at one time in the Northwestern University admissions office, I was aware of their high-quality student-recruiting program.

Fortunately, I was able to attract Jerry Reese from Northwestern in mid-1963 to head up our admissions office. I asked him to create a nationwide school-visitation program modeled after Northwestern's. I said to Jerry: "I don't care whether Ohio University is a third-choice 'safety' school after Harvard, Wellesley, Stanford, or other prestigious institutions. Even if turned down by their first or second choice schools, those out-of-state students would bring impressive credentials to the university, and the quality of the academic experience of Ohio students would be enhanced by exposure to talented young people from other sections of the country."

Jerry and his associates in the admissions office visited high schools and prep schools throughout the United States, and we did indeed attract many impressive young men and women. Within a few years, out-of-state enrollment reached more than 30 percent. With my encouragement, the admissions office staff looked for talent in the predominantly black high schools in the larger Ohio cities. At the time, we were the only public university in Ohio recruiting high-quality black students other than athletic stars. This was not an easy task, given community attitudes in the early 1960s. Visits from Nigerians through our USAID-sponsored program and the enrollment of an increasingly larger number of outstanding black students helped to change community attitudes, albeit not without tension.

When I was not off campus giving speeches, I frequently visited the dormitories to meet with students. In those informal "give and take" sessions, I tried to describe my vision of what Ohio University could become. In my first few years at Ohio, I occasionally stayed overnight to share with students the feeling of our overcrowded dormitory rooms. They always generously offered me the lower bunk.

In my sessions with students, I described our plans to create an honors college that would provide incentives to highly motivated students. The Ohio Fellows Program would offer special seminars as well as internships with leaders in government, business, and non-profit institutions. The Edwin and Ruth Kennedy Lecture series would bring prominent speakers to the campus. And then, of course, I described trustee Fred Johnson's vision for revitalizing southeastern Ohio and how leadership by the university could enhance the quality of life within the university and the community. When I returned to our home from those sessions with students, I was so charged up I found it difficult to go to sleep.

Throughout my tenure at Ohio, I sought out students of promise. Often, I discovered that I could lift their level of aspiration. Some who had planned to attend mediocre, regional graduate schools were persuaded to apply to a Harvard, Stanford, University of Chicago, or a Michigan graduate school. I wrote many letters of recommendation. I am proud of the many Ohio students who went on to distinguish themselves in various professions.

J. LESLIE ROLLINS had an uncanny ability to spot talent in young people and then motivate them to levels of accomplishment they did not realize they could attain. Many men and women who have led major corporations in recent years are products of cajoling and challenging by Les. He would find entry-level positions for them where mentors coached them to highly-successful careers.

I met Assistant Dean J. Leslie Rollins while a student at the Harvard Business School. He was a remarkable human being. As an undergraduate at tiny Buena Vista College, Les starred in football, basketball, and track. He took his graduate work at Northwestern and stayed on in the administration until recruited to the dean's office of the Harvard Business School. When Rollins reached retirement age, I persuaded him to join us at Ohio as a roving consultant without portfolio or salary. He continued to practice his magic upon students, lifting their levels of aspiration, and pointing them in the direction of leading graduate schools. Together with Robert Greenleaf, former vice president of AT&T and a seminal thinker and writer, he created the Ohio Fellows Program. Les and Bob identified in each freshman class young men and women of exceptional promise. John Chandler, who later became president of Claremont College, Professor Ed Whan of the English department, Lynn Shostack, and others assisted in the program.

The goal of the Ohio Fellows was to identify unusually gifted students across all majors and areas of study and provide them with exposure to the world outside the university environment and those who shape that larger world. Some faculty considered it subversive and a diversion of our financial resources, even though it was entirely privately funded by the Mellon Foundation and the Mead Corporation.

It *was* subversive. The Ohio Plan sent students to meet personally with world-renowned leaders in fields ranging from photography to business and government to engineering. The plan tried to show the student that, whatever his passion, his goals should not be limited; that he should look further than the borders of Ohio and dare to aim high. The plan funded student books and plays and even purchased a ton of structural steel so that a student sculptor could have the experience of creating large-scale work. Today, the Ohio Fellows' vision lives on in North Carolina as the Center for Creative Leadership, a very influential training ground for leaders in all fields.

Frank Zammataro, an assistant director of admissions and also consultant to the Ohio Fellows Program, helped in the establishment of the program. Frank Bordinaro, Robert Fallon, Michael Schott, Jon Rotenberg, Robert Walter, and Richard Brown are six of many Ohio Fellows who are successful business leaders today.

Another of Les Rollins's contributions to Ohio University was his identification and assistance in recruiting unusually bright young graduates from Harvard and other prestigious schools to join our administrative team. Michael Long, Walker Lewis, John Hodges, John Sevier, Mason Morfit, John Chandler, Janis Somerville, and William Haines were placed in various junior administrative posts, primarily within the areas reporting to Vice President Dr. James Whalen.

JIM WHALEN, who had headed the European program for the University of Maryland, was recruited in 1964 to become the first director of our Center for Psychological Services and associate professor of Psychology. Jim had received his doctorate in psychology at Pennsylvania State University. He had an extraordinary ability to win the loyalty and cooperation of his associates and he proved to be very popular with the students. When Dean of Students William Butler left to become a vice president of the University of Miami, I quickly replaced him with Jim Whalen.

The office had been structured with a dean of men and a dean of women, with little coordination between the two mini-empires. As the student body became more politically active, pushing for the elimination of women's hours and for coed dormitories and beer on campus, it became clear that we needed to strengthen and restructure our student-affairs office. The expanded office soon included admissions, financial aid, placement, health services, counseling and student personnel. As Jim demonstrated increasing competence and leadership, I appointed him vice president for administrative affairs and placed more and more functions under him, including student residence life, food services, the physical plant, and housing development. Soon after, he was promoted to executive vice president.

I needed action-oriented young people in my administration because we were in a hurry to bring about change. Jim Whalen, like Les Rollins, had unusual talent for attracting and motivating young administrators. He deserves great credit for placing able men and women in key positions and developing a loyal, energetic, and hardworking team. Once or twice a week, I gathered the group around the circular table in my office and we traded ideas and plotted strategies. They were a great stimulus to me, but more importantly they proved to be a strong motivating force among students. Several had offices on the second floor of Tupper Hall and soon became known as the Upper Tupper group. To some faculty and administrators, they were a threat—alleged to be "spies for the president." But that group of young administrators—all of whom are holding top-level positions today—contributed much to the sense of excitement and expectation that characterized Ohio University in the decade of the 1960s.

Joining Michael Long, Bill Haines, and Janis Somerville were Jim Henderson (the vice president for finance at Case Western Reserve University), Jesse Arnelle, the All-America football and basketball star at Penn State who worked effectively with black students (today a leading lawyer in San Francisco and chairman of the board of trustees at Penn State), and Bob Hynes (now director of residence and campus auxiliaries at Ohio University).

SOUND MIND/SOUND BODY

Athletic competition has always been important in the State of Ohio and at Ohio University. A former athlete myself, I believe that the teams representing a university are important in developing morale—

student, community, and alumni. In my experience, students who excel in academics as well as in athletics often become outstanding leaders.

Having played varsity baseball in college and having been since early childhood a fan of the Chicago Cubs, I was delighted by two events in the first few weeks on the job at Athens. Ohio defeated Ohio State in baseball by the lopsided score of 18–0; and I met Frank Baumholtz. I had not realized that the graceful Chicago Cub left fielder, who had been one of my heroes, not only was an alumnus of Ohio University but had been one of our greatest athletes. Frank has served as a trustee, chairman of the board, and a member of the Ohio University Foundation Board. Other pleasant surprises were that Coach Bill Hess's football team was invited to play in the Sun Bowl in Texas in December 1962 and our basketball team, led by Coach Jim Synder, defeated Iowa 62–54.

In June 1963, Brandon Grover, director of athletics, was scheduled to retire at the age of sixty-five. I then turned my attention to recruiting an athletic director who could establish Ohio athletics on a respectable national level. I did not have in mind becoming a "big time" power; that would have been impossible. I *did* want us to schedule well-known, prestigious institutions that would enhance our national visibility. This would be one more step in developing pride in Ohio University among alumni, students, and faculty.

I had heard about Bill Rohr, the basketball coach at Northwestern. Bill had built a successful program, but even more significant to me was his reputation among his peers as a solid, deeply religious, and personable human being. Marion and I invited Mary Ellen and Bill to the campus and we immediately established a rapport with them. Bill, having completed his most successful recruiting season at Northwestern, was reluctant to abandon his team, but after considerable efforts on our part, he and Mary Ellen accepted our invitation to join us at Ohio.

John Galbreath arranged a reception at his spectacular Darby Dan Farm, south of Columbus, to introduce Bill to the press. A large entourage of newspaper and television reporters was on hand, not only to meet Ohio's new athletic director but to take a peek at John's great horse Chateaugay, fresh off his triumphs in the Kentucky Derby and Belmont. Columbus Dispatch Sports Editor Paul Hornung—an Ohio State Buckeye enthusiast—wrote a glowing account of the press conference, concluding with a surprise tribute: "With a president who knows the names of the school's athletes and their records, who may be found almost in the huddle in football practice or on the basketball court, and who has the obvious dedication to excellence in athletes . . . with an athletic director who has proven quality and equal intense desire to move the school's athletic program ahead . . . and with a first-rate staff of coaches . . . the Bobcats obviously have every chance to make it."

In every way, Bill Rohr measured up to my expectations. Because of his national reputation, he was able to schedule football games with Tulane, Penn State, Maryland, Kentucky, Purdue, Kansas, Minnesota, Boston College, and others outside our conference. In basketball he scheduled games with Northwestern, Purdue, Minnesota, Michigan, and Indiana, all in the 1966/67 season. That year, I joked with him that we might win the Big Ten championship.

The 1963/64 basketball team, with a record of twenty-one wins to six losses, advanced to the finals of the NCAA Mid-East regionals. Along the way, Coach Snyder's team defeated Wisconsin, Louisville, and Kentucky (ranked fourth in the nation) by a score of 85–69. Sports Information Director Frank Morgan reported that "the 1963/64 team enjoyed the greatest season in the 57-year history of Ohio basketball." The Bobcats lost in the Mid-East finals to a great Michigan team that finished third in the national championships that year.

Several Ohio University athletes were recognized with All-America status. Elmore Banton won the NCAA championship in cross-country in 1964 and appeared in *Track and Field* magazine as athlete of the year. Darnell Mitchell, 1965, and Barry Sugden, 1964, were All-America in track; Harry Houska, 1964, having won a national championship in wrestling, was another All-American. John Frick, 1966, football, and John Eastman, 1965, soccer, gained similar distinction. In 1968, basketball player Wayne Young won Academic All-America honors. Harry Houska, who now coaches the Ohio wrestling team, won the gold medal in the Pan-American games, and in 1967 competed in the world championships in India. In 1968, the Bobcats football team (record 10 and 0) ranked fifteenth nationally and was invited to the Tangerine Bowl in Florida. In that game, basketball coach Jim Snyder's son, Todd, caught eleven passes for 214 yards, scored three touchdowns, and returned a kick-off for 88 yards.

The golf team, under Coach Kermit Blosser, won the Mid-American Conference championship in thirteen of fifteen years. In the 1960s Ohio athletic teams won the Mid-American Conference All Sports trophy in seven of nine years and eighteen team conference championships. Baseball coach Bob Wren (regular season record, 27 and 1 in 1965) developed several players who signed major league contracts. The most outstanding was Mike Schmidt, who won eight league home-run titles and, in 1995, was inducted into the Baseball Hall of Fame at Cooperstown. His teammate Joe Carbone is Ohio's baseball coach today. In the 1960s six Ohio baseball players were All-America and twenty-one signed professional contracts, six of whom made it to the major leagues.

There were other great performances: When the Convocation Center was dedicated in 1968, the Ohio basketball Bobcats defeated Indiana by a score of 80–70. In 1967, the football team defeated Kansas 35–15. And in the fall of 1969, Jim Snyder's basketball team began the season with seven victories, including wins over Purdue, Ohio State, Northwestern, and Indiana. The Bobcats climbed from tenth to fifth place nationally in the Associated Press poll and from twelfth to ninth place in the United Press/International Poll.

Having attended an Ivy League university, I am conditioned to be impressed by athletes who have academic talent. In my early years in the dean's office at Harvard Business School, I visited several colleges and universities every year to interview prospective students. One of my favorite stops was Princeton University, which in the 1950s had excellent athletic teams and outstanding scholar athletes. Charlie Caldwell, the football coach, was exceptionally good at recruiting players with superior academic records. Several of his football stars attended the Harvard Business School—Dick Kazmaier, George Sella, Dick Pivirotto, and George Chandler. Dick Kazmaier (one of Princeton's all-time great running backs, who won the Heisman Trophy in his senior year and was featured on the cover of *Time* magazine) was coached by Ohio's Bob Wren at Maumee High School. Dick turned down an opportunity to play professional football with the Chicago Bears, opting to attend the Harvard Business School. Dick and his wife, Patti, continue to be among our closest friends, and I served for several years on the advisory board of Kazmaier Associates. All of Caldwell's scholar athletes who attended Harvard Business School went on to lead business corporations. They demonstrated my belief that competitive athletics and a sound academic background contribute to leadership ability.

I certainly do believe this—that athletic competition helps to develop leaders. It seems to me that Americans are becoming increasingly self-centered—the "what's in it for me" syndrome. Our society borders on becoming splintered into interest groups each fighting for entitlements that allow each individual to pursue his or her own interests without the inconvenience of cooperative and shared concerns. In collegiate athletics, "teamwork" and "loyalty to teammates" is essential. A winning season requires each player to give up ego in the interests of the team. It has been proven many times that a team with spirit, harmony, and shared goals can outplay a collection of uncoordinated individual stars. A successful leader in any enterprise must create a similar environment of cooperation and goal sharing. The scholar-athletes I have described learned this lesson at an early age in athletic competition.

After I was discharged from the navy in 1946, as noted earlier, I returned to Brown University to complete my undergraduate degree, and working in the admissions office. While there, I met Joe Paterno, who is now the revered football coach at Penn State. Joe was applying to Brown. Bill Rohr and I arranged two games with the nationally ranked Nittany Lions squad, and Joe, being a consummate gentleman, did not run up the score on our Bobcat team.

The experience at Penn State triggered my thinking about the Mid-American Conference in which we competed. I was not altogether happy with the institutions represented in the conference. I took the lead in asking Marshall University to drop out of the conference after recruiting violations and the use of federal money to underwrite football scholarships. I thought about the possibility of creating a new conference with Ohio, Miami, and Bowling Green—leaving the Mid-American and inviting such universities as Vanderbilt, West Virginia, Pittsburgh, and William and Mary to form a new conference. I had hoped that we could associate in athletics with better-known universities, but aside from conversations with Bill Rohr, Bill Hess, and Jim Snyder, I did not carry that idea any further.

CHAPTER 4

The Core of the University—the Faculty

I CAN SPEAK glowingly of the faculty of Ohio University. From my first day on campus, I was impressed with their quality and dedication. We had a solid corps of faculty members committed to teaching and devoted to the university. Marion and I continue to stay in touch with several faculty families even though we have been away from Ohio for more than twenty-five years. There were, of course, some young firebrands on the fringe who continually pushed for unionization, but they never captured the central core of the faculty.

In his oral-history memoirs, John Baker expressed his concern that the standards for granting tenure to faculty members were not stringent enough. Having also been involved in Harvard's established policy of "up or out" (if one did not qualify for tenure at Harvard, the faculty member needed to look for opportunities elsewhere), I believed that we should carefully review our procedures for granting tenure. Many universities were placing too much emphasis on published research. I felt that we should include in our procedures ways of evaluating classroom teaching, counseling of students, and service on behalf of the university. I asked the deans and department chairmen to take a fresh look at our policies and standards of promotion.

Although we made great progress in pushing up faculty salaries, I would like to have rewarded our outstanding professors even more. I was concerned that in salary administration we seemed to be granting equal, albeit modest, increases to every individual. I suggested to the deans that they consider a "merit" salary policy. I asked them to recommend to me one-third of their faculty members for substantial increases, one-third for modest increases, and one-third for no increase. I was met with resistance from several of the deans. Some said, "I just cannot make that evaluation. I am willing to forgo an increase myself, but I insist upon giving all faculty members the same percentage raise. After all, all faculty salaries are still too low." Other deans did cooperate and applied more exacting measures of performance for faculty members in their departments and colleges. Much as I tried, we never accomplished a more sophisticated procedure in salary administration during my years at Ohio.

When I arrived in 1962, I was surprised that we did not have a faculty senate that would enable greater faculty participation in academic decision making. There had been in place since 1936 a Faculty Advisory Council but it had little responsibility for shaping academic policy. I discovered early on that the trustees had been cautioned by previous administrators not to give too much power to the faculty.

My position was that a university community consisted of at least five major entities: the faculty, the students, the trustees, the alumni, and the administration. Like the fingers of the hand, if all worked together, much could be accomplished. But if one finger was damaged or weak, a simple task such as buttoning one's collar was difficult, if not impossible. I believed that all of the elements in the university community should be strong and involved in decisions that concerned them.

It was not an easy task to persuade the trustees to establish and recognize a faculty senate. I spent many hours in one-on-one conversations with skeptical trustees trying to convince them that we would be a stronger university with more involvement by faculty through an established senate. The Faculty Senate was authorized by the trustees on November 17, 1964.

Perhaps it takes time for any group of people who have not had adequate representation to rise to the level expected of them. One of the disappointments during my tenure was that the senate did not address major issues that needed faculty input—the curriculum, the academic calendar, promotion and research policies, admissions policy, degree requirements, and so forth. Instead, their recommendations consisted of procedural and contractual issues concerning the faculty handbook, salaries, and fringe benefits. In his book *The Decade of the University*,* Meno Lovenstein observed, "Perhaps the most unfortunate consequence was that the traditional focus on procedures, even preoccupation with them, diverted the faculty from making imaginative contributions to the conception of Ohio University, contributions more appropriate to their calling and their talents."

On two occasions, I had to refuse to transmit letters of protest to the trustees or the board of regents because I felt the senate representatives had not done sufficient analysis of the issues involved, and their rigid positions would merely jeopardize the senate's reputation with the trustees or the regents. Happily, the Faculty Senate has matured with time.

To stimulate faculty research and publications, in 1963 we created the Ohio University Press, with Professor Taylor Culbert as its first president. Together, we appointed a distinguished group of faculty as members of the advisory board: Paul Kendall, William Snyder, Claude Kantner, Carl Shermer, John Cady, Edward Stone, George Hill, and William Huntsman. Within a few months, we recruited as director Cecil Hemley, a well-known novelist, editor, and poet, who while with the distinguished publishing firm of Farrar, Straus, and

---

* *The Decade of the University: Ohio University and the Alden Years* (Ohio: Ohio University Press, 1971).

Cudahy, cofounded the Noonday Press. In its first two years, the Press published twelve high-quality volumes that received critical approval in reviews. In 1968/69 fifteen books were published, followed by twenty in 1970. The Press published the complete works of Robert Browning under the general editorship of Professor Roma King.

We were blessed with having several exceptionally fine writers on the faculty. Rainer Schulte, assistant professor of English, created *Mundus Artium,* a bilingual journal of international literature and the arts of the world. Hollis Summers became nationally known for his poetry. Paul Kendall received acclaim for his biography *Richard the Third* and was selected as the first regents' professor, a chair established by the board of regents to recognize distinguished professors within the state universities and to assist in attracting eminent faculty from outside of Ohio. The university became known for its creative writers, and we were able to attract an outstanding group of resident writers, among them Daniel Keyes, Walter Tevis, Jack Matthews, and Norman Schmidt.

David Hostetler has become well-known for his unique sculptures. We became good friends, and I tried to help him by introducing him to Yousuf Karsh, Arthur Harris, and Foster Harmon, who helped assist him in gaining national visibility. His wife, Susan, is a genius in promoting David's work. I am happy I bought two of his pieces early on: they have increased in value like Intel or Microsoft stock.

In 1967, we recruited Professor Alonzo Hamby to the Department of History. Hamby is well-known nationally, particularly for his acclaimed books on Harry Truman. Several others who joined the faculty in the 1960s were eventually designated distinguished professor, as was Hamby: Jacobo Rapaport, Raymond Lane, and Roger Finlay in physics, Jack Matthews and Roma King in English, Wai-Kai Chen in engineering, Lowell Galloway and Richard Vedder in economics, Guido Stempel in journalism, and John Gaddis in history.

By 1969, approximately 75 percent of our faculty had been recruited during my tenure. Our deans and department chairmen did an outstanding job in recruiting talent from leading universities throughout the nation and in providing them with an environment favorable to their development as teachers and scholars.

I was constantly on the lookout for potential administrative talent among our faculty. In the mid-1960s, I had observed Assistant Professor William Holmes teaching an English III course on the university's television station. The next morning I appeared in his office to ask him if he had ever considered a career in university administration. Not too many months later, I appointed him director of our summer school session. Apparently he enjoyed the role, because he applied to the American Council on Higher Education for a one-year fellowship/internship with a university president of his choice. I was delighted that he chose to spend the year in close working relationship with me.

Professor Nicholas Dinos, who joined the faculty in 1966, was selected Ohio Professor of the Year in 1996 from a pool of twenty-five nominees representing twenty-one Ohio colleges. The award, sponsored by the Council for Advancement and Support of Teaching, recognizes each year individuals who bring "extraordinary dedication and scholarly approach to undergraduate teaching, as well as exceptional service to the students, institution, community, and profession." Before he came to Ohio, Professor Dinos worked for the Atomic Energy Division of DuPont, creating heavy water, used in nuclear reactors. He also spent several years designing reactors for the company.

For many reasons, including the desire to stimulate the economy of the area, we moved to strengthen our research capability in engineering, chemistry, mathematics, and physics. The research program in nuclear physics had been a bold gamble since the earliest days of its development. The university took a major step forward toward establishing the research program when a small Cockcroft-Walton accelerator was purchased in 1960. The department chairman, Charles Randall, originally intended the accelerator for use in undergraduate teaching, but in 1962 he turned it over to a new faculty member,

Roger Finlay, for experimentation in nuclear physics. In 1963, our proposal to the National Science Foundation brought $52,000 in research funds.

In 1967, the U.S. Atomic Energy Commission announced that an eight-million-volt tandem electrostatic accelerator would be made available. Twelve universities submitted proposals. We were eager to win out in the competition because the tandem accelerator would provide a basic tool for fundamental research in nuclear physics, both on the experimental and theoretical level. It would provide a one-hundredfold increase in capability over the smaller accelerator then in use. Big problem: a million dollars would be required to match the funds made available by the Atomic Energy Commission. We did not have it in our budget or in our capital appropriation from the state. Once again, I called upon my friend Stanley Mechem, president pro-tem of the Ohio Senate. I broached the subject of a special line-item appropriation and used my best efforts to describe how important the accelerator would be, not only to university research but toward building a viable economic base in southeastern Ohio. As often was the case, Stanley Mechem fully supported our efforts by quietly penciling in an additional one million dollars to our line-item capital appropriations. Shortly after the announcement of the AEC award, we received an additional $563,000 from the National Science Foundation to aid development in the entire physics area. Soon we were digging underground to build the facility to house the accelerator. The building was appropriately named for Distinguished Professor of Physics John E. Edwards. In October 1965, the Standard Oil Company of Ohio contributed a $200,000 satellite tracking system, which we installed on "Radar Hill" to supplement the resources placed there in 1963 to enable a seven-man team of faculty members to track the moon and satellites. The team, under the direction of Professor Richard McFarland, invited electrical engineering students to participate in the research activities. We invited the student editor of the *Post,* Joe Eszterhas, to join us on the plane to Cleveland and participate in the luncheon celebration with the executives at Sohio. Unusual for a student editor, Joe expressed his enthusiastic support in an ensuing editorial: "Ohio University has just scored another big victory. First there was Ike's visit, and then Beasley's gift [*sic*] and then Morton's endowment. And now another president, Charles Spahr of Sohio, had just announced that Sohio has given $200,000 worth of satellite tracking equipment to Ohio University. Moments before, we had become the owners of the world's only privately operated satellite tracking station."

CHAPTER **5**

The Changing of the Guard

THE UNIVERSITY WAS GROWING, and not only in numbers of students; the plant was growing, too. In June 1963, Ohio University's land holdings were increased by 65 percent when the legislature transferred to the university 235 acres of land from the Athens State Mental Hospital in exchange for the university farm at Hebardsville. Adjacent to the West Green, this acquisition would be used for additional dormitories, engineering buildings, and recreational facilities. In 1967, Otis Simpson, vice president and plant manager of the Royal McBee Corporation, contributed to the Ohio University Fund a complex of five buildings, including two large manufacturing plants, and ten acres of land adjacent to the campus. The gift was valued at between $4 and $5 million. Shortly thereafter, the U.S. Post Office building located in the middle of the campus was declared surplus when plans were made to build a new structure across town. When the building was offered to the university, the mayor of Athens claimed that the city had priority rights to the building and would give up its "claim" only if the university would give the city $400,000 or two acres of its land holdings. I asked the mayor to put his proposal in writing, which I then sent to Washington. The General Services Administration ruled the city's claim "out of order" and immediately transferred the old post office to Ohio University.

There could not be a successful expansion of the whole university —students, faculty, and physical plant—without a reorganization of the institution. During his last two years as president, John Baker was required to be off campus frequently. In his absence, a triumvirate consisting of Brandon Grover, Paul O'Brien, and Luverne Lausche administered the university. Brandon, known as "Butch" Grover, carried the title of assistant to the president as well as director of athletics. Paul O'Brien was the treasurer and chief financial officer, and Luverne Lausche was business manager. All three men were likable and completely devoted to the university. Lausche frequently strolled into my office unannounced, smoking a small cheroot, wearing his hat tilted back on his head, put his legs up on my table, and proceeded to chat. Paul was quiet, rather shy, and played his financial cards close to his chest. Grover, who had many close friends on Court Street, did not appear often in my office but was unusually polite and always addressed me as Mr. President.

When I arrived, there were in place three assistants to the president. There were no vice presidents, and there was no faculty organ of any importance. Overall, there was little coordination. The only group that appeared really administrative were the deans of the individual colleges, who ran their areas as they saw fit and with little outside interference.

Besides Brandon Grover, I inherited as assistants to the president Tom Smith and Marty Hecht. Smith, in charge of the summer school, had risen through the Department of Physics. He was respected by the faculty as an academic peer and a conscientious and deliberate leader. In fall 1962, I appointed him to the university's first vice presidency, that of academic affairs.

Marty Hecht had been a general assistant to John Baker. An Ohio alumnus, alumni secretary, and a long-time resident of Athens, Marty's personal knowledge of the state, the community, and the campus was extensive. He was completely dedicated and loyal to the university's welfare. I assigned to him the responsibility for carrying out university involvement in area development. Although I knew that I was putting him on the firing line and that he would encounter a goodly share of resistance in the state and local community, I was impressed with his efficiency and energy and his ability to push things through. As time went on, I gave Marty Hecht additional responsibility, in 1965 appointing him vice president in charge of university development, responsible for private and public fund-raising, university publications, public relations, and the aviation department, in addition to area development.

Other changes included, in 1967, Jack Ellis's being appointed executive director of the Alumni Association. Dean Ed Taylor of the College of Engineering and Technology reached retirement age and was replaced by Robert Savage, who had joined the university in 1964 from his position as vice president of research and engineering at the North American Coal Company. Before that he had been superintendent of engineering at the Battelle Memorial Institute and a professor of chemical engineering at the Case Institute. Dean Al Gubitz, who had led the development of the branch campus program, retired and was replaced by Professor Ed Penson of the College of Communication.

Dean Rush Elliott of the College of Arts and Sciences developed an enormous following among alumni physicians, most of whom had been encouraged by Rush Elliott to pursue medical careers. When he returned to teaching in 1966, a professorship was named in his honor, and Professor George Klare replaced him as dean.

Business and Financial Affairs

Although I had graduated from the Harvard Business School and as associate dean had overall responsibility for the budget and day-to-day financial administration, I discovered that it was almost impossible to get a grip around the finances of Ohio University. The university had been administered very conservatively; each dean had a tight budget, and there were a number of "reserves" set up for any eventuality. Over the years Ohio University had not been generously supported by the state. There had been many lean years, and the financial planning and administration reflected the caution that resulted.

As our student population grew, funding from the state became more generous. We also began to attract a substantial number of federal grants. Gifts from alumni, foundations, and corporations increased steadily. I became more and more frustrated by the lack of financial information, especially when planning annual budgets. I looked outside the university for a sophisticated Harvard Business School–trained financial executive. I was turned down by Dick Lindgren, who held a senior position in financial planning at the Ford Motor Company, and by Bob Vance, from California. Finally, I was able to recruit another experienced Harvard Business School graduate, Bill Converse. Bill lasted less than a year. He could not win the cooperation of the deeply entrenched business manager and treasurer.

Paul O'Brien, whose health had been deteriorating, gracefully accepted in 1966 the position of secretary of the board of trustees. Facing a $95 million construction program, including dormitories, a new library, the space arts building, the mathematics and science complex, and the Convocation Center, the task of overseeing these projects would be more than a full-time job. Luverne Lausche was asked to step into the role of university architect and director of engineering and planning. In addition, Alan Geiger, now secretary to the board of trustees, did a superb job in ensuring that new building construction was consistent with specified university architectural design. I then placed the entire financial and business management organization under James Whalen and appointed him executive vice president.

Academic Vice President Tom Smith was given the title of provost, and Robert Savage added to his responsibilities the role of vice president for research and industrial liaison.

The College of Communication

Ohio University was known for its outstanding School of Journalism. Over the years the school had educated several prominent reporters and editors. The school had been placed administratively under the College of Commerce, soon to become the College of Business Administration. Under the jurisdiction of the College of Fine Arts were the School of Hearing and Speech Sciences, the School of Interpersonal Communication, and the School of Radio and Television. When funding became available to construct a major building that could house the faculty and facilities of the various schools, I saw an opportunity to combine all of these entities into a College of Communication.

I recruited the director of McGraw-Hill World News, John Wilhelm, to become the director of the School of Journalism and the first dean of the new college. John was reluctant at first. "I don't have a Ph.D.," he said. "That's exactly why I want you," I replied. I wanted him to establish a practical, "real world" program in journalism, television, radio, and speech that would include summer internships and exposure of students to leading practitioners in those fields. John was attracted by the combination of the various schools under a College of Communication. "Schools of Journalism," he said, "have in the past been restricted to print journalism. When radio and television came along, they tended to fall into the Speech Department. At many universities this caused a split between the School of Journalism and the Speech Department and resulted in confusion and difficulty for the students."

The $4.1 million radio-television building housed the College of Communication, and soon a new Ph.D. program in mass communication was established. Several prominent communicators—Walter Cronkite, David Brinkley, Martin Agronsky, James Reston, and Marshall McLuhan among them—came to the campus to meet with students. Practical, day-to-day insights into the broadcasting industry were given by Bob Coe, who was recruited from his position as vice president of ABC-TV. Clarence Page, Matt Lauer, Joe Eszterhas, and Andy Alexander are today perhaps the best-known among the many former Ohio University students in the communication field.

John Wilhelm was instrumental in bringing to Ohio University in 1981 a remarkable collection owned by war correspondent, journalist, and author Cornelius Ryan. The collection, housed in Alden Library, includes manuscripts, maps, and photographs from World War II. Wilhelm and Ryan had served together as reporters in the European theater of combat. Cornelius Ryan is well known for his books *The Longest Day, The Last Battle,* and *A Bridge Too Far.*

The College of Fine Arts

Earl Seigfred, dean of the College of Fine Arts, was scheduled to retire soon after the new Space Arts building was completed. The new building, appropriately named for Dean Seigfred, housed the School of Painting and Allied Arts and the School of Architecture. It contained classrooms, photographic studios and dark rooms, an art gallery, a fine arts library, and a 225-seat auditorium. A faculty committee was established to identify, screen, and recruit a successor to Dean Seigfred. I was impressed with the professionalism of their nationwide search and the final candidate they recommended—Jack Morrison.

Jack Morrison was a well-known professor and administrator in the Theater Department at UCLA. When I interviewed him, I knew that we had found our new dean. And with his arrival on the Athens campus, we discovered an extra dividend in his wife, Jean Cagney Morrison. Jean had a vivacious personality and a contagious sense of humor. She was the younger sister of the famous movie actor Jimmy Cagney.

Jean was one of the most upbeat, optimistic persons I have ever met. Even when, some years later, she became seriously ill, I never heard her complain or appear discouraged. While Jack was recruiting faculty members and strengthening an already impressive College of Fine Arts, Jean hosted a local radio program, *Good News*. Every day she brought to her listeners stories of people of goodwill, neighborliness, and courage. Even in the darkest hours of student and faculty unrest in the late 1960s, Jean brought cheer to the Athens community. Our daughter, Anne, and the Morrisons' daughter, Mary Anne, became close friends, rode horses together, and to this day are each other's closest friend and confidante.

Jean and her brother Jimmy Cagney had summer homes on Martha's Vineyard. Unlike his screen image, Jim was a shy, almost reclusive individual who rarely accepted social invitations. We were pleased that he visited our homes in Ohio and Martha's Vineyard and invited us to sail with him on his Vineyard boat. He explained his reluctance to appear in public with a story from his early acting years. Upon his return by ship from Europe, he was walking down the dock in New York when an over-eager fan grabbed his necktie. As the knot tightened around his neck, Jim choked and almost fainted. The experience left him wary of strangers and groups of people.

Shortly after our family left Ohio to return to Boston (see chapter 10) the Morrisons returned to California. Jack and Jean eventually divorced, and Jean developed cancer. These setbacks did nothing to change her sunny disposition. She continued to bring cheer to every person who met her.

The College of Business Administration

Having come to Ohio from a business school whose objective was to train young men and women for leadership positions, I was concerned by the vocation-oriented, "trade school" thrust of the College of Commerce. It seemed to me that the curriculum had not changed since the school's inception in 1936. Lumped into the college were the Departments of Secretarial Studies, Home Economics, Agricultural Studies, and Accounting. I put pressure on Dean Paul Noble to develop a school that would prepare students for leadership positions rather than simply opening-level job opportunities. As a first step, we changed the name of the college to the College of Business Administration.

To provide stimulation and ideas from the "real world" of business, we created a visiting committee, which included among others Edward Hanley, the president of Allegheny Ludlum Steel Corporation; William Sneath, president of Union Carbide; Donald Power, chairman of General Telephone and Electronics Company; Thomas McCabe, president of Scott Paper; Robert Haigh, vice president of Standard Oil of Ohio; Warren McClure, publisher of the Burlington *Free Press*; George Putnam, chairman of the Putnam Funds; and Professor Georges Doriot of the Harvard Business School.

Dean Noble, a genial and well-liked person, was put in an almost impossible position. When he attempted to phase out secretarial studies, his faculty voted him down. The committee appointed to revise the business curriculum had concluded that everything was just fine and needed no alteration. Noble had recruited a bright, young faculty member from Northwestern, Harry Evarts, who wrote a report offering an alternate plan.

When Paul Noble in frustration left to accept a position in New York, I appointed Harry Evarts as acting dean. Evarts was not liked by the entrenched faculty; nine promptly resigned. The university was shocked. Fortunately, Harry was supported by the editor of the student newspaper, Joe Eszterhas. Quoting from the nationally published *Danforth Report,* Joe opined that "'bad teaching is a major problem, and it is important to emphasize that no college, not even the most prestigious, has escaped it.' The problem here has diminished with each year of President Alden's administration. New deans with new ideas, like Business Administration's Harry Evarts, unafraid to put their ideas into practice even at the cost of personal unpopularity, have done much to help." To digress a moment, Joe Eszterhas was no doubt the most talented, sophisticated editor of the *Post* during my tenure. He understood what we were trying to accomplish, and his editorials were balanced and supportive in contrast to those of editors in my last two years at Ohio. Today, Joe is widely known and sought after as a screenwriter in Hollywood. Following his box-office smash success with *Basic Instinct,* featuring actress Sharon Stone, he has been well rewarded. In one of his columns, he quoted from a speech I made at the Academy of Management in New York City: "To stimulate creative approaches to teaching, a college president must probe, needle and energize people. . . . Young faculty members must be given plenty of running room. They must not be stifled by well-entrenched and powerful faculty members. To borrow an expression from football, the president sometimes serves as a 'blocking back' when he sees exciting programs emasculated in committee deliberations."

In the business college crisis, Evarts's hand was strengthened as faculty members were brought in from outside the university. Richard French, recruited from a senior position in business, proved to be especially popular, both with students and his faculty colleagues. He added strength and credibility to the college. I supported Harry Evarts throughout the crisis and tried to bolster his tested morale in the face of abuse. In the next few months my faith was justified as the College of Business Administration moved ahead, and I formally appointed Evarts as dean of the college.

The Black Studies Institute

Although the issue of racial discrimination and social segregation was of concern before the 1960s, my tenure at Ohio coincided with a time when U.S. college campuses were both catalyst and laboratory for volatile social change and political turmoil sweeping the country. The Athens community was not much different from the rest of southern Ohio in its conservative attitude toward race relations.

Prior to 1960, the university had been slow to enforce its constitutional duty to integrate on-campus housing. Shortly after I arrived on campus, we adopted a policy of rooming students randomly, and in September 1962, we required all owners of off-campus rental units to comply with "Approved Housing Standards"—accepting student renters without regard to race, religion, or national origin.

In July 1963, I and several dozen other university presidents were invited to the White House to meet with President Kennedy on the issue of civil rights. It was clear that the federal government was stepping up its efforts to enforce federal laws on discrimination. Enforcing university regulations was not an easy matter. We discovered that several off-campus realtors had attempted to circumvent our requirements and we found it necessary to withdraw university approval from five landlords. A fraternity disregarded our nondiscrimination policy blatantly enough to have its charter revoked by the university's Committee for the Elimination of Discrimination in Student Organizations.

In early 1963, we hired Ohio University's first African-American professor, E. Curmie Price, to teach in our English department. By 1967 we had recruited seven more black faculty members, but I received turndowns from seven other prospects, reportedly because of the difficulty of obtaining satisfactory housing in the community.

In December 1963 more than two hundred students, faculty members, and townspeople formed the Athens Civil Rights Action Committee to help collect food, clothing, and other items to support voter registration projects in the South. Several civil rights leaders spoke on campus that year, including the secretary of the Southern Christian Leadership Conference, Rev. F. L. Shuttlesworth. He drew a large student-faculty audience. Among other black leaders, Carl Stokes, mayor of Cleveland, spoke warmly of the university's stance on civil rights, and Dick Gregory met in our home with several black students to discuss ways in which to improve our campus environment for minority students.

Black History Week became an established tradition as the university continued to help fund the visits of black activists, entertainers, and cultural groups focusing on African-American pride, contributions, and experiences in the United States. Black history and literature courses were introduced into the curricula of the History and English Departments.

As the civil rights movement gained momentum early in 1965, campus and community activity intensified. The Campus Affairs Committee approved a fund-raising effort in support of the civil rights march from Selma. More than a dozen Ohio University students went to Alabama to participate. When Martin Luther King, Jr. was assassinated in 1968, a campuswide memorial service was attended by more than four thousand students and faculty. I gave a lengthy tribute to the leader who had "exhilarated us all with his vision of a society based on love, justice and brotherhood."

Despite the university's public appreciation of racial issues, racial tension increased. Black students, led by student activist James Steele, formed the Student Action Coordination Committee to give black students a collective voice in university and community matters. In late 1968, a group of eighteen black students came to my office and presented a list of six demands that included the establishment of an Afro-cultural center, a black counseling program, and a black curriculum taught by black faculty members.

Black studies programs were being demanded by students on the West Coast and in the Ivy League, often accompanied by sit-ins or rioting, but at Ohio University black representatives met frequently with Executive Vice President Whalen, Provost Smith, Mike Long, and me. Ohio University was one of the first to establish a Black Studies Institute. Black students at Ohio University presented their demands in a dignified, constructive manner and did not link themselves with demands from other student leaders. I give much credit to black faculty members who worked closely with them—Ron Williams, Jim Barnes, and Jesse Arnelle. In late spring 1969, I authorized a commitment of $250,000 to fund the Black Studies Institute, beginning in the fall term.

CHAPTER **6**

Bringing in Resources

IN 1891, WILLIAM D. EMERSON, class of 1833, bequeathed $1,000 to the university as a permanent fund, the interest to be used as "a prize to the student or alumnus who produced the best original poem." *The Legal History of Ohio University* records no other private gifts in the 1890s or for most of the first half of the twentieth century. In 1946, John Baker launched the Ohio University Fund, enabling alumni and friends to make private gifts to the University, a pioneering effort among public universities in those days. During my years at Harvard Business School, I had been responsible for the Alumni Fund as well as the Corporate Associates program. To provide incentive for increased giving, I established various gift levels for which alumni making large contributions would be recognized. This practice is commonplace today, but it was an innovation in the 1950s.

I observed that private gifts to Ohio had totaled $279,987 in the 1960/61 academic year and I was convinced that we could find ways to increase the level of annual giving. We established the following categories: those who gave $500 or more became members of the 1804 Society; gifts of $250 or more qualified alumni for the Jacob Lindley Society; and $100 gifts merited Honor memberships. Names of contributors by category were published in the alumni magazine. Heartened by the response, we decided really to challenge alumni supporters by establishing the Trustees Academy, which recognized alumni whose gifts or pledges totaled $10,000. To encourage others to give at that level, Marion and I became the first members of the academy. We wanted to reward each member of the academy with a commemoration gift—one that could be discretely displayed but interesting enough to entice others to join. Phil David selected in New York a distinctive "Park Avenue milking stool." Visitors to our home inevitably asked about the unique little seat in front of our fireplace. We told them it was our most expensive piece of furniture. Even the student body caught the spirit of giving. At the June 1962 graduation exercises, the senior class president, Douglas Dunkle, started a tradition by presenting a $2,000 gift to the Ohio University Fund from his classmates.

In 1962/63 private giving had risen to $1,410,470, and by 1968 the Ohio University Fund was receiving $3 million in contributions and pledges. Generous support from alumni, business corporations, and foundations did indeed enable us "to blend the best in private and public education." During graduation ceremonies, held in the sweltering heat of the Campus Green, I would lose almost five pounds under my academic robes shaking hands with four thousand graduates, greeting parents, and attending the receptions following the ceremonies. Marion and I would return to 29 Park Place,* change into old clothes or pajamas, lie on the soft living-room rug, and listen to records of Frank Sinatra, Glenn Miller, Tommy Dorsey, or Count Basie. Little did we know that alumnus Richard Linke and

---

*Ohio University, like other universities, has maintained a tradition of providing a house for the president on its main campus. This arrangement, for the most part, is an excellent way for the president and the university community to stay in close touch.

Professor William Fenzel sat on Bill's side porch next door listening through the open porch door to our music as well. Dick later rewarded us by sending a wonderful collection of vintage 1940s–1950s records. In April 1963, Linke, a successful personal manager for well-known Hollywood personalities, brought to the campus Andy Griffith and several other stars for a performance to establish the Richard O. Linke Scholarship program. The following fall, Dick was honored at homecoming.

The CBS network featured in 1964 a television program called *Alumni Fun*. Ohio alumni John Galbreath (1920), bandleader Sammy Kaye (1932), and *Popular Science* magazine executive vice president John Whiting (1936) teamed up to defeat the University of Missouri, 650 to 550, and won $2,000 in scholarship funds for the university. During the 1960s and in the decades since then, many alumni have made substantial gifts to the university, but the most remarkable contribution in my early years at Ohio was made by a native of Athens, a member of the class of 1898. Charlie O'Bleness was a legend in Athens well before I arrived on the scene. For many years he had been president of the Athens National Bank and was rumored to have amassed a considerable amount of money. Apparently, he had saved it all, because he was the most frugal person I ever met. He lived alone in a tiny, not very tidy, second-floor apartment, surrounded by newspapers and cheap, worn furniture. He liked to play golf occasionally, and it was rumored that after his shower at the Athens Country Club, he would dry himself with paper towels to save the dime charged for a cloth towel. John Baker had advised me, "If you play your cards right, and if you and Marion will court Charlie O'Bleness, you might get $5,000 out of him for the university." I accepted the challenge and vowed that we would do even better.

We invited Charlie to several dinner parties, especially when we were entertaining a well-known visitor. Bob Hope came to Athens in May 1963 to head a benefit for the library. We seated Charlie immediately next to Bob Hope, but he missed most of the banter and Hope's humor because of his hearing problem. Late in the dinner, he turned to Bob and asked in his reedy, high-pitched voice, "Young man, where do you make your home?" Without skipping a beat, Hope replied, "On American Airlines."

After entertaining Charlie on many such special occasions, Marion and I decided that it was time to make our pitch to him. We invited him to join us alone for dinner. Marion had arranged lovely hors d'oeuvres to go along with strong drinks and a beautiful dinner. After he had eaten, Charlie often picked his teeth with a well-worn toothpick. He had set it down on his plate when dessert was being served, and the bus boy started to carry the plate away. "Just a minute, young man. I have further use for that toothpick," said Charlie.

We began to get nervous about our planned proposals as we moved into the living room. Without waiting too long, I presented what I often called my "financial plate of hors d'oeuvres"—a building with the donor's name on it, scholarship grants, faculty research funds, or an endowed professorship. Charlie immediately latched on to the idea of a professorship that would be named for him in perpetuity. "Boy! What the fellas at the Buckeye Cafeteria would think of that," he exclaimed. "By the way, how much would that cost?" I told him $500,000. Charlie turned white, then red, and didn't say anything for what seemed like several minutes. We worried that we might lose him right there in our living room. Then he burst out with, "By God! I'm going to do it."

The report in the *Athens Messenger* the next day announcing Charlie O'Bleness's first major gift made a page-one headline. The community was stunned. That gift changed Charlie's life. The reputed tightwad was greeted with warmth on the streets of Athens. He bought a new wardrobe and a car. The biggest shock was yet to come. At the age of eighty, he proposed to and married the woman who had been his secretary for most of his career at the bank. They bought and moved into a spacious house in the most attractive Athens neighborhood. The local joke was that they wanted to have enough room for children.

Charlie was not a reckless driver, but the Athens police issued an order forbidding the eighty-three-year-old to drive. We assigned a financial-aid student to chauffeur the O'Blenesses when they needed to leave their home. From time to time, however, Charlie would sneak out and drive the car himself. Once he was stopped by a policeman who took over the steering wheel and drove Charlie home. When he attempted to drive the car into the narrow entrance of the garage, he had difficulty. Charlie urged the policeman to get out of the car, took over the steering wheel, and cruised into the garage as smoothly as a professional driver.

Two or three years after his gift to the university, Charlie responded to appeals from the local hospital by making a gift of $750,000. The Sheltering Arms Hospital was renamed the Charles O'Bleness Hospital. I have often said that one of the great satisfactions in raising money is the joy that giving can bring to the donor. Charles O'Bleness's life was completely changed after his gift to Ohio university. It brought him respect, confidence, pleasure, and a completely new lifestyle.

Over the years I have had the privilege of associating with many public-spirited, generous supporters of various fund-raising efforts: Paul and Beth Stocker, John Galbreath, Ed Kennedy, Will Konneker, George Mathews, Warren Alpert, Tom Lee, Shoichiro Toyoda, Junichi Murata, Akio Morita, Tony Kobayashi, Tom Watson, Dick Salomon, Art Joukowsky, Gordon Cadwgan, Henry Sharpe—to name just a few. Paul Stocker, a trustee throughout my tenure, gave stock in his company totaling more than $24.5 million. Paul and his wife, Beth, demonstrated again and again their loyalty to Ohio University. All of these friends have inspired me to give as generously as possible to the annual gift and endowment funds of our colleges and the nonprofit institutions on whose boards I serve. One of my mentors, Henry Wriston, when he was president of Brown University, defined the financial obligations of a trustee: "Give ... get ... or get out."

Every fund-raiser has a story or two about promised gifts that didn't materialize. I recall reading some years ago about the elderly couple in the Pacific Northwest who had promised "to leave a sub-

stantial sum" to a small liberal arts college. For years they were lav-
ishly entertained by the president and appeared frequently at college
functions. When the couple finally died in their late eighties, they left
no will, no financial resources, and no written record of their promise
to the college.

My two experiences with "lost gifts" are different but are, perhaps,
worth telling: In 1964, then chairman of our board of trustees, Fred
Johnson, and I traveled to Lexington, Kentucky, to watch our basketball team play the University of Kentucky in an NCAA regional
game. We upset the Wildcats 85 to 69, which was impressive, but we
were even more impressed with the facility in which the game was
played. Our basketball gymnasium seated fewer than four thousand
for a student body of ten thousand, soon to grow to eighteen thousand on the main campus. Commencement exercises were held outdoors on the College Green, because no indoor facility could contain
the graduating seniors, parents, and well-wishers. The student newspaper complained that without an auditorium large enough to meet
financial guarantees, we could not attract to our isolated campus
big-name entertainment groups.

Fred and I were determined to build a convocation center that
would not only meet the needs of our rapidly growing student body,
but would also assist the community and the southeastern Ohio region in economic development programs. Plans were drawn for a
13,000-seat multipurpose center that would eventually cost $8.5 mil-
lion. (Today comparable facilities are costing hundreds of million
dollars to build.)

Perhaps the wealthiest citizen in Athens was Fred Beasley, an automobile dealer who had built a fairly respectable fortune in coal-
mining projects throughout the Appalachian region. Fred Johnson
and I determined that the projected facility should be named, the
Fred Beasley Center. Our plans called for an initial $1 million gift, a
transfer of $2 million from our dormitory and dining surplus funds,
and the balance to be financed by low-cost borrowing.

When our plans were announced, we were met by a storm of

protest from faculty members. They insisted that any funds we raised should go toward improving faculty salaries or building a new library. The student newspaper reversed its previous position and complained about the "new temple for basketball." During my tenure at Ohio, we built facilities costing more than $100 million—classroom, library, laboratory, and dormitory facilities—but the center was far and away the most controversial.

Our project was given a huge boost when Fred Beasley promised to provide the $1 million pledge we were seeking. An appropriate opportunity to announce Fred's pledge publicly took place a few weeks later. Former President Dwight Eisenhower came to the university to speak and receive an honorary degree. At the ceremony we announced Fred's planned gift, and we invited Fred and his family to our home for a private celebration luncheon with President Eisenhower. The Beasley family and Marion and I were enthralled as the former president entertained us with stories from his World War II experiences, his presidency, and his childhood. I am certain it was a peak experience for Fred Beasley.

About a year later, before the building of the center was completed, we were preparing for the dedication ceremonies that would recognize Fred's generous gift. Bob Mathews, his son-in-law, visited me in my office. "I'm distressed to tell you this, Vern," he said, "but Fred has had some serious reversals this past year. His coal-mining projects have gone belly up, and he just cannot fulfill his pledge to you."

Having weathered bitter criticism over the building of the center, the loss of Fred's pledge only heightened the flood of protest from faculty and student leaders. By then we were only a year away from dedicating the new library and in the process of moving the river—the one that flooded and closed down the campus every spring. But this did not assuage the anger of those opposed to the new facility.

Today, thirty years later and named the Convocation Center, the building is spoken of with pride by all members of the university community and is featured as a showpiece in campus publications.

When I now visit the campus and listen to many people taking credit for the building, I am reminded of President Kennedy's wry comment: "Success has many fathers; failure is an orphan."

During the twelve years I worked at Harvard Business School, Marion and I became close friends of Leigh Stevens, a well-known engineering consultant who visited the school frequently as a distinguished lecturer. Leigh was a pioneer in introducing time-and-motion studies to U.S. industry, and he counted among his clients several of the most prestigious corporations. Dean Donald David invited Leigh to lecture several times each year and to counsel with individual students during his week-or-more visits to the campus. Marion and I frequently entertained him in our Wellesley home and were the beneficiaries of his colorful stories about U.S. business as well as his efforts to introduce contemporary agricultural expertise to rural India.

With the retirement of Dean David and our move to Ohio, Leigh Stevens's visits to the Harvard Business School campus became less frequent. We invited him to Athens, believing that his exchanges with students would be as interesting and valuable as they were to students at Harvard. One evening after Marion and I had shared dinner with Leigh, we relaxed with him over nightcaps in our home library. He confessed to us that with the change in leadership at Harvard Business School he didn't feel useful and as comfortable as he had under Dean David. He welcomed an opportunity to spend more time at Ohio University.

Leigh reminisced about his early years as an engineering consultant, recalling the difficult years of the Great Depression—the 1930s. One of his clients did not have the cash to pay him for his consulting help, so they fulfilled their obligation by deeding over to him some twenty thousand acres of land in South Carolina. After acquiring the property, Leigh persuaded Frank Lloyd Wright to build a magnificent home on the site. "I've been wondering what I should do with the property when I die," he said. "Do you suppose Ohio University would be interested if I leave it in my will as a gift? Perhaps you could use the site for executive development programs or other off-campus activities."

Both Marion and I practically jumped out of our chairs. Of course, we'd be interested. Leigh seemed pleased to have resolved an issue that apparently had been troubling him for some time. He agreed to get together with his lawyers in New York and prepare the appropriate papers, transferring the South Carolina property to Ohio University upon his death.

The next day—the very next day—I received a telephone call in the late afternoon informing me that Leigh Stevens had collapsed and died of a heart attack; we had lost not only a friend but also what would have been a fabulous gift.

THE EDWIN AND RUTH KENNEDY LECTURES

In 1960, Trustee Ed Kennedy had established the Distinguished Professor Award, which annually recognized one of Ohio University's outstanding teachers and provided a significant incentive to excellence in the classroom. The following year he provided a fund to honor Ohio's retiring president and encourage faculty research. Appropriately, the fund was named the John C. Baker Fund.

In 1962, Ed Kennedy and I met to discuss the possibility of yet another gift to enrich the academic environment of the university. We agreed that he would provide the resources to enable us to invite scholars, public officials, and outstanding men and women of affairs to speak with and meet students and faculty. In its first year, the Edwin and Ruth Kennedy Lecture Series brought to the campus Margaret Mead; Arnold Toynbee; Justice William O. Douglas; Harold Taylor, president of Sarah Lawrence College; Charles Frankel, professor at Columbia University; and Robert Carr, president of Oberlin College. In the following years, other notable figures spoke on campus in the Kennedy Lecture Series: Pearl Buck, Oscar Handlin, Paul Tillich, Senator Charles Percy, Henry Steele Commager, Adolph

Berle, physicist Isidore Rabi, and James McGregor Burns. Upon each occasion, Marion and I gave a dinner party for the speaker and faculty guests before the lecture, and as often as possible, student groups met with the Kennedy lecturer after the speech. The visit of every Kennedy lecturer was a stimulating occasion and I will describe our experience with four of them.

When Chief Justice William Douglas came to the campus to speak in the series, the woman in charge of the university guest house asked me to help her solve "a serious problem." "The Justice has brought a young woman with him, and they want to stay in the same room," she said. Solving such "major problems" is the burden of presidential leadership.

In May 1964, Paul Tillich, the well-known theologian, arrived on the campus to speak as a Kennedy lecturer. Never having met the good reverend, we were concerned about whether we should serve cocktails. We concluded that we should; otherwise, faculty members who were accustomed to our style of entertaining would think we were being phony. When a student waiter asked the Rev. Tillich whether he would like to have orange juice or some other soft drink, the theologian bellowed, "No, I want bourbon, no ice, in a tumbler, and this much"—stretching his thumb and forefinger about three inches. Tillich downed three of those tumblers of bourbon before dinner, while Marion and I wondered whether we would have a Kennedy lecture after all. He did brilliantly, giving a lecture that inspired and illuminated the audience. Years later, when we read his biography, written by his wife, recounting his racy escapades when a guest at various people's homes, we were relieved that we had not invited him to stay overnight.

Another distinguished lecturer who had not planned to stay overnight in our home was Margaret Mead; however, the flooding Hocking River provided us with a rare opportunity to become well acquainted with her. To combat the flooding (prior to relocation of the river in 1969) we had connected our recently constructed dormitories with elevated crosswalks. This permitted on-campus access, but all highways leading into Athens were completely flooded and inaccessible, and throughout the three days of our isolation, Margaret Mead held court in our living room. With her two-pronged, six-foot walking stick angled across her lap, she entertained faculty and students with stories about South Pacific tribes, gossip about colleagues, and good-natured banter. Marion was later quoted in a *Time* magazine article describing Mead's visit as "refreshing as a cold shower."

Senator Charles Percy not only spoke in the series but remained on campus for two days of meetings and discussion with students and faculty. He was impressive in his interchanges with a wide variety of people on the campus. We gave a dinner party and invited him to stay overnight in our home. When he left for Washington, my wife discovered that he had left some of his belongings. A few days later she received a letter:

> Dear Marion:
> My secretary was somewhat hesitant to bring into me your note together with my pajamas and necktie, but being a perceptive and intelligent person, she presumed, correctly, that the circumstances under which they were returned were perfectly honorable and could be explained.
> Being so forgetful you would think I was the proverbial professor rather than a presumably alert candidate for public office!

Early in my tenure at Ohio I decided to place plaques on the outside wall of Memorial Auditorium commemorating the visits to campus of distinguished leaders. Each plaque contained a brief excerpt from that person's speech or writings. Robert Frost's read: "What we do in college is get over our little-mindedness." Arnold Toynbee said, "Civilization is a movement and not a condition, a voyage and not a harbor." Carl Sandburg's plaque read: "Man will never arrive, man will always be on the way." Following President Johnson's address, we placed his challenge on a plaque: "Let your young hearts armed with new weapons join an old battle against ancient enemies; the enemies of poverty and disease, illiteracy and strife . . . with your courage and your compassion we will build the Great Society."

Some day perhaps a lonely student might wander over to Memorial Auditorium on a quiet evening and read the inspiring words spoken on campus many years before. That student might be deeply moved and inspired while reading the twenty-five plaques. Those words could even change the direction of a life.

CHAPTER 7

Joining the War on Poverty . . .

and Reaching Overseas

MICHAEL GILLETTE headed the Lyndon Baines Johnson Library's Oral History Program and is currently the director of the Center for Legislative Archives at the National Archives in Washington, D.C. He interviewed me in preparation for his oral history volume, *Launching the War on Poverty*. The inside cover of his book includes the statement: "Today, the welfare programs of the Great Society are criticized as a failure of liberal idealism; but these firsthand testimonies demonstrate that the strategies of the original poverty warriors were rooted in the American work ethic and were designed to encourage self-help instead of dependence."

The following gives a sample of my oral history conversation with Michael Gillette:*

---

*Michael Gillette, *Launching the War on Poverty: An Oral History* (New York: Twayne Publishers, 1996).

Alden: I was invited in the winter of 1964 to Hawaii to speak at a convention. It seemed like a marvelous quasi-vacation, because I had been going at my job eighteen hours a day, seven days a week. I looked forward to giving my speech and relaxing on Waikiki Beach for four or five days. I had given my speech and had been on the beach no more than half an hour when I was paged for a call from the White House. I picked up the phone, and after a long wait President Johnson came on with an invitation to fly immediately to Washington. Then he said, "I'd like to have Mr. Shriver explain what this is all about." Sargent Shriver said, "We want to talk to you about being part of an exciting new program we're developing." I replied, "Well, yes, I can be in Washington next week sometime." Shriver said, "What do you mean, next week? We expect you tomorrow." I said, "I had planned to stay here a little bit longer." He said, "No, you've got to come right away. After all, it's the president of the United States inviting you."

So I got on a plane and flew all the way back to Washington and then sat around a day and a half waiting to be seen by Lyndon Johnson and Sargent Shriver. They said they wanted me to drop everything at the university immediately and come to Washington to chair the force planning the Job Corps portion of the War on Poverty. I responded, "Look, I've been at this university only two years, and we have a number of very substantial programs just beginning. I just can't run out on people." Shriver said, "Well, maybe you can be part of the task force for a period of time, and then you'll be able to leave and join us full time." I replied, "That's not possible. I really doubt whether I can take any time at all, even spending a day or two a week in Washington."

Sargent Shriver then flew down to Florida and talked to the chairman of the Ohio [University] board, who was then John Galbreath. Shriver told him that it would be important to the university that I chair the task force. John Galbreath called me and said, "You know, I think this will be difficult for the board of trustees and for the people of Ohio to accept, being as conservative as they are. But if you feel that you really want to do it and should do it, I think the board would okay your going there for maybe a couple of days a week for the next three months or so." He went on to say, "I gather from what you said to Shriver that there's no way that you'd leave the university to take on the full-time responsibility as head of the Job Corps." I said, "That's true. I will make whatever inputs I can to the task force, and I will do those things that Mr. Shriver described to me, but obviously, I am not going to be a candidate for the directorship of the Job Corps."

So I flew to Washington a couple of days a week for a period of about three months. I would get up about five in the morning, fly to Washington, work all day long, talk with Shriver until well in the evening, and then work all the next day before flying back to Ohio late at night.

I would guess that the reason Sargent Shriver asked me to become involved was that I had gone to Harvard Business School and worked there on the faculty and in the administration for twelve years. I also served on some corporate boards and knew the business community very well while being a member of the academic community. He apparently wanted somebody who was comfortable in both worlds, because the Job Corps looked to him to be a combination of the practicality of business with the research and teaching inputs that the academic world could give.

Do you recall what President Johnson said to you at that first meeting and the circumstances of the meeting?

Alden: It was not a long meeting. It was in the so-called Fish Room. With the president were Mr. Shriver and a black man. I've forgotten his name, but I don't think he ever became a member of the task force. He probably was a visitor whom the president was trying to impress with his plans for the War on Poverty. President Johnson reminisced about his youth, his teaching experiences, and his very early concern for poor people. He said that he had been dirt-poor himself, that he had always wanted to do something for poor folks. He went on to say that he had talked with Sargent Shriver about a program that would eradicate poverty in our lifetime. He described various elements of it—community action, the VISTA volunteers, and a job-oriented program that would be modeled after the CCC camps, only they would be better. He spoke in generalities. It was a brief meeting, and then I went off with Sargent Shriver to the first building we occupied.

I did not get too deeply into the detailed planning of the Job Corps camps or the logistical work that had to be done with the Department of Defense or Labor. Bob McNamara and Pat Moynihan were both friends of mine from Harvard days, so in the initial meetings I took our small team over to talk with them. But then John Carley or Wade Robinson or other members would carry on the day-to-day detail work with their staffs. I perceived my role— and I assumed Sargent Shriver agreed—as an outreach to the businesses and academic communities. I also knew several leading sports figures who could help us make the Job Corps camps attractive to young people. I spent some time running around the country talking to business leaders, to academics, to the press, inviting them to share their ideas with the task force.

Many Republican-oriented businessmen were skeptical of the War on Poverty. I visited several business leaders, trying to explain that the Job Corps was practical, businesslike, and focused on the problem of poverty. I shall never forget my interview with Neil McElroy, the chairman of Procter & Gamble. Because he was a graduate of Harvard and the Harvard Business School, I thought that he would be one of the more understanding and liberal businessmen. I was wrong. I argued, "Do you have any idea how much money we're spending on kids who have dropped out of school, have gotten into lives of crime, and are now locked up in prisons or detention homes? We are spending millions, even billions of dollars on these lost kids. What if we had a program that would take unemployable youngsters out of predominately black neighborhoods, or hollows of Appalachia, and first of all bring them up to a decent condition of health, then give them some basic skills, so that they could at least read and write and learn how to use a telephone or cash a check—just those elementary skills that we take for granted? Now, what if we were able to take these kids out of their dead-end environments and, as Lyndon Johnson said, no longer give them a 'handout' but give them a 'handup'? What if millions of them could be made employable, find jobs, and have spending money? How much more Crest toothpaste could you sell? It's a very practical problem. We plan to take these lost young-sters off welfare, out of detention homes, out of dead-end situa-tions, and make them more employable."

McElroy's response was, "Well, I've heard from President Eisen-hower and others that this is a boondoggle, so that's good enough for me."

But happily enough, there were several businessmen who took an interest, and we set up an advisory board of business leaders. I helped Mr. Shriver put together that list, and we invited them to meet with us from time to time in Washington. They served as an advisory group, but more importantly, they were emissaries to the rest of the business community.

When we began to talk about where the Job Corps camps should be located and who should run them, we discovered early on that academic people wanted to use them as research laborato-ries. They were looking for grants from us so they could study these kids, like specimens. We were disappointed that few acade-mics had practical ideas for meeting our goal: making unemploy-able young people healthy, skilled, and useful to society. So we decided that several Job Corps camps would be run by business corporations. There was a business recession in 1964, and in many companies there were sophisticated Ph.D.s who really didn't have an awful lot to do or were about to be laid off. It occurred to me that running a Job Corps program could be attractive to Xerox, Litton, CBS, or other companies. Looking at the record, some of the best Job Corps camps were run by goal-oriented, well-orga-nized business corporations.

The only times I saw the president were, once, when he initially talked to me briefly about serving. Secondly, one time Representa-tive Gerald Ford [of Michigan] attacked the Job Corps on the floor of the House, calling it a boondoggle and a waste of money. Sargent Shriver was told about it by Wilson McCarthy. I happened to be in Sarge's office at the time, so he grabbed me and said he was going over to the White House right away to talk to the presi-dent. We were ushered into the president's office, and Sarge was hopping mad about Gerald Ford's attack. That's when the famous statement was made: "Don't worry about Gerald Ford, because he can't fart and chew gum at the same time." It was polished up and reported as: "Gerald Ford can't walk and chew gum at the same time." Maybe the president said it again in a different context, but I was in the office when he said that, trying to calm down Shriver.

We were concerned that the public would think that this was a program only for black kids, for ghetto kids. So we emphasized in all our speeches that there were hundreds of thousands of young people trapped in the hollows of Appalachia or in other rural areas, and that this was not just a black program; it was a white and black problem. We were afraid also that the public would believe that the Job Corps was designed primarily for youngsters with prison records, [for] juvenile delinquents or drug pushers. We planned to take kids with poor records, but they were not going to be the only ones in the program.

We also talked about the poor health of kids. We discovered that many were going to need an awful lot of remedial work on their teeth, for example. We talked about the number of young people in high schools who could not read at grade-school level. We invited representatives of publishing firms to discuss teaching tools that would be needed.

Do you know how Otis Singletary was chosen to head the Job Corps?

Alden: Otis at the time was [chancellor of the University of North Carolina at Greensboro]. He was not on the original list of people I gave to Sarge. I knew Otis, but I thought that it would be impossible to wrest him away from the University of [North Carolina]. I think that Sarge must have gotten his name from one of the representatives or senators from [North Carolina]. Sarge asked me about Otis, and my response was that I thought Otis was a fine fellow but he probably couldn't be persuaded to take the job. But Shriver talked him into it.

Did Shriver feel that the Job Corps director should be a college president?

Alden: Yes. Shriver felt all along that the program had to have prestige in the eye of the public. The Job Corps was not going to be just another outfit where we would get a government veteran from the bureaucracy to run it. He wanted to have the Job Corps identified as an educational opportunity for people. He could have had a school superintendent or a school board member, but I think that Sarge really wanted to give the program a little bit of distinction by saying a university president would run it.

In those days, people were much more in awe of university presidents than they are today.

WITH A STRONG business advisory committee, the Job Corps took young men and women out of urban and rural slums and placed them in job training centers or conservation camps run by business corporations and universities. These young people, trapped in lives of poverty, failure, frustration, and disappointment, were described by James Conant, former Harvard president, as "social dynamite." Most were unemployable, without reading and writing skills and often in poor health. We made certain that the Job Corps program would be businesslike, practical, and focused upon the goal of preparing the young men and women for employment. It is one of the few Great Society programs still functioning today.

The distinguished *New York Times* writer Fred Hechinger wrote in the May 3, 1964, *Times*:

> Last week, Dr. Vernon Roger Alden, president of Ohio University and the new part-time Job Corps planner under President Johnson's proposed Economic Opportunity Act, hammered out a comprehensive plan that could turn that Act—backbone of the War on Poverty—into something of an educational revolution. Since the educational experiments—even the good ones—and their impact on educational deficiencies have usually been too little and too late, Dr. Alden has drawn up a blueprint that would give the experts and theorists a chance to make their work nationwide, continuing, pragmatic, and as unconventional as necessary.

While I was working part-time with President Johnson and Sargent Shriver, I was invited by the Junior League of Columbus to speak about the War on Poverty. I assumed I was going to meet with bright, active young women but was surprised to discover that husbands had also been invited—doctors, lawyers, dentists, businessmen—all from conservative, suburban Upper Arlington. I talked about the need to assist young people from the ghettos and rural poverty areas, not with handouts but with practical, businesslike training programs. I have never since encountered a more hostile audience. I left the meeting feeling that I had been branded a wild-eyed Communist.

My involvement with the War on Poverty did open me up to attack from legislators opposed to the program. Ohio Republican Congressmen William Harsha and "Pete" Abele both expressed concern that I had "tried to pressure them into voting for the bill." Congressman Abele, from our congressional district, was especially critical of me in a press conference that resulted in articles in most of the Ohio newspapers over a period of several days. I felt I had to respond: "We are not interested in the politics of these bills," I said. "We want the financial assistance that can help the people in our area find jobs and our communities to prosper economically." I pointed out in my press conference that Congressman Abele had "voted against accelerated public works, the Area Development Act, Aid to Education, and the Appalachian Program, all pieces of legislation specifically designed to aid depressed areas such as Southeast Ohio."

Senator Stephen Young (Ohio) labeled Abele's criticism of me "amazing." He announced to the press that "Abele was dead wrong in his highly partisan comments regarding this far-sighted educator." A Portsmouth, Ohio, columnist claimed that "every citizen has a right to pressure his congressman for issues he is interested in. . . . Over 300 years ago another Alden was advised to 'speak for yourself.'"

Pete Abele was defeated in the next election and replaced by Democrat Walter Moeller. My image among conservative Ohioans improved somewhat when I traveled around the state as chairman of the Ohio Cancer Crusade, accompanied by National Chairman Gregory Peck.

FEBRUARY 18, 1964, marked the 160th anniversary of Ohio University. A week-long celebration was planned, highlighted by the dedication of a Memorial Room in Baker Center. Fred Johnson contributed a collection that included each of the flags that represented the United States since its colonial beginnings. Ohio Medal of Honor recipients were recognized in a special ceremony. The highlight of the program was a presentation by Astronaut John Glenn from nearby New Concord, Ohio.

A few months before his assassination, I met with President John Kennedy at the White House. I invited him to speak at our anniversary celebration, and he agreed. After the tragic events in Dallas, I felt it was inappropriate to invite President Johnson immediately, and I did not feel confident that he would accept. Almost three months after the February anniversary date, I had worked closely enough with President Johnson on the War on Poverty to believe it was worth a try. With the help of Bill Moyers and Jack Valenti, I was able to persuade President Johnson to visit the campus and announce his plans for the Great Society. Several days before the president's arrival, the Secret Service installed the "hot line" telephone in our home. The night before our convocation, the Secret Service called to say that they had picked up—not far from our home—a man sitting in a car with a rifle across his lap. Twenty minutes later the agent called to report, "No problem. The man is simply keeping tabs on his wife who is visiting some other guy."

The helicopter carrying President Johnson landed in the Ohio University football stadium, where he was met by our trustees, Governor Jim Rhodes, and university administrators. The president, the governor, and I climbed into a top-down convertible to lead a parade of automobiles from the stadium to the Campus Green. Along the way, the president frequently jumped out of the car to doff his ten-gallon hat, shake hands, and to sign whatever he was offered, including the bass drum of the local high school band. When President Johnson approached the podium to give his Great Society address, I noticed that his cuff links had been swiped and the backs of his hands were scratched and bleeding. Never before or since have I ridden in an open car with a president. It's a frightening experience.

The president spoke on the College Green, packed with 25,000 students, faculty, and Athens residents. Two United States senators, including Senator Gore of Tennessee (now deceased), five congressmen, four cabinet members, several state officials (including twenty members of the governor's cabinet and staff crowded in. His daughter, Lynda Bird, wearing Ohio colors, green and white, and Franklin D. Roosevelt Jr. were also members of the platform party. We did not provide chairs: that helped the Green to accommodate the turnout. The president's speech was transmitted off campus via the moon from our research facilities on Radar Hill. In his characteristic manner, President Johnson alternately whispered and shouted his plans for "the Great Society." He used the Ohio campus as the first forum outside of Washington (contrary to the claim of the University of Michigan) to announce his program before setting out on a tour of the Appalachian region.

The president began his speech by explaining: "Since this began as a poverty inspection tour, I want to clarify our presence here. The faculty opinion not withstanding, I do not believe that Ohio University has any poor students. As the father of a college daughter dressed in green and white today, if I wanted to inspect pockets of poverty, I would go and inspect the parents instead of coming here."

President Johnson went on to say: "Under Dr. Alden's leadership, Ohio University is setting a national standard of leadership in attacking the problems in area economic development, and I am proud to announce today that a contract has been signed in the Area Redevelopment Administration to establish a regional development institution here." In challenging the students, he said: "There is in front of you young people today the promise of a greater tomorrow. It is a tomorrow that is brighter than yesterday, and it is a tomorrow that is more challenging than today. This is not a time for timid souls and troubling spirits. We have it within our power to find the best solutions to the worst of problems, and we intend to do just that."

Reflecting on the president's visit, I read in the next day's Athens Messenger a lovely tribute to Marion entitled, "Portrait of a Lady," written by a person who identified herself only as Lynn:

> It's the business of great men's wives to stay in the background and to be "the woman behind the man." But, it's equally important for these women to present a striking figure, a lovely, poised and pretty one, to the public.
>
> These women must be striking, but not shocking, gracious and poised, but not pressing, elegant but not arrogant, intelligent, but not intellects. . . .
>
> The task, sometimes regarded an impossibility, is not an easy one, but when it is achieved, which is not so often, the result is pure perfection.
>
> One example of this perfection is our own Marion Alden, who seated behind and to the left of her husband, Dr. Vernon R. Alden, yesterday, wore a light grey coat dress with pink accessories. She was stunning in a pale pink billowy turban–styled beret.
>
> She talked pleasantly with Mrs. James Rhodes who sat to her left and extended her hand to Washington dignitaries (who seemed most anxious to meet the charming first lady of Ohio University) until the program began.
>
> Though she is striking, she has so mastered the art of being unnoticed that it is difficult to know exactly what were her reactions to all that went on during the addresses at the program where President Lyndon B. Johnson spoke. Undoubtedly, she listened intently to the words of her husband, Ohio University's president, to Gov. Rhodes, to the short speech by Lynda Bird Johnson and to the words of the president.
>
> Dr. Alden introduced our President . . . his wife introduced true ladyhood.

This tribute to Marion reminds me of other testimonials to her outstanding abilities. When John Glenn spoke on campus that February, our son David had been born just five days before. Marion, in her usual fashion, made preparations for the luncheon, reception, and activities for the spouses. Having just returned from the hospital did not slow her down a bit. John Glenn has ever since called her "the Pioneer Woman."

Throughout the time we lived in Athens, Marion entertained in our home 3,500 to 4,000 people every year—for breakfast, lunch, tea, dinner, or nightcaps. She supervised the cook and the busboys, created the menus, kept careful lists of guests, and graciously hosted every visitor, while at the same time raising with great care four young children. Never has she lacked for energy, imagination, and devotion to her responsibilities. I take pride in knowing that the university got two people for the price of one. She never received a salary.

Experienced as an interior designer, Marion completely refurbished 29 Park Place, drawing compliments from townspeople, faculty, and visitors. She loved music and theater and found the resources offered by our excellent School of Music and Theater especially rewarding. Frequently, I held meetings in our living room with the senior and younger administrators. I believed in proactive administration, trying to anticipate problems or opportunities. She enjoyed participating in those discussions and often made significant contributions. She traveled with me to alumni gatherings, spoke eloquently when called upon, and in every way exemplified the ideal university president's wife. I shall be forever grateful for her support. There is no greater satisfaction than working together and sharing the same goals in building and strengthening an institution.

OUT OF MY ASSOCIATION with the White House in the War on Poverty there came insights into national political life. In that spring of 1964, President Johnson was preparing his run for his second term in November. There was much speculation in the press concerning his selection of a vice-presidential running mate. Bobby Kennedy was the choice of the media and the liberal wing of the Democratic Party. Johnson met the issue head on by telling Kennedy that he would not be his choice. That same evening, I was scheduled to have dinner privately with Sargent Shriver. He was late. When he finally arrived, he explained that he had been with the president and that he, too, had been told he would not be a candidate for the vice presidency.

For several weeks there was speculation in the press about Johnson's choice. He kept the rumor mills active by stating that his running mate might be a "congressman or Governor or even a university president." When the president made that comment, my family and I were driving from Ohio to Martha's Vineyard for a brief vacation. The telephone in our Vineyard cottage was ringing off the hook when we arrived. No doubt several senators and governors were being swamped by the press at the same time, but the telephone calls quickly stopped when the selection of Hubert Humphrey was announced a few days later.

Few presidents have had the energy and drive that Johnson had. Marion and I were invited on April 27, 1966, to a White House formal dinner honoring the prime minister of Denmark. Following dinner, the president danced with almost every woman in the room. At midnight, Lady Bird Johnson retired for the evening, but the president kept on dancing until 3:00 A.M. We were told that he then rushed with friends to Andrews Air Force base to catch a plane to Texas.

President Johnson has been vilified by many for failing to win a controversial war and, simultaneously, support a huge domestic economic program. He will be remembered for the passage of a sweeping civil rights bill and other major legislative initiatives, which even the popular President Kennedy had not been able to push through Congress. Barbara Jordan, the black Texas congresswoman who gained fame in the Watergate hearings, served with me on the board of the Mead Corporation. She said that "Lyndon Johnson did more for my people than any president since Abraham Lincoln." In my conversations with President Johnson about his early Texas childhood, his relationships with minorities, and his family, I found him to be one of the most fascinating individuals I have ever met.

Sargent Shriver, head of the Peace Corps under his brother-in-law John Kennedy, came to the campus on July 7, 1962, to announce a $400,000 grant to enable Ohio University to train Peace Corps volunteers for service in Western Cameroon. More than one hundred Peace Corps volunteers were in Athens to prepare themselves for service in Cameroon and another forty for India. We gave a party for 250 guests in the garden at 29 Park Place. Ohio was the first university to grant academic credit for returning Peace Corps volunteers.

Since 1958, the university has been involved in U.S. government-sponsored educational programs for newly emerging nations. Ohio was the first U.S. university to participate in teaching programs in Western Nigeria. By mid–1968, thirty-eight of our faculty members had taught in western, eastern, and northern Nigeria. Ten Nigerian faculty members and thirty-five students, sponsored by the United States Agency for International Development (USAID), were on campus in 1963 and 1964. Under the leadership of Professor Milton Ploghoft, our project grew into the largest and most unique U.S.-sponsored education project in West Africa.

Marion and I traveled to Nigeria with trustee Ed Kennedy to review our programs in Lagos, Ibadan, and Kano. The Ford Foundation announced a grant to establish, in cooperation with Ahmadu Bello University in Zaria, a multipurpose teachers' college in Kano, to help train more than ten thousand teachers for primary schools. The Nigerians who served as drivers took great pride in their Ohio green and white uniforms, which also were the national colors of Nigeria.

Ed Kennedy, who collected and contributed an unusually valuable collection of Southwest American-Indian blankets to Ohio University, had earlier purchased a large number of pieces of Nigerian art. These, too, were given to the university, and are displayed on the third floor of the library. We were entertained at elaborate receptions in each of the provinces by emirs and chieftains in colorful regalia.

We always arrived precisely at the time given on the invitations, and then sat around for an hour or more waiting for our hosts to arrive. One evening I spoke to a group of around one hundred Nigerian students gathered under a tent illuminated by only dim lanterns. I included in my remarks a quotation from Henri Bergson, "To exist is to change, to change is to mature, and to mature is to go on creating oneself endlessly." Apparently, the quote struck a sensitive nerve, because a tremendous roar and cheering erupted among the students.

The success of our venture in western Nigeria eventually led to similar USAID-sponsored programs being conducted by Harvard, Indiana, and Wisconsin. I was invited to travel to Nigeria once again with the presidents of those institutions to visit and inspect each other's programs, including newly established efforts in Benin, eastern Nigeria.

Russell Millikan, a savvy, politically-wise member of the College of Education faculty, was appointed head of our Center for International Programs. Russ negotiated contracts with USAID for our programs in Nigeria and Vietnam. Professor Norman Parmer, an authority on Malaysian culture, was responsible for the Center for International Studies, assisting departments in planning and developing courses relating to Africa, Latin America, and Southeast Asia. The African Studies Program was headed by Professor Alan Booth, and the Southeast Asian Studies Program was chaired by Professor Paul van der Veur. Instruction in Housa and Swahili languages was offered together with fifty other courses in the African Studies Program. Faculty in the Southeast Asia Studies Program offered instruction in Chinese, Malay, and Indonesian languages, along with several other courses in the social sciences and humanities, some of which were already offered by Professors John Cady and Wid Elsbree.

A popular and successful interdisciplinary master's degree program was launched. Its graduates entered government and industry as well as prestigious Ph.D. programs. An undergraduate interdisciplinary bachelor's program was added and a publication series was begun as well. These academic programs were enhanced by the expansion of undergraduate study-abroad programs, led by Professor Richard Danner and Marjorie Stone, and the growth in the number of our foreign students, especially from Nigeria, Malaysia, and China, whose needs were administered by Geoff Woods.

The Government of Malaysia made it possible for faculty and staff of the Mara Institute of Technology, located in Kuala Lumpur, to receive training at Ohio University. Eventually joint degree programs were developed, and several hundred Malaysian students came to Athens to study.

WITH USAID SUPPORT, in 1963 we established a teaching program in South Vietnam. Under the French system, the schooling provided to young people was a narrow, French, secondary education, taught in French. Our objective was to replace this program, available to only a few, with a system patterned after the comprehensive U.S. high school, taught in the Vietnamese language with Vietnamese texts and materials and open to many Vietnamese young people. With the conclusion of the war in Vietnam, it was hoped, a comprehensive school system could be established that would prepare a wide spectrum of young people with the skills needed in the democratic society that was expected to be in place when Communist forces were defeated. Six Ohio faculty members were sent to work closely with Vietnamese teachers at the Universities of Hue, Saigon, and Can Tho, training teachers for secondary schools and establishing twelve model high schools in South Vietnam. Professor Donald Knox headed the program, succeeded by Professor William Inman. Gilbert Stevenson and Marguerite Appel were also key members of the Ohio team. Under the USAID grant, thirteen students from Vietnam studied at Ohio University.

The owner of the local school-supplies store publicly expressed concern that the university was accepting and wasting "good taxpayer dollars in foreign programs." I suggested to Russ Milliken that we not purchase supplies for our Nigerian and Vietnam programs from our complaining store owner for a month or two. It did not take our critic long to discover that most of the USAID funds were being spent locally.

In 1964 I traveled to South Vietnam to confer with our faculty members and to meet with U.S. and Vietnamese government officials. Charles Benton, the chairman of *Encyclopaedia Britannica*, accompanied me and presented a $150,000 gift to our program. While in Saigon, I visited an orphanage on the outskirts of the city—to be greeted by hundreds of tiny, flag-waving orphans gathered under a huge banner: "Welcome President Alden."

While in Saigon, I received a telephone call from the commander of our armed forces in Vietnam, General William Westmoreland. I had met the general in the late 1950s when, at the Harvard Business School, I conducted the program for newly appointed college presidents and their spouses. General Westmoreland, at that time commandant of the United States Military Academy at West Point, and his wife attended one of our sessions at Harvard. I was impressed with the general's intelligence and sincerity and we became good friends. Early in my Ohio University presidency, General and Mrs. Westmoreland invited Marion and me to a football game, on a brilliant fall afternoon, at West Point. Talk about a rabid fan and cheerleader for his team! Few could outdo Westmoreland. Touring the battle areas with the general in his jeep was an unexpected opportunity. In combat dress, General Westmoreland was an impressive figure—trim, with a square jaw and steely eyes—every inch a commander. "We must win this war," he said, "but even more important we must win the hearts and minds of the Vietnamese people." He described to me, and I saw firsthand, the programs he had developed to carry out that mission. We talked about community development and the discipline and standards of conduct he was requiring of the men who served with him. I was impressed and convinced of the "rightness" of our commitment to assist the Vietnamese.

In the mid-1960s we invited to the university campus—in addition to President Johnson—Secretary of Defense Robert McNamara, Secretary of State Dean Rusk, General Maxwell Taylor, and George Ball. Although by then the Vietnam conflict was a controversial matter, they all spoke without causing campus disruptions and were able to participate in constructive dialogue with faculty and students. When Dean Rusk visited the campus, Distinguished Professor John Cady came to my office to inquire whether I would be embarrassed if he presented a letter to the secretary of state protesting U.S involvement in Vietnam. Dr. Cady was one of our country's leading experts on Southeast Asia—an author of several books on the area. I was proud of the civilized manner in which he and other faculty members expressed their views on that complex issue.

In November 1967, the university's associate professor of English, Harrison Butterworth, on sabbatical leave, was seized by U.S. Marines as he swam ashore at Da Nang from the Quaker yacht *Phoenix*, which was attempting to deliver medicine to South Vietnam, having been rejected by the North Vietnamese. Hoping to turn the event into a controversy, *Columbus Dispatch* reporters pressed me for my reaction. My response was, "no comment, either favorable or unfavorable —we have no tradition of harassing our professors. Certainly if university action were called for, none would be pursued without due process." End of a nonstory.

By 1968, the mood on campus had changed in the aftermath of the Tet and the earlier My Lai massacre. There was turmoil on campuses throughout the United States. George Romney torpedoed his chances to become the Republican candidate for the presidency with the statement that he had been "brainwashed" while visiting Vietnam. When he made that comment, public sentiment in the United States had already turned against the war.

Whether the United States should have intervened in Vietnam in its effort to halt the spread of Communism throughout Southeast Asia is a question that will continue to be debated and perhaps never resolved. But when General Westmoreland had responsibility for overseeing our country's military commitment, I believe he conducted the military operation with integrity and with the noblest of intentions.

IN 1969, the United States Information Agency recognized Ohio University with a special citation, expressing appreciation for our efforts in Africa and Southeast Asia. The chairman of the board, Fred Johnson, Russell Milliken, and I traveled to Washington for the ceremony. The congressmen and senators from Ohio had been invited to attend. Few showed up. However, much to my surprise, Senator Ted Kennedy dropped in for the ceremony and made some very flattering remarks. Photographers covering the event took pictures of Fred, Russ, and me with the Massachusetts senator. I privately wondered what staunch Republican Fred Johnson was thinking. He had been Ohio Senator Robert Taft's campaign manager at one time and deeply involved in Republican politics. Much to my amusement, when I visited Fred in his Columbus office a few weeks later, he had the framed photograph of Ted Kennedy and the Ohio University trio hanging on his wall.

CHAPTER 8

Developing Southeastern Ohio—
and a Change in State Financing

ATHENS AND THE UNIVERSITY were desperately in need of facilities for visitors. The Berry Hotel on Court Street was in poor shape and much too small to accommodate the influx of families, student and faculty prospects, and others traveling to our growing university. I expressed these concerns to trustee John Galbreath and asked him to consider building a modern hotel/inn on an edge of the campus.

As he had so many times before, John Galbreath stepped in to help meet a critical institutional need. His company immediately began to plan the Ohio University Inn, but the route from planning to building was more complex than any of us had anticipated. As land was acquired at the foot of the Athens State Hospital, the home of a faculty member stood in the middle of the most desirable site. Galbreath agreed to acquire land overlooking the university and move the professor's house to this more attractive location but the faculty member was on leave overseas, making negotiations more complex and time-consuming.

When that obstacle was cleared, an even more daunting challenge faced us. To be economically successful, the new inn would need a license to serve liquor. A referendum would be required to legalize the sale of spirits south of the Hocking River. It didn't take long for the bar owners on and near Court Street to express their concerns that the new facility would cut into their business. It was rumored that some of the bar owners were handing out inducements to residents of South Athens to vote against the referendum. One tavern owner became so incensed that he telephoned me in the middle of the night, slurring his words, and threatening my life, or at least "running me out of town" when a new administration took over the statehouse in Columbus. The vice president for development, Marty Hecht, who did a yeomanlike job in overseeing the Ohio University Inn project, received similar threats.

When word of this reached John Galbreath, he requested clarification from Ohio Supreme Court Justice William O'Neil to determine if the entire community would have to vote on whether Athens would be dry. The existing rule of adjoining precincts called for both precincts to vote when a precinct opted to go from "dry" to "wet." After a review of the precinct boundaries by the Ohio Department of Liquor Control, the vote for the Ohio University Inn's liquor license was determined to include the licenses of the Court Street bar owner. Faced with the prospect of losing their licenses, the same bar owners rushed to "persuade" South Athenians to vote in favor of the petition.

The Ohio University Inn was finally built and has been a lively hospitality center for alumni, parents and other visitors to the community. And, of course, the bars are still in business.

At the same time we had other needs that were met by private developers. The Tishman Company of New York built the nine-story private Bromley Hall to house students as we raced to finish West Green and build facilities on South Green. An enterprising local business firm built six multistory apartment buildings on the fringe of the campus to accommodate our rapidly increasing faculty and graduate student growth. The Lakeview Manor Apartments, as they were called, were augmented by a community center, providing bowling alleys, a billiard room, indoor miniature golf, a public dining room, and additional rooms for private functions. We later rented space in these apartments to provide for much needed offices. Several other apartment complexes were built on the hills at the edge of town. Altogether, about $25 million was spent by private investors who helped the university meet its demands for space.

THE UNIVERSITY AIRPORT on East Side Athens offered flying and navigation instruction to students. The air fleet consisted of five single-engine planes and a DC-3. Ohio University, as did a few other Midwestern public universities, provided air transportation services to university administrators, faculty, and distinguished visitors. Francis Fuller ably directed the program, and David Vaughn supervised student copilots in transporting the university president and others who found that highway access to Athens was inadequate. Halden Connor, one of our talented student pilots, is today an enormously successful business leader in Texas, the key player in the development and expansion of Fort Worth. Joan Mace returned to the university in 1963 as a pilot and instructor. She received the university Medal of Merit in 1992 and has recently been elected to the National Alumni Board.

We soon discovered that the demand for air transportation was so heavy that I asked Fran Fuller to inform me of any business corporations advertising the sale of aircraft. When in due course I was alerted, I then asked the corporation to make a tax-deductible gift of their aircraft to Ohio University. We received our first DC-3 from the Mead Corporation. General Motors gave us a Lockheed Lodestar, and the Pittsburgh Plate Glass Company and Detroit Steel each gave us a DC-3. Other companies contributed planes, some of which we sold or used for spare parts for our Beechcraft and DC-3s.

The politicians in Columbus were not too happy with our aviation program, although they willingly accepted rides to Athens when they visited. In July 1967, the state auditor ordered tighter controls on the use of university aircraft. In his press release, he listed the twelve planes that had been given to us by the federal government or private corporations. He included the names of prominent visitors who had been flown to the campus: Notre Dame football coach Ara Parseghian, TV star Garry Moore, Secretary of State Dean Rusk, and newscasters David Brinkley and Martin Agronsky. He criticized the trustees' chairman, Paul Stocker, for using university planes to attend trustee meetings, ignoring the fact that Paul could save a whole day of travel from Lorain, Ohio, each way. The auditor's press release reported on fund-raising trips to Florida and the East Coast, but in fairness he pointed out that private gifts in 1966/67 totaled $3.7 million, compared with $218,000 in 1961/62, and that federal grants for the same years increased to $10.4 million from $484,000. After the story was run in several Ohio newspapers, we did not hear from the state auditor about airplanes again.

It soon became apparent that our East Side airport was too small to handle visitors in jets. Jets were having to land in Columbus or Parkersburg. Too often in bad weather we had to be diverted to Parkersburg or Charleston, West Virginia. Once Fran Fuller and I had skidded off the slick runway and piled into a huge snowbank; the aircraft was damaged but we were unharmed. The Federal Aviation Administration in 1967 gave us a $487,000 grant to acquire land in nearby Albany and build runways that could handle jet aircraft. The site would also provide facilities to expand the important aeronautical research being conducted for NASA by Professor Richard McFarland and his associates in the Department of Electrical Engineering.

Martin Hecht, assistant to the president (later to be vice president) deserves enormous credit for the university's efforts to develop the economy of Athens and southeastern Ohio. Assisted by grants from the Area Redevelopment Administration, Marty organized development committees in each of the sixteen southeastern Ohio counties. The College of Business Administration launched studies of potential tourist-trade development and a program of assistance

to small businesses. The combined efforts of the volunteer commit
tee members stimulated new business investment—public and private projects—totaling more than $15 million in 1963.

Yet an early effort to recruit industry to the area failed. The president of a major corporation on the East Coast, a personal friend, had
been persuaded to bring a team of executives to the area to assess
possibilities for establishing a $20 million research center. The pros-
pect, after scouting the community, was reluctantly unable to commit himself and outlined four reasons for the decision: first, the water
supply was inadequate; second, the community did not possess service facilities adequate for an extra one thousand people who would
have been brought to Athens; third, the highway system leading north
and west was abysmally poor and would be unable to support heavy
transport flows; and fourth, the community airport was not adequate
for even light executive jets.

A few months later, Dr. Robert Weaver, administrator of the Federal Housing and Home Finance Agency, announced on campus an
urban planning assistance grant to the City of Athens to finance
studies designed to improve water supply, fire protection, highway
access, and land subdivision regulations. An urban renewal grant of
$1,250,000 enabled the university to acquire substandard housing to
clear the way for building the South Green dormitory complex.

A group of Athens citizens and university architecture students
rallied under a program sloganed "Let's Clean Up Court Street." In
response to their interest, Mayor Raymond Shepard appointed a
citizens' advisory committee, with Bill Roberts, university space-
utilization officer, as chairman. University Planner Alan Geiger, who
was teaching an advanced course in architecture, organized a group
of students who completed a comprehensive study in campus planning. Roberts and Geiger arranged for the students to use downtown
Athens as a field for their second study. The group suggested what
might be done with lighting, signs, and graphics in the shopping area.
They reviewed the city's plans for a new parking garage, a bus service, and the projected growth rate of Athens. Some experts estimate

that the students' work would have cost the city $50,000 if it had been done commercially.

In working with the community, we were fortunate to have several individuals who provided strong moral and financial support: Dr. Ted Sprague, Tad Grover, Bill Lavelle, Joe Yanity, John Jones, Carl Clifford, Jim Anastas, Charles Kirkwood, and Rev. Bill Black. The publisher of the *Athens Messenger,* Kenner Bush, was committed to the development of southeastern Ohio as well as the university. Through personal leadership and with editorial support, he was enormously helpful throughout our tenure at Ohio. Since that time he has played a significant role in leading economic development statewide. Kenner Bush is currently a member of the State Investment Committee.

One month before the celebration of Ohio University's 160th anniversary, we established the Institute for Regional Development (IRD). This nonprofit research organization was given free use of university facilities and charged with identifying practical, solution-oriented direction toward economic development in southeastern Ohio. IRD worked closely with the five-hundred-member Southeastern Ohio Regional Council in providing management and research service to small area industries, identification and promotion of tourist centers, planning of public facilities, and development of national and historic resources.

IRD was initially headed by Harvard graduate Mason Morfit, son of television star Garry Moore. Working with him were Peace Corps alumni Tom Gee and Mike Valentine and a niece of Ambassador Henry Cabot Lodge, Emily Alexander. Ward Schram spearheaded IRD after Mason Morfit left to enroll in graduate work at Stanford. In efforts to reduce poverty in the twenty-eight-county region, the program utilized resources from Upward Bound, Neighborhood Youth Corps, Vista, and Rural Action for Better Consumer Development. The state's natural resource director complained in the Columbus newspapers that "Ohio University has pushed through in just three days a $107,000 grant from the Federal Aviation Development Administration on behalf of the Institute for Regional Development, while my department has had applications for ARA-financed projects pending more than a year."

Congressman Wayne Hays, from Belmont County, played a pivotal role in several of our successful funding efforts. Because he chaired the house committee that approved all office support and perquisites for congressmen, he enjoyed and exercised tremendous clout on appropriations. He persuaded Secretary of State Dean Rusk to visit the campus during the height of the Vietnam War. At the Rusk convocation, we conferred an honorary degree upon Wayne Hayes in recognition of his many services to Ohio University and our branch in Belmont County. With the help of Sargent Shriver, we received from the Office of Economic Opportunity a $600,000 grant to establish a Center for Economic Opportunity and a Community Services Center. Both centers provided opportunities for graduate and undergraduate students to use the Appalachian areas as a laboratory for learning and research and for practical job opportunities. Teacher aides, funded by Upward Bound, brought Appalachian students to the campus for five-week sessions, working with university students, and, subsequently, five-week sessions in their own communities, teaching younger children what they had learned.

Lest it be suggested that by participating as vigorously as we did in economic development we were neglecting the primary concerns of the university, the opposite is true. To me it seemed obvious that the university had to assume this responsibility as we faced the pressures of enormous growth in the 1960s. Southeastern Ohio's poverty and underdevelopment had placed us at a disadvantage in attracting support and recruiting talent. No other organization or group of individuals had ever taken on this leadership responsibility.

In my inaugural address, I predicted that Ohio University "would be asked to enroll as many students in the next ten years as we had in our entire 159-year history." In September 1962, 9,600 students enrolled on the Athens campus and 4,000 additional students registered on the seven branch campuses. I suggested that our total enrollment in 1973 might reach 26,000, but urged that the student population on the main Athens campus be topped off at 18,000. We did not wish to become a huge, monolithic campus such as Ohio State.

Working closely with former President Baker, Dean Al Gubitz had pioneered the development of the branch campus program. In 1962, the Portsmouth branch launched an urban renewal program, acquiring five city blocks and a building for daytime classroom operation. The Ohio University Development Committee in Chillicothe raised more than $350,000 in a drive to purchase a campus site. The Mead Corporation contributed a substantial home to serve as administrative headquarters. In May 1963, the county commissioners of Muskingum County made available 179 acres of choice land in Zanesville for the development of our campus there.

Throughout the 1960s, state appropriations through bond issues enabled us to build classroom, library, and laboratory facilities on the campuses in Chillicothe, Portsmouth, Zanesville, Belmont County, and Lancaster. Maintaining a close working relationship with the main campus, each regional campus offered two-year academic programs. Students were able to move into their junior year at Athens without the usual problems encountered when transferring from one independent institution to another. Along with concerts, lectures, and entertainment that the university made available to the branch campuses, the communities developed local choruses, theater groups, art leagues, sports teams, discussion programs, and task forces to meet specific regional needs.

Not far from the Belmont County branch campus stood a beautiful 454-acre tract of timberland that included fifty acres of the only virgin forest left in Ohio—Dysart Woods. In 1967, Ohio University was given possession of this rare jewel, which was designated by the U.S. Department of Interior as a national natural landmark useful as a land lab.

Governor Rhodes had promised the electorate that he would reform the state's higher education system by establishing a board of regents to coordinate planning and financing of the state universities. Under his plan, the regents "would make studies and formulate a master plan for higher education." They would recommend to the director of finance and the legislature "operating funds, capital improvements, the establishment of new programs and new degrees, the use of personnel and facilities, admission and enrollment, enrollments on residential campuses, undergraduate and graduate programs, special professional programs, and research." I testified at the legislative hearings when the board of regents was being considered and expressed my concern that Ohio University, originating in a resolution of the Continental Congress and given certain autonomy, would lose it with the creation of the regents. Privately, I was concerned that the move to establish the board was a power play by Ohio State University.

I felt more sanguine when John Millett, president of Miami University in Oxford, was appointed chancellor of the board of regents in 1963. I had known John before moving to Ohio; he had served on the board of our Institute for College and University Administrators, and he and his wife, Catherine, had attended our sessions at Harvard.

The governor's plan for establishing a board of regents also called for expansion of the individual boards of trustees. Ohio University, with seven members, was required to expand to nine. By statute, the majority of the Ohio board must be graduates. Over the years this worked to our advantage. A governor could not pack the board with his "cronies." Fortunately, with the expansion, the requirement that a majority of trustees (five out of nine) be alumni would not be lost.

John Millett was as much aware and concerned as I was about the inequity in operating support between Ohio State and the other state universities. The formula provided for $900 for each student at Ohio State and $500 per student at the other universities. At one of the meetings of Millett's staff, I presented figures showing that $900 for each of the 35,000 or more undergraduate students at Ohio State resulted in a $7,000 subsidy for each graduate student.

It appeared that an incentive was built-in for Ohio State to continue to increase its huge undergraduate population in order to subsidize the rest of the student body, while the other universities struggled to support *all* students at little more than one-half of the fee per student. I argued that each state university should receive the same amount per undergraduate student, plus a larger subsidy (but the same at each university) for master's and doctoral candidates. A special grant could be made for the medical program at Ohio State, but state support for all other students should be equitable among all public universities. The regents recommended to the legislature a program calling for X dollars for all freshmen and sophomores, Y dollars for juniors and seniors, and Z dollars for graduate students. Special provision was made for the expensive medical program at Ohio State. When the recommendation was approved by the legislature, it became clear that Ohio State was not controlling the regents' agenda.

Progress was also made on extending opportunities to develop graduate programs at Ohio University. In 1939, Ohio State had persuaded the legislature to rule that no programs beyond those at master's degree level would be initiated at any state university other than OSU. John Baker had cracked through that barrier, but even so there were only four doctoral programs at Ohio University in 1962. Between 1962 and 1969, we were permitted to expand doctoral programs in thirteen additional areas.

In 1966, the Rhodes administration was planning a major bond issue to benefit not only higher education but community colleges, vocational schools, and Ohio's transportation system. At the same time, efforts would be made to utilize the physical plants more efficiently and to facilitate the possibility of students transferring from branch campuses to any of the Ohio four-year institutions. In July 1966, the state university presidents were given a memorandum by

Chancellor Millett setting forth reasons for a common academic calendar for all the state-assisted universities. We were told that the chances of passing the bond issue would thereby be enhanced. It was suggested that steps be taken to adopt a quarterly calendar by September 1968.

Having asked our faculty without success in 1962 to consider moving to a quarterly calendar, I welcomed the chancellor's suggestion. Not only would it provide an opportunity for students to substitute a summer quarter for a midwinter quarter, this could place Ohio University students at an advantage in finding vacation-time jobs. Students might opt to stay out of school during the fall or winter quarters and not compete with all other college students for summertime jobs. It would also require all faculty members to take a fresh look at their course offerings. A curriculum revision can bring new vitality to the classroom experience. In meeting with the faculty, I described the benefits of the regents' plan as having a fourfold objective: (1) to equalize state assistance to the state universities; (2) to give Ohio University the opportunity to build up its graduate program; (3) to permit a selective admissions policy; (4) to convert all state universities to a quarterly calendar. Evidence that we were making fuller and more efficient use of facilities, I emphasized, would make it possible for the regents to persuade the legislature to increase appropriations. I estimated that support of the plan could well increase our appropriation by $6 million in the first year.

Two days after my meeting with the faculty, the chancellor announced that "all units of the state system of higher education would not only convert to the quarter system but accomplish this change by summer, 1967." The faculty's reaction was one of shock. Voices were raised concerning the shortness of the changeover time and that "a closer look should be taken before there was any change at all." Provost Tom Smith and I convened several faculty meetings to discuss the proposed calendar change. Several faculty members, most notably Professor Carl Shermer in engineering, spoke in favor of the change, citing examples of benefits to students and to utilization of the physical plant. A larger number of faculty were opposed, arguing that the regents, supported by the Ohio University administration, were snatching away their academic freedom, making decisions arbitrarily on academic matters that the faculty considered "sacred." Students, stirred up by inflammatory articles in the *Post*, fanned the flames; but they had no legitimate complaint since they were unfamiliar with the quarter system, and therefore were relatively unqualified to judge it in advance.

At Bowling Green State University, the faculty issued a statement that Chancellor Millett had acted in an "arbitrary, cavalier and dictatorial manner." Ohio was the only university that had agreed to comply with the chancellor's mandate. As criticism from the other universities mounted, Millett waffled on his directive, asserting that he had merely made a "suggestion" for change. He released a statement to the *Post*: "I warned all state university presidents that they should be alert to the possibility of going on a common calendar, but by no means said it was a certainty." The *Post* suddenly jumped onto the side of the university, reprinting Millett's earlier statement that "Ohio University must make plans leading to a quarterly calendar to become effective in July 1967." The article was accompanied by a cartoon showing Millett with two faces—two mouths and two different "lines," one to the presidents and the other to the press.

The furor on campus began to die down and we proceeded with plans for the changeover. The very next year, the board of regents did, in fact, mandate a common calendar for all state schools—except one. The exception was Miami University, which Millett had headed. In his last year as president, he had pushed through a modified trimester system. He granted Miami additional time to make the shift, explaining that they had hardly had time to become accustomed to the trimester schedule.

CHAPTER 9

The Dawn of Turmoil

THE TRANQUIL MOOD on the Ohio campus abruptly changed in 1967. I am indebted to Lynn Shostack of the Ohio Fellows Program for the following perceptive analysis of the mood on U.S. college campuses in the late 1960s:

> Though the specific issues varied from campus to campus, every mainstream university in America was rocked by evidence of confusion, frustration and social change taking place during the Sixties. A hundred theories have been put forth as to the reasons for educational chaos; yet whatever the underlying causes, certain characteristics were similar in case after case, be it black student violence at San Francisco State and Cornell, SDS-inspired destruction at Columbia, Free Speech at Berkeley or student-police confrontation at the Democratic Convention in Chicago. Whatever the issue, and in some cases it seemed the issues were manufactured to meet the need, these upheavals seemed to have

in common: assault on a figure or organization representative of established authority; a complete rejection of communication and compromise; an emotional, sometimes hysterical, atmosphere; and finally, a disillusioning and uneasy resolution. Evidence of academic turmoil was so widespread during the Sixties as to deny the possibility that one or two schools were uniquely to blame. It was a reflection of national growing pains and national evolution. . . .

Though specific issues have been rallying points for student rebellion, at its base the cause appears more fundamental and more emotional. The first large-scale student eruption was the Free Speech Movement at Berkeley in 1964. Yet the three previous years seem to show a unique series of events which set the stage for this first action. Certainly the presidency of John Fitzgerald Kennedy contributed immensely. His insistence on critical judgment, on idealism and on active pursuit of goals made him a hero among the youth of the nation. President Kennedy's image as a "dragon-slayer" led thousands of young people into the civil rights cause, the Peace Corps, and politics. His liberalism may not have initiated the New Left, but it opened the doors of possibility. During the first national student demonstration, the Washington Peace March of 1962, President Kennedy dispensed coffee to picketers and maintained that the right of free speech overshadowed and repudiated any thought of reprisal. That same year saw the formation of the SDS based on the idealistic concept of "participatory democracy."

By 1963, student optimism and idealism was at its peak; the signing of the nuclear test-ban treaty and pending civil rights legislation indicated true reform. As suggested, at this time students appeared more concerned with societal issues than with the university. The death of John Kennedy was especially traumatic for the college population; and although Lyndon Baines Johnson actually initiated more far-reaching social legislation than Kennedy had, the image was not the same. It appeared that the old, entrenched "wheeler dealers" had taken over, and President Johnson did not project the "call to youth" that Kennedy had so vigorously expounded.

Yet the year after the assassination was relatively quiet; students still volunteered for poverty-area work, Peace Corps duty and ghetto efforts, partly due to the ideal implied in the War on Poverty. Then in the fall of 1964, Berkeley erupted, demonstrating the feasibility of direct action techniques on the campus. By 1965, student groups had swung further to the left, because of increased hostility to the Vietnam War on the part of college-age men, and because of creeping disillusionment with the "system" and any hope of reforming it peacefully. Feeling blocked from national participation, students focused on a closer "establishment"; i.e., the university itself. The next five years only increased antagonism between students and the "system"; the list of campuses involved is both lengthy and encompassing.

In addition, a Third World movement of black students became more vocal and made more violent demands for cultural and social reparation in ethnic education. This is but a partial exploration of events and reasons, yet it serves to illustrate the schism which had grown between youth and the nation. Though the majority of young people were not militantly involved in any confrontations, they stood silent as violence was done. And in many cases, they were mobilized by more radical elements who were able to capitalize on the underlying frustration of the majority. In the latter half of the 1960s college had become a political arena as well as an educational debating ground. The university structure was ill-equipped to deal with these changes, as event after event illustrated.

Student concerns about the war in Vietnam and the threat of being drafted into the armed forces contributed to the souring of the atmosphere on campuses. The assassinations of President Kennedy, Robert Kennedy, and the Reverend Martin Luther King Jr. were shocking blows to student and faculty morale. Student riots forced the resignations of Clark Kerr in California and James Perkins at Cornell. Riots at South Carolina State College resulted in two dead and forty injured. The National Student Association reported 221 major demonstrations on 101 campuses between January 1 and May 15, 1968.

Yet the student mood on the Ohio University campus did not

turn ugly until 1969. Amusingly, a small group of students identifying themselves as members of the Students for a Democratic Society (SDS) knocked on our door at 29 Park Place in the mid-1960s. Marion invited them in for a chat. Expecting that she would be flattered, they announced that they had selected Ohio University for "colonization." Apparently, they found little interest on our campus at that time because there is no evidence they ever moved in. Kent State was not so fortunate: it is clear in reading about the tragic events of 1970 that the SDS had occupied near-campus housing.

The Ohio student newspaper, the *Post,* became increasingly critical and outspoken in early 1967. Concerns were expressed about crowded living conditions, women's hours, parietal rules, and the prohibition of alcohol on campus. It took a strike of nonacademic employees to galvanize student action and sharp, often savage, criticism of university leadership by editors of the *Post.*

Representatives of the American Federation of State, County, and Municipal Employees (AFCSME)—a branch of the AFL-CIO—appeared on campus importuning our 1,300 nonacademic employees to join the union. The AFL-CIO, losing membership nationally, looked upon the state educational system as a prime target for organization. Although state civil service employees were prohibited from striking by the Ferguson Act, this law had never been tested in court.

In order to open the doors to statewide unionization, the AFCSME had to set a precedent of recognition at but a single state university. Its choice of Athens and Ohio University for the effort was shrewd and calculated. Athens was geographically isolated and could not draw outside labor in the event of trouble. This meant that any success in organizing or striking would show quick and dramatic results, and that just the threat of such action could be a potent tool for forcing recognition. Furthermore, there was a tradition of unionism in the mining communities of southeastern Ohio dating from the 1860s. People in the area respected picket lines—in fact, they feared crossing them because of the history of violence that accompanied mine workers' strikes over the years. Furthermore, we were vulnerable because of my earlier involvement with President Johnson's War on Poverty and our efforts to improve economic conditions in Appalachian Ohio. How could I deny our own employees, they argued, what we were freely advocating for high school dropouts?

The community at large showed little concern, even as the fuse was lit. November 1966 saw a minor test: sixteen meat cutters and drivers called in "sick," evoking an unfortunately high-handed response from Business Manager Luverne Lausche, who implied to the workers that they may have "gotten away with it" once, but were not likely to do so again. That month, two hundred rank-and-file employees signed payroll deduction cards pledging their support to the AFCSME.

The union immediately demanded that the university authorize a "check off," deducting union dues from employees' wages and turning them over to the union. If the demands were met, it meant official recognition of the union's legal representation of employees. Rules of the Inter-University Council (IUC), representing the presidents of each of the state universities, required that member institutions not request an official opinion of the attorney general on any matter of statewide significance, unless such action had been approved by the council.

Ohio laws stated that in legal disputes state universities could be represented by only the attorney general or his designated representative. Attorney General William Saxbe appointed Athens lawyer Earl Bridgewater to advise us on the legality of the check-off demand. Bridgewater, in his brief, cited a 1947 Ohio Supreme Court decision, *Hagerman vs. City of Dayton*, which ruled that a "check-off is contrary to the spirit and purpose of the civil service laws of the state . . . and labor unions have no function which they discharge in connection with civil service appointees."

Attorney General Saxbe, though in absentia, made it clearly known to the members of the Inter-University Council that a state university could not lawfully give deductions to a union. He also cited the Ferguson Act prohibiting civil service employees from striking. The council voted against the check-off partially from fear of ramifications at their own institutions and partially because of the strong pressure from Columbus. Ohio University was left with no alternative but to resist the union demands.

The real action began on Saturday, March 4, 1967, when I received the news that seventy-six of the university's nonacademic workers had voted to strike and requested the union's assistance. The next morning churchgoers were greeted with the first evidence of the coming siege as fifty picketers took posts around the university.

The Student Congress, morally committed to the workers' plight, voted to support the strike and passed resolutions opposing student interference in it. Conspicuously jumping on the bandwagon, a group of about a dozen faculty members announced the immediate formation of a teacher's union, which was also AFL-CIO initiated. The *Post* came out with an editorial supporting the strike. A large number of workers left their jobs in sympathy with their striking counterparts. Students began rallying to the cause, stirred on by a handful of self-appointed leaders and strident articles in the *Post* urging students not to be "scabs" by taking jobs as substitutes for the striking workers.

By the fourth day of the strike, tension had reached an explosive level. Strikers had begun a series of anonymous telephone calls intimidating and threatening their nonstriking coworkers. Students grew restless and unhappy as the strike began to affect food distribution, maintenance of dormitories, and the continuance of classes. Simultaneously, the Hocking River was approaching its springtime flood stage. As the waters rose higher, the atmosphere grew more strained. One of the radical student leaders raced about campus shouting, "The word is resist . . . resist anything that helps put the university back on an even keel."

Vice President Whalen and I continued to meet with the Faculty Senate and Student Congress. We went to Memorial Auditorium for an open meeting with the student body, answering questions for more than an hour from the two thousand students assembled. All of these efforts proved futile. The student body president persuaded the 250 student board-jobbers to stage a one-day boycott in support of the strike. Despite overwhelming pressure, we complied with the Inter-University Council's ruling not to seek direct assistance from the attorney general and to abide by the legal advice of Saxbe's representative as valid and indicative of the state's position.

Then came the most crippling blow of all. Attorney General Saxbe was campaigning in Cleveland for the United States Senate seat. In Ohio's largest labor union constituency, he casually remarked that recognition of a union was legal and could be granted by a university president. Bridgewater, his attorney representative in Athens, had decided to leave town for what was described by a friend as "the first winter vacation of his life."

The following morning three thousand students held an emotional demonstration outside of Memorial Auditorium, demanding capitulation to the union. Although a restraining order had been issued by the Athens courts, the pickets remained at their posts. In the midst of the disastrous hurricane of events, I was determined to resolve the issue, whatever the outcome. There would be no more strategies, no more vacillation, and no further disintegration of Ohio University. I requested a meeting of the executive committee of the board of trustees. Chairman John Galbreath set up the meeting in Columbus with the attorney general for Tuesday evening the following week. I sent telegrams to the other state university presidents explaining the urgency of our situation and indicating that our board would seek a direct ruling from the attorney general without waiting for Inter-University Council approval. I invited their comments and suggestions. None came.

With five days remaining before the meeting in Columbus, the atmosphere on campus became steadily worse and more explosive. Volunteer workers were near exhaustion, food supplies were dwindling, and a flurry of threatening telephone calls increased the tension on campus. A new rumor spread that the new heating plant would be dynamited.

An official inspection of the university resulted in the assessment that the campus could not sustain itself until Tuesday, and probably not even beyond Sunday. As a choice between voluntarily closing the school and being forced to by breakdown, the executive committee favored the former. At 4:00 P.M. the decision to advance spring recess by two weeks was aired over the university radio station.

The effect on the student body was electrifying. In a humiliating desertion of both its firebrand leaders and the disadvantaged strikers, the student body fled. Within a matter of minutes, the telephone boards were hopelessly tangled; lines wound around the banks, which were caught in a one-city depression, staying open to provide traveling money for unprepared students; lines stretched more than a block from the travel agency; and bumper-to-bumper lines of cars crawled out of Athens in all directions.

While preparing for the crucial meeting in Columbus, I was buoyed by a vote of support from the Faculty Senate and a petition signed by 237 members of the faculty: "We, the undersigned faculty members of Ohio University, believe that President Vernon Alden has consistently tried to act in the best interests of Ohio University and that he has been motivated by a desire to be fair to all parties concerned. We wish to go on record expressing our confidence in the president's good will and competence to work out solutions to the current problems."

After eleven wearying and sometimes terrifying days, the Tuesday (March 14) meeting in Columbus finally took place. Early in the evening, several administrative officers and I met with members of the executive committee of the board of trustees. Governor James Rhodes was in Japan with a group of touring Ohio industrialists, but he was represented by Director of Finance Richard Krabach. Attorney General Saxbe and his assistant, Donald Colasurd, completed the group. Saxbe began by arguing that he saw no reason why the board of trustees could not recognize the union, but that the

Little Vernon, brother Don, and
sister Janet in their 1920s finest.

Mother and Father Alden.

A newly minted Naval officer
in 1943 about to enter Japanese
Language School.

Son Jim gives his approval before Dad leaves to preside over Commencement.

A breakfast conference with daughter Anne.

Marion inspecting garden flowers for the Peace Corps reception.

The neighborhood youngsters get together. That's tow-headed Jim between Maya Lin and Anne. Rob on the far left uses a hands-on approach.

Rob at the farewell dinner.

David, Jim, Anne, and Rob with former President Eisenhower.
My mother's favorite photograph.

A memorable visit with former President Eisenhower.

Ohio University celebrates its 160th anniversary with the dedication of
the Memorial Room in Baker Center at which trustee Fred Johnson and
astronaut John Glenn spoke.

Meeting with Trustee Chairman John Galbreath.

Trustee Paul Stocker examines a Japanese print and antique Noh mask box.

Planning the Job Corps program with Sargent Shriver and volunteers
Stan Musial and Jesse Owens.

President Barnaby Keeney of Brown presents me with an honorary degree at my alma mater.

I missed this shot in the basketball game between the Harlem Globetrotters and the Ohio University Athletic Department.

About to experience dive-bombing in an Air Force jet.

Greeted by hundreds of South Vietnamese children upon visit to Saigon orphanage.

A conference between Nigerian teachers and Ohio University faculty members.

Bob Hope on campus for a library benefit.

Supreme Court Justice William O. Douglas before his presentation in the Edwin and Ruth Kennedy Lecture Series.

President Johnson announces his Great Society program at Ohio University in May 1964.

Walter Cronkite visits the Ohio University campus. Provost Tom Smith in the background.

Trustee Chairman Fred Johnson at the ground-breaking for the rerouting of the Hocking River.

With Russell Milliken and Trustee Fred Johnson being greeted by Senator Ted Kennedy following USAID's recognition of Ohio University's overseas programs.

Secretary of Defense Robert McNamara being welcomed at the Ohio University airport by Trustees Wayne Brown, Paul Stocker, and Joseph Hall.

David being congratulated by his father after winning the 100th Anniversary Pie Race at Northfield–Mount Hermon School—a victory over Olympian Frank Shorter.

Together with Neil Armstrong in meeting with directors of Lloyds of London.

The family celebrates after the the Japanese Emperor conferred upon me "The Order of the Rising Sun."

A meeting with the Emperor of Japan.

Greeting the newly wed Crown Prince and Princess at their reception in the Imperial Palace in Tokyo.

The old and the new — with President Robert Glidden.

Announcing the establishment of the "Vernon and Marion Alden Chair" for the cello at the Boston Symphony Orchestra.

Host Michael Long greets friends gathered for a dinner honoring Marion and me at the Lotos Club in New York.

Sandy Elsass, Jane and George Mathews.

Bob Axline, Lynn Shostack, Bill Haines, and Jean Axline.

Sargent Shriver addresses dinner guests.

Catey Long, Robert Fallon, and René Glidden.

check-off of dues was explicitly illegal. One without the other was unacceptable to the union. After lengthy and sometimes heated discussions, Richard Krabach, who had power and influence in the governor's cabinet well beyond his director of finance title, said heatedly to Saxbe: "You cannot keep a major university shut down forever. I'm suggesting to this board that they recognize the union and authorize the check-off—and you can sue them if it's illegal." Saxbe conceded his original stance and approved the check-off of dues. In a public conference later in the evening, the executive committee accepted my recommendation that the check-off be granted. The strike was over.

After such trauma, we came to an unsatisfactory and temporary truce: the union maintained a threatening attitude and promised to repeat its demands later when the employees had recovered their stability; the university was unable to bring the union to any firm commitment of cooperation or future standards. In the state, my position with both the IUC presidents and Columbus had been weakened. But worst of all, my close and trusting relationship with students had been seriously damaged. When the university opened after the advanced spring break, and we were prepared to resume regular operations, I made the following observations at a university convocation: "It seems clear that we on this campus have been the focal point of a drive to organize the nonteaching personnel of the universities in the State, and the ramifications extend far beyond Athens. Furthermore, this is a new experience for all of us. Those of us who, for the past few days, have invested all of our waking hours (plus many hours we should have been sleeping) have tried to do our best. Nevertheless, in retrospect, we can clearly see where we might have done things differently." My speech continued:

> I have learned much in the past few days: a strike is a little bit like a war—it is much easier to prevent it than it is to take the action that stops it. We were faced with a many-sided issue. First there is the question of justice: what is right for the complainants who precipitated the issue by striking; and what is right for the many

who are affected by their actions? Then there is the question of law: which presumes to define the rules of justice, but which, at its root is political. And then, this is a university: and we are involved in a controversy where the ground rules for dealing with it—the union strategy, the legal approach, the administrative experience are derived primarily from private business—a radically different kind of institution. The questions I have brooded over most have been these: What is just, what is legal, and what is the University in dealing with these issues—if one must compromise, what is it most important to preserve?

However, the question that has been most on my mind as I have had brief periods of reflection these past few days is, What is the University in the light of these recent events? As I brooded on this question this past week, I was plagued by the thought that I had spent my working life in educational administration without ever having realistically faced this question. I became sharply aware that the modern university, which is the lineal descendent of the medieval university, seems not to have examined this question. I have asked myself, where is the theoretical design to which we may turn to resolve the questions we now have? And I had to concede that I have never seen one. I don't believe it exists and I fear that the vulnerability of the University to our recent threats is rooted in this lack of a comprehensive theory of university design that will serve as a point of reference for any constituent of the University on any issue that may arise. In an emergency such as we have just come through, I suspect that the scars we carry that will interfere with our work for some time to come would not be of much consequence if we had a fuller agreement, in advance, on the nature of our institution and its place in society.

It was heartening to read the reaction of columnist Phil Skardon in an article entitled "Labor Day": "The talk was the measure of the man. There should be sympathy; for the university was ill-equipped for the war. But there should be admiration too, for few have spoken so cogently about a conflict of rights—on the one hand, to organize, and on the other, to educate."

When I wrote this chapter (in 1996), I felt great sympathy for

Richard Levin, president of Yale. At the time, he was trying to negotiate a strike—a strike that was concluded later that year—that had been going on for more than ten weeks and included an appearance of Jesse Jackson leading a group of four thousand union supporters shouting "Work With Dignity" at the graduation ceremonies. Yale experienced a six-day strike in 1968 and has suffered through an eight-week strike in 1971, ten weeks in 1974, thirteen weeks in 1977, ten weeks in 1984, and a four-day strike in 1992. Yale's experience underscores my comments on the vulnerability of universities.

CLOUDS ON THE HORIZON

A few years ago an alumnus sent me a copy of a letter, dated January 14, 1968, he had written to me while a student at Ohio:

President Alden,

Upon receiving my bill for this present quarter my room-mates and I were trying to decide what the $35 student fee was to go for. We decided that it paid for the free sports' events, use of Baker Center (which we rarely use), use of the library, and whatever else we use but do not pay for.

Now the situation has arisen that there is about eight inches of snow on the ground. Our question is why are the sidewalks on the West Green not cleared off? For all the money we "shovel" out to this school I think it is your responsibility, as our beloved leader, to see that we get what we are entitled to.

I expect a reply to this letter. Many of the students are fed up with the way they are used for their money. My address will be enclosed.

Larry Smith
234 James Hall

He also sent me a copy of my reply, dated two days later:

Dear Larry:

Thank you for your letter expressing concern about the condition of the sidewalks on the West Green. As you may know by now, we had a total of 19 inches of snow in Athens during the past few days. Because most of our employees were snowbound on Sunday, we were able to bring in only eight people to clear sidewalks and parking lots that day. However, on Monday and Tuesday I feel that our people did a remarkable job of clearing sidewalks, streets and parking lots around the University. This morning, Tuesday, I toured the West Green and was quite impressed with the job they had done.

As a matter of fact, I am more proud of how they are doing than of how you are doing academically. I hope that you can do a somewhat better job in the next couple of quarters and still be with us next year.

Sincerely yours,
Vernon R. Alden

In 1968 we were threatened with another strike by nonacademic employees, but this time we were much better prepared. Personnel Director Ward Wilson planned to fill some seventy supervisory positions through competitive examination. The union insisted upon seniority as the criterion.

At the first threat of a strike, we took precautionary measures. Extra workers were hired to staff cafeterias and maintenance positions. The university was one week away from final examinations, but we planned not to be placed in the position of having to accede to the union to avert a campus shutdown. A list of electives was worked out between student leaders and the Faculty Senate so that, in the event the university were to close, students would be able to leave without enduring any penalty in grades or attendance requirements.

The union overplayed its hand. Unlike the previous year, it seemed obvious that the student body was not about to rally behind their grievances. The university had beaten the union's strategy with claims (claims that were legally correct) of illegal proceedings by the union. On the evening before the threatened strike, they reversed their position and backed down.

At the level of power, it seemed that the issue had been resolved. The university would remain open as usual, however tense the truce.

However, the students were again approaching an emotional out-burst. They did not have the least interest in the union's grievances, but they had been conditioned the year before to equate "strike" with "vacation." In 1967 they had convinced themselves that it had been "student power" that had led to the closing of the university. Some had already sent their clothes home; many were packed and pre-pared to leave the campus when the news came that the union had decided not to strike. After all of our careful preparation, we found ourselves outflanked, not by a union, but by an unstable, unpre-dictable, and uncontrollable student body.

At approximately 9:00 P.M. on Sunday, March 19, a group of stu-dents began shouting outside dormitories around the campus for the students to come out. To the shouts of "We want a strike." and "Let's go home," the fast-increasing crowd surged from the East to the West Greens, gathering numbers and building up emotional in-tensity. About 1,000 of the 16,500 students on campus were involved. Initially, the chants were good-natured; after hollering for a few minutes outside the president's home, the group moved to the town's main intersection and sat in the middle of the street. Then the mob began to get ugly. Word was passed to the effect that, "If we raise enough hell, we can go home."

The crowd headed toward the construction site of the new library and climbed atop the partially built floor. Firecrackers were set off and shouting students began throwing rocks and construction ma-terials across the street at our home. Marion and I and our four young children huddled in the safety of our second-floor hallway while bolts and bricks crashed through our front windows. Three students tried to climb through an upstairs window but were chased off by campus police. A student bystander was hit in the eye with a thrown rock. Vice President Whalen and members of his staff bravely moved about between the library and our home, trying to bring order to the mob. Quickly outrunning our small campus police force, the crowd swept onto the main campus, breaking win-dows and walkway lights along the way. By midnight the police had dispelled most of the crowd. The following day, the student newspaper editorialized: "It wasn't good. Rioting never is good. People getting hurt never is good. Buildings damaged never is good. Cops—who don't make trouble but only have to deal with it—getting hurt never is good. So, to get it on the record, we didn't like what happened last night—in front of Cutler Hall, in front of Baker Center, at Court and Union."

Yet the *Post* went on to draw conclusions. It put words in the mouths of the student body; to give a "cause" to coincide with its own year-long advocation of more shows of student power. This sounded a keynote for student leaders, who had been no part of the spontaneous demonstration, to take over and make it their own:

> An objective analysis is needed. And we will try to provide one—as we see it.
>
> Why did it happen?
>
> It happened because students wanted to go home this week. They were planning to go home. And then all of a sudden, they couldn't go home. It was a SUNDAY night.
>
> It was cold and RAINING.
>
> It was 2,000 ANGRY students.
>
> Why angry? Just because they couldn't go home this week?
>
> Well, that's part of it. Then there are all the other things, too. Women's hours. Beer in the dorms. The pressure of the quarter system. Long lines. The feeling that everybody is using you, that no one really cares about what you want or what is best for you. THE INABILITY TO HAVE ANY INFLUENCE OVER DECISIONS THAT AFFECT STUDENTS' LIVES!!

The *Post* continued its attack upon the university's "in loco parentis" policies, many of which were in the process of modification under the skillful leadership of James Whalen and his staff. The *Post* editor conducted an ugly and vicious personal attack upon me, and a small group of student leaders ran from meeting to meeting trying to stir up campus protests. To reach as many students as possible, I appeared on the university's television station with a prepared statement:

We stand solidly, with the backing of the Board of Trustees and the Governor of Ohio, to keep this University open. We do not intend to allow the disruptive actions of some to permanently damage the central purpose of this institution. . . . No university in America has expended more energy and more resources in the process of achieving a new relationship among the various elements within the University structure. . . . We have but one responsibility—to keep Ohio University open so that the vast majority of students, who have clearly shown their genuine desire to proceed with their degree programs, may do so.

I digressed from my prepared remarks to add: "Any student who is so tired of the pursuit of an education at this school, is free to go home whenever he pleases, but to expect academic credit for nonperformance is absurd." Apparently, my remarks were picked up by commercial television stations throughout the state and were carried on the six o'clock news in most of Ohio's major cities. We were deluged with telephone calls and letters of support from citizens who were clearly fed up with the student insurrections taking place throughout the country. At the same time, the governor sent the Ohio National Guard to the county fairgrounds in case they would be needed on campus.

The next day, the Hocking River began making its annual pilgrimage to dry land, and it appeared that this flood would be an especially serious one. An NBC television commentator remarked with a certain appropriate humor: "A labor union tried to close Ohio University and failed. Then the students tried and failed. Now God is trying to close the University but President Alden seems to be holding his own." The publisher of *Parade* magazine had apparently listened to NBC-TV and telephoned me requesting that I write a cover story for the magazine, beginning with the quote. My article appeared a week or so later and was given the title, "Will Peace Come to the Campus?"

The Hocking River reached its highest point in the university's 164-year history, inundating the area with record flood water. A plea from nearby towns saw students drop their "cause" and travel by the hundreds to stricken communities to help pile sandbags along with troops from the National Guard. Mayor Earl Hilleary of nearby Nelsonville was quoted by the *Dayton Daily News*: "Had it not been for the help of about 500 Ohio University students, it was obvious by noon that the river would have completely flooded the town."

CHAPTER **10**

On the Move: Back to Boston

THE SUMMER OF 1968 was a peaceful one. Construction of new buildings continued, and faculty and administrators went about their tasks without interruption. For the first time in my tenure at Ohio University I began to think about the future and reflect upon what had or had not been accomplished at the university. I was deeply hurt by the assault upon our family by the rock-throwing students. My overriding goal had been to create an environment that would meet student concerns and lift their levels of aspiration. I found myself the target of a vicious attack by a small cadre of student leaders and the editors of the student newspaper, who felt that the university was not changing rapidly enough. Vice President Whalen and his team were moving as quickly and as creatively as any administrative organization in the nation to change our "in loco parentis" culture. I had quietly struggled with the faculty to upgrade and open up the curriculum and had spent countless hours with trustees who were not overly enthusiastic about changes in parietal rules. Being a congenital optimist, I was confident that the much larger, but silent, number of students supported and appreciated our efforts.

In correspondence with me, Lynn Shostack, now a prominent New York real-estate developer, made some interesting observations about leadership:

> Does a life spent wielding power make one more optimistic or more pessimistic? Does ambition fulfilled lead to humility or arrogance? Have you found (as I have) that being a leader not only acquaints you intimately with your strengths and weaknesses, but also with the fact that to be a good leader you must give away all credit, accept all blame and never, never ask for sympathy or expect understanding? Do you believe that leadership is like a fiery crucible—that it burns away all pretense, all illusion and either leaves one tempered and strong or turns one to cinders?

I was not prepared to answer her perceptive questions in the summer of 1968, but I did, for the first time, begin to think about life beyond Ohio University. In my second year as president, I had been visited by Professor Guy Dodge, of Brown University, a member of their presidential search committee. He asked me whether I would consider being a candidate to head my alma mater. Without any reservation I explained that much remained to be accomplished at Ohio University, and I would not consider leaving. I gave the same answer to President Johnson and Sargent Shriver when they twisted my arm in 1964 to accept the directorship of the United States Job Corps.

After a lengthy and flattering front-page story in the *Wall Street Journal* describing our efforts at Ohio and my experiences in Washington, in 1966 and 1967 I received several telephone calls from executive search firms representing large U.S. companies. Investments by American corporations typically follow emerging products or trends—electronics, computers, environmental concerns, international outreach, and so on. With the enormous growth of higher education in the 1960s, the development of advanced management programs, and the prospect of using new technology in undergraduate and adult education, many corporations moved to acquire a position in the emerging "knowledge industry." Because of my background as a graduate of the Harvard Business School, a director of companies, and a university president, I was asked by several corporations to head up their education subsidiaries—Xerox, IBM, CBS, Westinghouse, and Raytheon among them. Despite attractive salary offers, stock options, and so forth, I declined those invitations because I felt that we still had much left to complete at Ohio University.

Late in the summer of 1968 my family and I traveled to our Martha's Vineyard vacation house. While there, I received an invitation that I felt I had to consider seriously. Mr. Ralph Lowell—known affectionately as "Mr. Boston"—was retiring from his distinguished career as chairman of the Boston Safe Deposit and Trust Company and its recently formed holding company, the Boston Company. Lowell had invited me to become a director of the Trust Company several years before, and I had regularly attended meetings of the board, even while at Ohio. Much to my surprise, the directors invited me to return to Boston to serve as chairman of both entities. The prospect of stepping into the communitywide responsibilities in which "Mr. Boston" had distinguished himself proved to be irresistible. Three of our four children had been born in Boston and before long they would be attending college.

When I had made my decision, I met first with Fred Johnson, our board chairman, to tell him of my plans to leave. It was not easy to tell Fred I was leaving: from the very beginning, he had captivated me with his vision for the university and southeastern Ohio. Before I gave him the details—and with him still unaware that Lowell was soon to retire—his response was, "I know you've had several attractive offers over the years, Vern, but I was hoping that you'd stay on for several more years and then return to Boston to succeed Mr. Lowell, who spoke so highly of you at the fifth anniversary celebration." When I told him the specifics, he couldn't argue with my decision.

Together, Fred and I had accomplished the wildest of our dreams. We were even moving the restless Hocking River. People could no longer poke fun and question our sanity.

At our formal board meeting on September 11, I promised the trustees that I would remain as president for another academic year and return to Boston after the June commencement in 1969. It was not easy to read my statement of resignation to the group of nine trustees who had been so supportive and helpful during our years at Ohio:

> My decision to leave Ohio University next June, after seven and one-half of the most exciting and satisfying years of my life, is based upon the unusual opportunity in Boston and my awareness that the optimal long-range growth of institutions is in cycles of development, with each stage calling for different qualities of leadership.
>
> I believe that we are at a turning point and that the University can best continue its forward thrust if the trustees have an opportunity to assess the present achievement, set new goals and priorities, and select a new president for the next period, which I am sure will be one of great service to the young people of Ohio. There is a special kind of spirit and dedication to service at Ohio University which was in the institution when my distinguished predecessor, John Calhoun Baker, passed his mantle on to me. I have tried to nourish this spirit, build upon it, and keep it contemporary within these fast-moving times. The task has been rewarding because of the wonderful people among its trustees, faculty, administrators, nonacademic employees and students whose hopes and dreams I have shared.

The *Athens Messenger* generously commented in an editorial:

> The Alden years have been seven years of utterly fantastic growth. Never in our long history have such demands been placed upon this institution and the where-with-all been made so available to finance this growth with such speed. Consider these figures bracketing the years of Alden's tenure:

Since 1962 enrollment on the main campus here at Athens has more than doubled, and on the university's five branch campuses enrollment has nearly tripled. Graduate enrollment here has increased four times.

The faculty has jumped from 341 to 736. What were maximum salaries at associate and full professor levels in 1962 are today minimum salaries.

Ohio University's operating budget has jumped from $13 to $49 million; physical assets have grown from $40 to $120 million.

University construction has totaled over $82 million, and private developers—almost unheard of here prior to 1962—have invested at least $20 million in university related construction projects.

This is not the total story, of course. These are merely head count and dollar-and-cents figures that affect, but certainly do not describe, the real essence of a university, the capability to provide a meaningful educational experience for youth in today's and tomorrow's complex world.

And yet these figures bracketing the Alden years do serve to measure if only by way of example, the hurdle that this vibrant institution has jumped in such a short period of time. It is also noteworthy that in a very real sense Athens has jumped this same hurdle too. Just how many communities of 15,000 population, relatively isolated from metropolitan population growth centers, have enjoyed anything like what has been Athens' as well as Ohio University's experience?

The *Ohio Alumnus* magazine and Professor Meno Lovenstein's book *The Decade of the University* recorded additional accomplishments during our tenure:

The size of the Athens campus increased by 750 acres, including 141 acres of airport land—a growth of 88 percent

Capital funds from Ohio, the Federal government and bond issues resulted in an increase in assets from $40 million to $153 million ... with a ten-year expansion program to be completed in 1973 totaling $205 million

Private gifts increased from $279,000 in 1962 to $3 million in 1968

The first endowed faculty chairs were established—named for Charles O'Bleness, Robert Morton, and Rush Elliott

New benefits were extended to the faculty—sabbatical leaves (forty-seven professors were on sabbatical leave in 1969) and remission of three-quarters of tuition fees for children of faculty members

Scholarships and loans to students increased two and one-half times, financial aid grants and loans totaled $3.3 million in 1968/69, and work-study and student jobs brought the total to $7.5 million

In our last year at the university, Marion and I traveled to several Ohio University alumni clubs throughout the United States. Our good friend Bill Jerome, the president of Bowling Green University, presented me with an honorary degree at the June commencement. Other recipients that day were Bob Hope and Cyrus Eaton. The exercises were held outdoors in the Bowling Green stadium. As the ceremonies were about to begin, a torrential rain poured down upon the robed assembly. Bob Hope shouted to President Jerome: "Hey, prez, you'd better call it off before we all go down for the third time."

May 23, 1969 was designated as "Marion and Vernon Alden Day" at Ohio University. A concert, a library dedication, and a banquet were attended by our family and the university community. In a surprise announcement by Fred Johnson, the trustees' chairman, the new library was named the Vernon Roger Alden Library. This was a special honor to me because I deeply believed that an excellent library performs a central role at a quality university. At the banquet, citations were presented from the student body, the faculty, the alumni, the military units on campus, and the Senate of the State of Ohio. At the June commencement, held in the Convocation Center with 13,500 people attending, the trustees awarded me the honorary degree doctor of humane letters. They also conferred upon me the Founder's Citation, which at that time had been awarded to only two other recipients in Ohio University's history. In my final annual report, I made the following observations:

> Although these years at Ohio University have been exciting and rewarding, they also have brought crises, problems and disappointments. Our dreams and hopes have been larger than our capacities. Conflicts from time to time appeared to obscure our purposes; misunderstandings have sometimes detracted from our basic goodwill, and impatience was often the measure of difference between the goal and what was immediately possible. In these frustrations we have been cheered by the thought that nothing of significance is ever achieved without difficulty . . . and we were attempting significant things.
>
> In 1962 we were confronted with state-wide efforts to impose limitations upon the University in inviting outside speakers. Ohio University stood almost alone in successfully combating legislation which would have restricted the freedoms of our students and faculty. Even today there are those inside and outside the University who would deny us the benefits of that climate of freedom which we have fought so hard to preserve in the state of Ohio.
>
> In 1967 Ohio University was selected as the primary target for a state-wide effort to unionize nonacademic employees. We had to endure a ten-day strike and its attendant turmoil on campus. Since then a climate of trust is being established between the local union and our administration, resulting in a two-year, no-strike agreement reached last fall.
>
> The American college and university student is properly concerned about the relevance of the academic curriculum today, concerns which are being expressed on almost every campus throughout the nation. Although innovative programs have been introduced at Ohio University, efforts to involve students in serious discussion of academic change have oftentimes resulted in disappointment. Nevertheless, the Committee on Educational Inquiry, headed by Professor Meno Lovenstein, produced a remarkable report recommending significant changes at the University.
>
> A university in a free society exists to prepare the leaders and

sharpen the wits of followers and critics. Leadership, after all, is one of the most ephemeral of all the arts; there is no better place for students to learn this art than at a university.

At Ohio University we have understood that mission of the university, and I believe that during these years we have all moved closer to that vision.

While a transition from a certain and ordered approach to a more open one is bound to be difficult in any institution, I am confident that when we all have made our adjustment to it we will find university life much richer, a much more creative force, and a model of achievement, tolerance and humane social intercourse for the larger society. I am genuinely sorry not to be staying on to see this achieved, but I shall be watching from a distance, with interest, enthusiasm and respect for those who will one day make Ohio University what I have always believed she should be . . . a truly distinguished university.

Shortly after I returned to Boston, Provost Tom Smith resigned to accept the presidency of Lawrence University in Appleton, Wisconsin. Executive Vice President Jim Whalen took on the presidency of Newton College in Massachusetts. After successfully merging the college with Boston College, he accepted the presidency of Ithaca College, which he led with extraordinary distinction for twenty-two years. Tom Gee, who has an incredibly shrewd political sense and had been so helpful in attracting federal funds, accepted my invitation to join me at the Boston Company. He later became president of Southern Vermont College.

Dean Harry Evarts became the president of Bryant College in Rhode Island; Dr. John Chandler became president of Claremont College in California; Dean Ed Penson became the president of Salem State College in Massachusetts. A year later, Professor William Holmes became the president of Simmons College in Boston. The chairman of the presidential search committee at Simmons College in Boston had asked me to recommend a candidate for their presidency. Clearly, Bill made a great impression upon the trustees, faculty, and student representatives who interviewed him. Bill provided outstanding leadership at Simmons for twenty-three years.

Between September, when I notified the trustees I would be leaving, and the June 1969 commencement, I traveled to Boston one day a month to attend the Boston Company board meetings and to look for a new house. The housing market was fairly depressed, so it did not take long to find a place that would suit our needs—a lovely, old Victorian home overlooking the Brookline Reservoir. We bought it from Tudor and Tenley Albright Gardner. Tenley, a medical doctor, had been an Olympic figure-skating champion.

On one of those visits to Boston, Alan Weinberg, the president of the Ohio University alumni club in Boston, and I dedicated a plaque on the site of the original Bunch of Grapes Tavern, where the idea of the American Western University—now Ohio University—was conceived in 1786. The State Street Bank occupied the site, which is less than a block from the Old State House where the massacre sparking the Revolutionary War took place. The president of the bank, several Ohio alumni, Dean George Klare, and Professor William Holmes joined Alan and me in dedicating the plaque.

What I feel I must call a final note to my tenure at Ohio University came in the 1970s. Marion, the children and I spent two weeks vacationing on the Caribbean island of Antigua. Driving along an island dusty roads, I spotted and picked up two young hitchhikers. Introducing myself, I said, "My name is Vernon Alden." "What a coincidence! We're going to a university with a library by that name." Of course, I didn't say a word, but I invited them back to our cottage for a Coke and a sandwich. Before too long, Marion let the cat out of the bag. "My God!" they exclaimed. "We thought you were dead."

RETURNING TO BOSTON

I HAD SPENT the 1950s working at the Harvard Business School and the 1960s at Ohio University. The 1970s would be at the Boston Company. Each decade was a chapter in my life, and each of my job responsibilities opened up new challenges and opportunities. The surge of veterans into colleges after World War II was followed in the

1950s by the growth of graduate schools such as the Harvard Business School. The postwar baby boom resulted in an explosive growth of all colleges and universities, including Ohio, in the 1960s. In the decade of the 1970s, the Boston Company quadrupled its assets, led by the new entities and new levels of income created by friends I recruited to the company—Tom Courtney, Ed Rudman, and Tom Walsh. It became the nation's fifteenth largest investment-management firm.

The Boston Safe Deposit and Trust Company had served well the families of Boston for a century, but government restrictions had limited its activities to Massachusetts. The creation of the Boston Company permitted us to acquire investment counseling firms throughout the United States and to develop new entities such as the Boston Consulting Group, the Financial Strategies Group, Institutional Investors, Rinfret-Boston Economic Advisory Services, and an oil and gas investment subsidiary in Texas. *Business Week* magazine, in a lengthy article, described the Boston Company as "a string of matched pearls—a group of mutually-reinforcing, self-sustaining companies."

As the new chairman, I was determined to establish a board of directors which would truly reflect our national and international outreach. During my twelve years at the Harvard Business School, I had become acquainted with many leaders in U.S. business. I was delighted when the chief executive officers of Armco Steel, TransWorld Airlines, Continental Oil, Royal Dutch Shell in the United Kingdom, and the Dole Company in Hawaii all accepted my invitation to join the board.

I also had my eye on Lee Iacocca, who had already gained a national reputation with his leadership in developing the Mustang automobile at Ford. Lee had accepted an invitation to speak to our students at Ohio University and had presented the engineering school with a Mustang engine. When I invited him to join our board, he replied, "Mr. Ford doesn't allow us to take on any board assignments."

I asked Lee if I could talk with Henry Ford. When I did see Mr. Ford, I said that I knew that he was grooming Iacocca for the top position at Ford. "He knows all about automobiles, and he's a super salesman, but how much does he know about finance and investment policy?" I asked. "Participation on our board will give him this additional dimension, 'almost as good as a postgraduate Harvard Business School education.'" Lee was allowed to join our board, and he turned out to be a first-rate director. He never missed a meeting, his questions were sharp and perceptive, and he continually entertained the board with his wit.

While we administered in trust the funds of many individual families and private foundations in Boston, we were not known for our ability to manage pension funds for major U.S. corporations. I became acquainted with Tom Courtney when he was a student at The Harvard Business School. Tom, representing the United States, had won two gold medals in the 1956 Olympics, in Melbourne, Australia. Knowing that he applied the same drive and commitment to management of financial assets, I recruited him from his position as senior vice president of MacKay Shields Investment Corporation. Tom headed up a new subsidiary called Institutional Investors to specialize in managing national pension funds. He, in turn, recruited John Wise from Fidelity and Grayson Murphy from Endowment Management. Within the next few years, the group developed more than thirty national accounts, managing more than $500 million.

WHEN THE TALL SHIPS visited Boston in the bicentennial year, 1976, we invited customers and special guests to view the parade of ships from our lofty perch overlooking the harbor. An uninvited guest arrived at the luncheon on the forty-second floor of the Boston Company building. He introduced himself as Roberto Calvi, president of Banca Ambrosiano, claiming that he represented several wealthy clients. He asked whether we would be interested in managing their investments amounting to "several hundred million dollars." He implied that a good chunk of the money belonged to the

Vatican. In addition to the pope and cardinals, he dropped the names of several wealthy Europeans.

The catch was we would be required to pay Calvi up front with a "finder's fee." He was a glib talker, but we were reluctant to put down any money until we knew much more about him and his clients. After he returned to Italy, Calvi telephoned us several times but did not share much information beyond his desire to have a finder's fee.

In 1981, I read in the *New York Times* that Roberto Calvi had been found hanging from the Blackfriars Bridge in London. There was speculation about whether his death was suicide or murder. A flurry of newspaper articles linked Calvi with scandals at the Vatican and the death of Pope John Paul I, who served only thirty-three days of papal rule in 1978. In 1929, Mussolini and the Vatican signed the Lateran Treaty and the Concordat making Vatican City a sovereign state within Rome and independent of the Italian government. At the same time, Mussolini transferred millions of lira to the church. In the early 1970s, the Vatican, needing experienced financiers to invest the funds, turned to Calvi and Michele Sindona. Soon the church became embarrassed to discover that illegal U.S. securities were being bought from the Mafia.

In 1980, Sindona was convicted in the United States on sixty-five counts of fraud. Extradited to Italy, two years later he was poisoned in his cell while serving a life sentence for murder. Roberto Calvi was convicted by an Italian court in 1981 for illegal currency transactions. It was later that year, with $400 million still unaccounted for, he was found hanging from the bridge over the Thames.

The speculation about the death of Pope John Paul I has been kept alive by Francis Ford Coppola's movie *The Godfather III*. Was the pope murdered by poisoned coffee? Were Sindona and Calvi involved, John Paul I having vowed to stop their illegal activities? Or did the pope die of a heart attack as reported? In any event, I am relieved that the Boston Company never became involved in managing the investments being pushed by Roberto Calvi.

For many years I had been fascinated by the organizations that the Rockefeller, Mellon, Ford, and Kennedy families had put in place to manage the assets of their families. I was aware that there were families with more modest wealth who needed the assistance that lawyers, money managers, and financial analysts provided to those wealthier families. I suggested that we establish a division that would evaluate the assets of families, give advice on estate planning, manage their resources, and enable them to invest in tax-shelter investments if desirable. We should have something like a "financial Mayo Brothers clinic" for families, less wealthy than the Rockefellers and the Fords, who needed overall investment and estate planning advice. I recruited Ed Rudman and Tony Pell to head up a "financial strategies" unit. Analysis of the needs of individuals and families soon revealed that we needed subsidiaries that had experience and expertise in investment in oil and gas, real estate and other nonconventional areas. At that time, there was a window of opportunity that made it possible for clients to convert low-cost-base investments into a diversified portfolio without having to pay capital gains taxes. I persuaded several of my long-time friends to invest in our Financial Strategies group.

The first clients of the Financial Strategies Group were John Glenn, George Webster, a fellow director of McGraw-Hill, the Kerr family of the Kerr-McGee Company, and Eppie Lederer, known more familiarly by her pen name Ann Landers.

I met Eppie and her husband, Jules Lederer, in the early 1950s through the Young Presidents' Organization (YPO), which I served as a consultant. Despite her hectic schedule in writing the widely-read Ann Landers column, both she and Jules participated in almost all YPO programs, and we became close friends. Eppie later generously accepted invitations to the Ohio campus to carry on dialogues with students.

Marion and I were invited several times to dinner at the Lederers' attractive apartment in Chicago. On almost every occasion, Father Ted Hesburgh, the well-known president of Notre Dame, was also a guest. It was clear that Eppie relied heavily upon Father Hesburgh's wisdom and knowledge in crafting replies to some of her letters.

Eppie and Jules planned to celebrate their thirty-fifth wedding anniversary with her sister, Abigail, and her husband, who were also celebrating their thirty-fifth. "We were married at the same time," explained Eppie, "because we couldn't afford more than one rabbi." The celebration was to be on Martha's Vineyard. When they arrived at an Edgartown inn, Eppie telephoned our summer home in Chilmark announcing that they'd like to call on us. I thought that it might be pleasant to pick them up in our Mako boat and provide them with a closeup view of the Vineyard beaches en route to our place. A big mistake! The water was rough and the wind was fierce. By the time we arrived in the shelter of Menemsha harbor, the beehive hairdos of both Eppie and Abigail were completely blown apart.

A few years later, Eppie telephoned me from South Bend, Indiana, where she was conferring with Father Hesburgh. "I need to see you," she said, "but let's not meet at your home or your office. How about the Harvard Club?" When we met, she revealed that her husband, Jules, and she were planning to divorce. After long discussions about her investment situation and how the news should be made public, I replied with tongue in cheek, "Eppie, your readers are in for two major shocks. One, Ann Landers is getting a divorce, and two, Father Ted Hesburgh is leaving the cloth to marry Ann Landers."

Eppie Lederer is an exceedingly generous person. She has been active in the affairs of the Harvard Medical School and has made substantial financial contributions. In the last year of President Derek Bok's tenure at Harvard, she was honored at the Faculty Club surrounded by friends who came from throughout the country—including Father Hesburgh.

FEW PEOPLE ARE aware that John Glenn has financial resources sufficient to qualify him for participation in the Financial Strategies Group. When John was preparing for his launch at Cape Canaveral, he met a refugee from the holocaust, Henri Landwirth, who had become wealthy as the owner of several Holiday Inn franchises. Henri generously offered partnerships in his motel ventures near Orlando to John Glenn and other astronauts. As a result, John was able to build a modest fortune. When I became chairman of the Boston Company, he asked us to manage his personal funds.

John is normally a calm, self-assured, unflappable individual, in public as well as in private. Only once did I see him on the verge of losing his cool. He was receiving letters in his office from several women in Florida—all of them unknown to him. Some letters were amorous in tone, some bitterly complaining of improper advances, others demanding money. John turned to the FBI for help in determining the reason for this strange flurry of mail. They tracked down a Glenn look-alike posing as John in Florida pickup bars.

In 1970, John decide to run for the U.S. Senate but lost in the spring primary. On February 15, 1971, he wrote to me saying: "An unfortunately large campaign debt had been incurred by the committee supporting me. . . . I am reminded of Will Rogers' ever increasingly pertinent observation, 'In politics these days, it take a lot of money to get beat with'!" He invited me to a huge fund-raising dinner in Cleveland on March 20, 1971. It was entitled, "An Evening with the Stars" and featured Andy Williams, Art Buchwald, Alan King, Ethel Kennedy, and other celebrities.

In 1974, he ran again for the Senate and was elected, carrying all eighty-eight Ohio counties with a margin of more than a million votes. He was reelected in 1980 with the largest vote margin in Ohio history—more than 1.6 million votes. Two years later, riding on the crest of his popularity and national visibility, he declared for the presidency. With my assistant at the Boston Company, Tom Gee, we put together a fund-raising committee in Massachusetts. Except for the State of Ohio, we raised more money than all other state committees. John traveled to Boston several times to assist us in our efforts. Unfortunately, other candidates overtook him in the race, and he was again left with a large debt.

Many politicians simply ignore their debts and expect lending institutions to swallow those liabilities. Straight arrow that he is, John was determined to make good on his campaign debt. We held additional fund-raisers in Boston, in Ohio, and a memorable one at the home of Pamela Harriman in Washington. So far as I know, John is still working to make good on those obligations, even though he has held his Senate seat three times since that presidential campaign.

ONE OF OUR subsidiaries was called Rinfret-Boston, headed by the colorful, widely quoted economist Pierre Rinfret. On one of my trips to New York to visit with Pierre, the city suffered the worst power failure and blackout in its history. Returning to the Waldorf Astoria where I was staying, I discovered that the lobby was crowded with people holding candles. None of the elevators was working, but I was determined to climb the stairs to my room on the thirty-fifth floor. Halfway up, I encountered a tiny, elderly lady sitting on the stairs, too exhausted to continue to her suite in the Waldorf Towers. I offered to carry her up the remaining flights of stairs. When we arrived at her room, she thanked me and identified herself as Mrs. Douglas MacArthur.

When Senator Ed Muskie of Maine announced his intention to run for president of the United States in 1972, Pierre Rinfret wanted to meet Muskie, hoping that the Rinfret-Boston firm might be hired as economic consultants for the campaign. He asked me to introduce him. We arrived in the senator's Washington office for our two o'clock appointment only to be told that we would have to wait a couple of hours because "the senator is taking a nap." We wondered whether he had the physical stamina for the presidential campaign. He subsequently withdrew from the campaign after the famous weeping incident in Maine.

To head up our marketing area, we recruited Tom Walsh. I had interviewed Tom in 1959 when he showed up in the admissions office of the Harvard Business School, leaving his training to become a Jesuit priest. He had scored a perfect 800 on the law school aptitude test and was about to enter the Harvard Law School. Dean Les

Rollins and I were impressed with his sly wit, his sparkling personality, and his devil-may-care attitude. We persuaded him to enroll at the Business School. In the 1960s, he had a spectacular record working in the investment field. I was convinced that we needed him at the Boston Company.

Soon after we hired Tom, he made several trips to Iowa, meeting with legislators and pension fund managers. He returned to Boston with an $800 million contract to manage the state employees' pension fund. Tom could make a three-week trip to the West Coast and sell a year's worth of business. In the evenings he played piano at the Bay Club in downtown Boston. He played by ear, never having taken a lesson in his life. He attracted quite a following, especially among young, attractive women, charmed by his music and his personality.

Today, Tom Walsh is a golf fanatic. He rarely plays a round of golf, but he is on the practice tee for hours. For years he has been creating a book and video about golf form, and he gives lessons and golf tips to anyone who will stop and listen for a few minutes.

The Boston Safe Deposit and Trust Company continued to be our largest and most prestigious subsidiary. I traveled to Cleveland to persuade Henry Russell to become president of the Trust Company. Tim, as he was known, had a warm, likable personality. Having served as president of the Harvard Alumni Association, he had many friends not only in Boston but throughout the United States. He provided excellent leadership to our flagship property.

The Boston Company created the well-known Boston Consulting Group (BCG) around one person, Bruce Henderson, and a secretary. I had known Bruce while working at the Harvard Business School. He was a rising executive at Westinghouse Air Brake. With a facile mind and the ability to think and strategize conceptually, he was restless at Westinghouse. The Boston Consulting Group provided him the opportunity to develop one of the world's outstanding consulting groups.

One of Bruce's first recruits was Bill Bain, a development officer at Vanderbilt, Henderson's alma mater. Bill had not gone to a graduate business school but had a flair that appealed to Bruce. He treated Bill Bain like an adopted son. After three or four years of working at BCG, Bain decided to launch his own consulting firm. He announced his idea to William Wolbach, president of the Boston Company, and me. We were intrigued with his plan and offered to finance his venture as we had done with the Boston Consulting Group. When Bruce Henderson found out about our tentative offer, we almost had to scrape him off the ceiling. Bruce often administered the group by tantrum, but he enjoyed fierce loyalty from his colleagues. Needless to say, we had to withdraw our offer to Bain.

Walker Lewis, who had worked with me at Ohio University, asked my advice about his adding a Harvard MBA to his Harvard College degree. I advised him not to invest in the expensive Harvard Business School program and at the same time forgo two years of income; instead, I suggested he should meet Bruce Henderson, and I offered to introduce him. Walker quickly became one of the young stars in the Boston Consulting Group. He subsequently established his own group, Strategic Planning Associates, in Washington, selling it for an attractive capital gain after a period of years.

Ira Magaziner was an outstanding student leader at Brown University during the hectic late 1960s. He is credited with having worked successfully with the faculty and administration in developing Brown's well-known "new curriculum," which has made Brown one of the most sought-after universities. Ira became a Rhodes Scholar, and upon his return from England became involved in community development in Fall River and New Bedford, Massachusetts. Frustrated with his lack of management skills, he came to Boston to ask my advice about attending the Harvard Business School. For the same reasons I gave Walker Lewis, I deflected his question and introduced him to Bruce Henderson. Ira, too, became a star at BCG and eventually founded his own consulting group— and, like Walker, sold the company for a sizable gain. Today, of course, he is a member of the Clinton administration, known for his and Mrs. Clinton's efforts to launch a revolutionary health plan.

Another area of business I introduced to the Boston Company was the financial management of professional athletes. In the early 1970s, with salaries of athletes skyrocketing, it appeared that they needed financial planning and asset management similar to what we offered through our Financial Strategies Group. I invited Red Auerbach and Dave Cowens of the Boston Celtics to serve on the advisory board of the new unit. I also persuaded my friend Willie Mays to join us.

Willie Mays and I first met at the American Airlines Celebrity Golf Tournament in Puerto Rico. In the first round, Willie and I were paired with Joe DiMaggio and Baltimore Orioles pitcher Jim Palmer. Joe Namath was supposed to be in the foursome, but he was reported to be under the weather. The match included, therefore, three baseball stars and me. As we approached the eighteenth green, Willie asked: "If you have a few minutes, I'd like to have you join me in my room. I know you're the chairman of the Boston Company, and I'd like to have your advice."

Willie confided that he would be retiring at the end of the season, or sooner if his legs did not hold out. He said that his baseball pension would amount to no more than $50,000 per year, and that he needed at least three times that amount to maintain his lifestyle. We seemed to have established some sort of special rapport that afternoon, and I promised to do everything I could to help him.

As a member of the board of directors of Colgate-Palmolive, I knew that Willie Mays could help us at the Colgate Games, an annual track meet in Madison Square Garden predominantly for black young women in New York, many of whom had gone on to great college performances, including Olympic Games participation. Colgate agreed to a $50,000 per year stipend for Willie Mays to represent them at the Colgate Games as well as at sales meetings, golf tournaments, and so forth. Two other companies I approached agreed to similar representation by Willie for salaries of $50,000 per year.

Willie was surprised that I was able to deliver so quickly on my promises. He asked me what he could do to express his thanks. I said, "Why don't you join us for dinner in Brookline so that my four children can meet you?" Willie arrived, and we had an evening full of chatter and laughs. He loves to talk and giggle with friends he can trust. At the end of the dinner, he slyly pulled out a little package, presenting it to me "as a token of his appreciation." It was a beautiful platinum-band watch, surrounded by sapphires and diamonds, which had probably been given to him on some special occasion.

Before his career ended, Willie was traded to the New York Mets. When he announced that he was retiring from baseball, a special evening was planned for him at the Mets Stadium. Willie invited me to the game. He hit a home run down the left field line. I asked him if the pitcher had served up an especially "fat" pitch. Willie simply giggled in his usual manner. The tributes to Willie Mays were amazing. He was given three cars, a trip around the world, golf clubs (he already had about fifty sets), and other special gifts. After the game and the cascade of praises and presents, Willie was surprisingly subdued. He said, "I want to get away from the crowd. Why don't you join me for dinner?" We dined alone—away from the autograph seekers and sycophants. Willie was very quiet and reflective, even sad. The next day, we went to the Mercedes showroom on Park Avenue to look at one of the cars he had been given. He acted like a small boy who had been given too many presents at Christmas.

I see Willie Mays from time to time when he has an autographing session in Boston, and I usually telephone him on his birthday. I was pleased to read in his autobiography:*

> I was enjoying myself at an off-season golf tournament run by American Airlines in Puerto Rico. There are a dozen events like that every year, in beautiful settings where you get the best food and suites. I was playing with a businessman named Vern Alden, and he asked me this question, "Willie, what are you going to do when you get out of baseball?"
>
> I didn't know; I had played baseball from the time I was four-

---

*Willie Mays with Lou Sahadi, *Say Hey! The Autobiography of Willie Mays* (New York: Simon and Schuster, 1988).

teen, and now I was beginning to wind down my career as a ball player. So I went upstairs and thought about it for a while. Then I called Vern and I said, "Mr. Alden, you better explain what you mean." We talked for a while, and we narrowed it down to public relations. He gave me the names of five companies, including Ogden and Colgate and a textile company down south. I wound up working for Colgate for twelve years, along with Ogden and the textile firm.

After a year working with professional athletes, we concluded that this was not an area that could ever be profitable. Tending to the needs of the athletes was more than a full-time job for the two Boston Company officers in charge of the unit, and fees charged for management of their investments did not even cover the overhead costs. We gave the small unit to the individuals managing it.

ALTHOUGH I HAD plenty to keep me busy at the Boston Company, I was invited from time to time to take on a special consulting assignment. One of the most interesting such experiences was working with Nicholas Salgo. Salgo was a highly successful entrepreneur before being appointed ambassador to his place of birth, Hungary. His company, the Bangor Punta Corporation, was among the first conglomerates, a collection of several enterprises in different fields of business.

Nick Salgo was constantly on the alert for new ideas, an avid listener, and a probing interrogator of any person who might be helpful. In the early 1970s, he put together a small personal think-tank group that included Buckminster Fuller, Peter Drucker, the brilliant architect I. M. Pei, and me. Why I was invited to join that all-star group, I'll never know. We met about every other month and were flown about the country in Nick Salgo's jet plane to visit his various factories and offices. While in the air and over meals, we talked about a vast array of topics, including what the world would and should be like in the year 2000. Each of us was offered an annual stipend of $25,000, a fairly handsome amount for part-time consultation in the early 1970s. We could take the amount in cash or in Bangor Punta stock. All of us except Bucky Fuller opted for stock: he insisted on cash. With the depressed stock market of the mid-1970s, the stock owned by the other three of us was worth much less than when given to us, and we had paid income taxes on the full amount.

Bucky Fuller had curious eating habits. At every dinner he ordered only a piece of steak—well done—no vegetables, no starches, nothing else. One night after dinner he challenged me to a foot race. I told him that I had been a runner in college so should give him a head start. He took a very small one, but he darn near beat me in the twenty-five-yard race.

Buckminster Fuller is best known as the creator of the geodesic dome, but his grasp of history and his knowledge of disparate fields of study was awesome.

As expected of me, I spent a substantial amount of time on nonprofit boards and traveling to visit with clients and prospects for the Boston Company. I was asked to join the boards of McGraw-Hill and Colgate-Palmolive and became increasingly involved with Japan. Robert Wood, president of the University of Massachusetts, asked me to chair a commission to develop a plan for "the future of the state university system in Massachusetts." Peter Edelman provided staff support and several leading citizens worked with us in developing a master plan.

Friends can perhaps identify other shortcomings of mine, but my greatest weakness is the inability to say no when approached for a good cause. I was invited to serve as a trustee of the Boston Symphony Orchestra and the Museum of Science, as well as an overseer of the Museum of Fine Arts and the Children's Museum. Harvard College, the Fletcher School of Law and Diplomacy, and MIT asked me to be a member of their visiting committees. Each of the preparatory schools our children attended invited me to be a trustee, and I served at various times Dexter, Winsor, Beaver Country Day, Carroll, and Northfield Mount Hermon Schools. General Doriot persuaded me to work with him on behalf of the French Library of Boston, where I have served as chairman of the executive committee for more than twenty years.

In 1973, Governor Frank Sargent appointed me chairman of the Massachusetts Arts Council when the entire budget was less than $100,000. Working closely with Executive Director Louise Tate, followed by Anne Hawley, we were able to persuade legislators to increase annual appropriations to $18.6 million. We continually had to persuade legislators that the arts were not merely the province of little old ladies on the North Shore or Brookline. We underwrote studies that demonstrated how much the arts contributed to tax revenues by attracting tourists and companies whose employees prefer to live in a community where culture is alive. During a thirteen-year span, I was reappointed chairman by Governors Dukakis and King. Senate President William Bulger was the leading force in the increased level of funding by the state.

My alma mater, Brown University, elected me a trustee. In 1971 I was appointed to the senior governing board—the board of fellows —which I served through 1986. While on the Brown Corporation, I was chairman of the admissions and financial-aid policy committee and chaired the presidential search committee that selected Howard Swearer as president. Because three of our four children attended the university, Brown has received the largest share of our annual gifts and the capital gifts we have made. Our elder son, Robert, was an outstanding distance runner at Harvard, and our third son, David, as early as his freshman year, received the Most Valuable Runner award on the cross-country team. Marion and I established a trophy awarded every year to the winner of the Brown-Harvard cross-country meet, and we contributed funds for the indoor running track at Brown.

The Boston Symphony Orchestra has provided special pleasure to both Marion and me. When asked to provide endowment for an orchestra chair, we selected the cello because our son Rob learned to play the cello while a youngster in Ohio. Early in my term as a trustee, the symphony was planning a concert tour to London and Paris. The trustees deliberated at length about possible sources of funding for the trip. At that time, business corporations were not an obvious source of support. Knowing that the Colgate-Palmolive Company had major business interests in the United Kingdom and France, I asked the trustees to give me a few days to seek out funding from the company. The proposal very much appealed to our Colgate CEO, David Foster, who authorized complete funding for the trip. This was the symphony's first corporate-supported tour. Since then, of course, other corporations have provided even larger support.

The late 1970s was not a happy time for the stock market, and the performance of the Boston Company's management of personal portfolios drew criticism from several individual customers. Mead Johnson, founder of a pharmaceutical company bearing his name, had become a client upon reading the "String of Pearls" *Business Week* article. Mead demanded stellar performance and was not reluctant to express concern when his substantial portfolio did not reflect it. After frequent visits with him at his seafront home in Palm Beach, I twice had to initiate a change in managers of his account. I found myself spending more time placating large customers and less time on day-to-day management concerns.

In an article in *Boston Magazine,* John Spooner described the stock market in the early 1970s: "In the seventies, people cared desperately about their falling stocks during the first year of decline (1972). During the second year (1973) people became almost used to the lousy prices. It had become like a lengthening war, and we were already used to the seven-year struggle in Vietnam. By 1974 . . . Wall Street had imploded; brokers, now called financial consultants, left the business by the thousands. They couldn't make a living."

In 1973 we were confronted with a worldwide oil crisis. The OPEC nations dictated oil prices which skyrocketed. Inflation forced up interest rates until they reached an astonishing 20 percent. Competition between financial service organizations escalated, and new forms of risky investments were created. The Savings and Loan scandals were to follow in the 1980s.

The 1973 and 1974 bear market, from peak to trough, racked up losses of 45 percent over the course of nearly two years. It was one of the biggest declines in the hundred-year history of the Dow Jones Industrial Average. In his book *Grand Expectations*,* Brown University professor James Patterson observes that "the sluggishness of the economy widened the gulf between grand expectations and the real limits of progress, undercutting the all-important sense that the country had the means to do almost anything, and exacerbating the contentiousness that had been rending American society since the late 1960s. This was the final irony of the exciting and extraordinarily expectant thirty years following World War II."

A major problem developed in our Institutional Investors Group (Tom Courtney, John Wise, and Grayson Murphy). The group had purchased 440,000 shares of an insurance stock called Equity Funding. Raymond Dirks, a Wall Street insurance analyst, telephoned Jerry Zukowski, the insurance specialist in our Institutional Investors Group. Dirks wanted to know if Zukowski thought it was possible Equity Funding was keeping two sets of books. Dirks had been told this by a former Equity Funding employee. Courtney went to New York City the next day for a client meeting. He also met with Dirks. Dirks went over the former employee's accusations and noted that the person spreading the rumor had left the company two-and-one-half years earlier. Courtney left Dirks's office and immediately called the Boston Company's lawyer from Goodwin, Proctor & Hoar. He read off all the information Dirks had passed on from the former employee, and our attorney said that there was no problem. Because that individual had left Equity Funding more than two and one-half years earlier, there was no problem of insider information, and Courtney's group was free to sell the stock. They did.

The Securities and Exchange Commission (SEC) subsequently conducted an investigation, and other firms brought suit against the Boston Company. It was later discovered that another affiliate, John

---

*James T. Patterson, *Grand Expectations: The United States, 1945–1974. Oxford History of the United States,* vol. 10 (New York: Oxford University Press, 1996).

Bristol and Company, had been a buyer of some of Institutional Investors' sales. Later Dirks, through the Freedom of Information Act, found that the former Equity Funding employee had told the same story to the chief enforcement officer of the SEC, Stanley Sporkin, two weeks before he had told Dirks. Sporkin called a former SEC man who had actually gone to work at Equity Funding, and was told there was nothing to the story of the disgruntled former employee. The SEC eventually cleared the Boston Company of all charges.

When Tom Courtney was recruited to the Boston Company in 1970, he and his associates rapidly built Institutional Investors into a major subsidiary. Perhaps it was this success that precipitated a major problem. Courtney, Wise, and Murphy had been given a contract for 40 percent equity in the subsidiary when they joined us. As Institutional Investors became increasingly profitable, the Boston Company president, Bill Wolbach, wanted to consolidate the subsidiary. He needed 80 percent of the stock to accomplish this. With 40 percent owned by the three principals, he took the position that only Courtney's stock ownership had been authorized and that the shares owned by Wise and Murphy would have to be given back, which would give the company its necessary 80 percent to consolidate Institutional Investors with the parent company. Tom Courtney quite appropriately indicated that he would honor the commitment to his associates, and when the issue could not be resolved it went to an arbitrator, as called for in the contract.

During the arbitration, each of the company's senior officers appeared before the arbitrator. When asked, I testified that our commitment to the officers of Institutional Investors should be honored. When the arbitrator ruled in favor of Tom and his associates, they were paid off and asked by Bill Wolbach to leave the company. With hindsight, perhaps if I had not been so much involved with the external relationships of the Boston Company, I could have prevented this precipitous decision before it was a fait accompli.

Bill Wolbach was a complex person—brilliant, shy, generous, but oftentimes abrasive in his relationships with people. He had dropped out of Harvard College and spent most of his working life with the Boston Safe Deposit and Trust Company and the Boston Company. Ralph Lowell had served as president of the Trust Company for many years. His son, John Lowell, and Bill Wolbach were in competition to succeed Mr. Lowell. Bill was selected as president of the Boston Safe Deposit and Trust Company and developed plans to create a parent entity, the Boston Company, that would enable expansion beyond Massachusetts and into new financial vehicles.

When the board of directors invited me to join the company, we followed the Lowell-Wolbach tradition. Neither of us held the title of chief executive officer. Bill, with his impressive knowledge of investment and trust management, devoted most of his energies to internal operations. I spent most of my time on external relationships, recruitment of management, and attention to clients. From time to time, I disagreed with Bill on major issues.

The Equity Funding problem, with the concerns raised by the Securities and Exchange Commission, required a knowledgeable attorney who could spend full time negotiating with the SEC and the private companies suing the Boston Company. Dwight Allison, a bright lawyer with substantial investment knowledge, was a partner of Donald Hurley, our senior director, in the firm of Goodwin, Proctor & Hoar. Dwight was recruited to deal with the SEC and the class action suits so that management could handle the day-to-day affairs of the company.

In 1975 three of our Boston-based directors—Georges Doriot, Sidney Rabb, and George Olmsted—reached retirement age. Each was a solid member of the board and would be missed. In November 1976, Lee Iacocca resigned from the board.

As the Boston Company continued to grow and become more complex, it became clear to Bill Wolbach and me that we needed a chief executive officer who could manage the many areas of the company with a firm hand. Not having long-time knowledge and experience in the investment world, I did not wish to assume the responsibilities of chief executive. And I felt that Bill Wolbach did not have the temperament and personality to be our leader. Together, we agreed that we would ask Dwight Allison to become president and CEO. I volunteered in December 1976 to become chairman of the executive committee so that Bill could move into the chairmanship.

Dwight took over his new position with a strong hand. He was determined to make the company more profitable by selling off or closing some of our affiliates and reducing the number of people working in the Trust Company, in research or in middle-level management positions. In July 1977, our Seattle-based affiliate, Kennedy-Boston Associates, became embroiled in litigation with the company. The Boston Company became a leaner, more legalistic, but less-exciting company. In August 1977, two of the outstanding directors I had recruited, Bill Verity, chairman of Armco Steel, and Herb Cornuelle, president of Dole in Hawaii, felt that they had contributed as much as they could and resigned from the board.

Shortly thereafter, the litigation growing out of the Equity Funding matter was settled. Dwight began to acquire a fairly large financial interest in the company, and his long-time friend and business partner, Robert Monks, also accumulated substantial blocks of stock. At the same time, several of Monks's friends and neighbors in Maine were purchasing Boston Company stock.

In the meantime, a fellow Brookline resident, Governor Michael Dukakis, was having conversations with me about his desire to attract foreign business to Massachusetts and to stimulate the sales of the state's products overseas. As we continued the discussions, he proposed the establishment of a foreign business council, comprised of a dozen or so Massachusetts executives. He invited me to chair the council. I was intrigued with the possibility of opening up another chapter in my career—one that would involve much more international activity. In September 1977, I informed Dwight Allison and Bill Wolbach of my discussions with the governor, and we agreed that I would inform the board of my plans to leave the company. At our November board meeting I advised the directors that I planned to accept the governor's invitation. I told them: "Because I wish to devote the next several years to public service before I retire from active responsibility, I shall not stand for reelection at our annual meeting next May 1978."

About a year after I had left the Boston Company, I began to hear rumblings from former colleagues there. Dwight Allison and Robert Monks and his friends had continued to accumulate large positions in the company's stock. Tim Russell was removed as president of the Boston Safe Deposit and Trust Company and was replaced by Allison, who also continued as CEO of the parent company. Robert Monks replaced Bill Wolbach as chairman of the Boston Company. In September 1980, Ed Rudman and Tony Pell, who had built the Financial Strategies Group into one of the most prestigious and profitable affiliates, left to establish the firm of Pell Rudman. Many of their clients, including the Alden family, transferred their funds to the new entity, which today is one of the nation's most successful investment and trust entities.

In February 1981, Allison announced a proposed merger between the Boston Company and Shearson Loeb Rhoades, Inc. Two months later, Shearson and the American Express Company announced a proposed merger. The Boston Company was subsequently acquired by the Mellon Bank of Pittsburgh.

CHAPTER **11**

Moving into the International Arena
—and More Politics

UPON JOINING THE Massachusetts Foreign Business Council, I insisted that I would serve as chairman without pay because I did not wish to give up my corporate board memberships; I believed that they would be helpful in carrying out my new responsibilities. Frank Morris, the chairman of the Federal Reserve Bank in Boston, offered me free office space in their attractive new building.

Howard Smith, the state's secretary of economic affairs, proposed that we launch trade missions to Japan, China, and Europe and that we create programs to make Massachusetts more hospitable to investment and tourism from abroad. Our first trade mission was to Japan—October 13–25, 1978. After careful screening of Massachusetts companies that were seriously interested in doing business in Japan, we selected a twenty-member delegation, led by Lt. Governor Tom O'Neill III. Our materials were prepared in Japanese, and we held several briefing sessions for participants before embarking upon our mission.

I had asked my long-time friend Noritake Kobayashi to assist us with introductions to several leading companies and corporations. On our first evening, Koby invited us to a hostess bar—the typical setting for relaxing and getting to know a person better in an informal environment: after rounds of sake and chitchat with lovely hostesses, new acquaintances let down their hair and develop the chemistry that Japanese hosts hope to accomplish with strangers. Howard completely misunderstood. He was aghast. He must have thought that he was being led into a house of ill-repute. He stormed out of the room, and we had to follow him. Koby, of course, completely understood, was not offended, and because of my many years of friendship with him, opened up doors to Japan that usually take months and years to pry open. Representatives of Digital returned to Boston with a multimillion-dollar order, and a Japanese firm, Rigaku, planned to open a new plant in Danvers.

In the many, many times I have traveled to Japan, I never tire of the long, fourteen-hour flight: I busy myself with reading and writing and catching enough sleep to accommodate myself to the sudden change of clock time. As the plane glides across the eastern coast of Japan en route to Narita Airport, the sun has just set, and the early-evening afterglow is reflected from the fresh water on the rice paddies and the sand traps of the golf courses below. Cars, from that altitude looking tiny, with headlights blinking like fireflies through the wispy ground fog, creep along the sinewy highways of Chiba Prefecture. After the long bus ride into Tokyo, I find myself immersed in a fantasy land of cascading neon and rippling electric signs, a myriad of winking and tumbling kanji and katakana characters. Since its opening more than thirty-five years ago, I have stayed at the Okura Hotel, and I am invariably greeted at the door by a man in proper cutaway coat—"Welcome home." After checking into my room, I usually cash in my "welcome drink" coupon in the top-floor Starlight Lounge, watching downtown Tokyo spread out for miles in a blanket of twinkling lights.

I usually find myself wide awake at four o'clock in the morning and watch CNN news until sunrise, when I can venture out for a morning run. I run down the hill past the American embassy and on to Sakurada-dori Avenue. The streets are empty, and only an occasional sleepy pedestrian comes into view. Along the way, I pass tree-lined parks, stone gardens, Buddhist temples, and dozens of tiny shops. There is something about the early morning light that intensifies all colors—the green grasses, pink and white cherry blossoms, wet gray stones, and brilliant-red temple columns. Need I say again how much I relish visiting Japan?

My fascination with Japan dates back to World War II. Shortly after the attack on Pearl Harbor, I enlisted in the Navy V-12 program at Brown. From there, I was sent to the Columbia University Midshipman's School. Upon receiving my commission as an ensign, I was given orders to report to a minesweeper in the North Pacific. The USS *Goshawk* operated out of Adak in the Aleutian Island chain. Every time we went out on patrols the waves were ten feet high and the williwaw winds beat the small ship with incredible intensity. I became dreadfully seasick every time we were out at sea.

One evening while on patrol we received a message indicating that I had been selected for the navy's Japanese-language program at the University of Colorado. After a year or so of intensive instruction in reading, writing, and speaking Japanese, I reported to the aircraft carrier, USS *Saratoga*. When the war ended, most language officers were ordered to join the Occupation Force in Japan. The navy apparently lost track of me, and I remained on the *Saratoga* until it sailed out under the Golden Gate Bridge to become one of the targets in the atomic bomb test at Bikini Island. Had I been part of the occupation, I might be living in Japan today with a Japanese wife along with many of my language-school classmates.

My first visit to Japan occurred in 1959 when I taught in the Keio University–Harvard Business School Advanced Management Program. The following year I again taught in the program. Since 1960 I have visited Japan more than sixty times, assisting U.S. companies wishing to do business in Japan, on speaking assignments, or working on projects involving Japan-U.S. cultural affairs.

Marion and I have maintained a lifelong friendship with the families of Noritake Kobayashi, Reijiro Hattori, Nobuyuki Nakahara, Yaichi Ayukawa, Seizo Ota, and Shoichiro Toyoda. Just after a tiny electronics company adopted the name Sony, I was taken by Professor Kobayashi to meet the founders, Akio Morita and Masaru Ibuka. This was many years before Mr. Morita developed the Walkman, but I was impressed with the tiny recorders and radios already in production. I wish that I could have bought stock in the company then.

In 1960, I became a member of the Japan Society of Boston, just a year before we moved to Ohio. Shortly after we returned to Boston in 1969, I rejoined the society and soon was asked to serve as president. At the time, the society had a very small budget and one part-time administrator. One of our major accomplishments was to secure a gift of a Japanese house (named Kyo-no-machiya) from the City of Kyoto, the sister city of Boston. Located in the Children's Museum, the house and its exhibits are visited by thousands of school children every year. As a birthday present to Marion, I made a gift to name for her the tiny garden behind the house: the Marion Alden Garden.

The U.S.-Japan Friendship Commission was established when Japan made a substantial contribution to the U.S. Treasury upon the reversion of Okinawa to Japan. Congress had the good sense to establish the commission to underwrite exchanges of students, professors, and artists between Japan and the United States. I was asked to become a member of the advisory council. At one of our first meetings, I suggested that support of Japan societies would be a meaningful way to promote friendship and mutual understanding. I added that the Boston society, working with the Children's Museum, the Museum of Fine Arts, and the various universities with Japan-related programs could be a model for such funding. The commission board agreed and voted to support not only the Japan Society of Boston but two other Japan-America Societies as well. As a result, in Boston we were able to hire Pat Givens as a full-time executive director, expand our program offerings, and increase our membership and corporate support.

The Japan Society of Boston was established in 1904, the first such society in America. In the late 1800s, Bostonians had a lively interest in Japan. Whaling-ship captains plied the Pacific Ocean and returned to Boston with art objects that decorated many Beacon Hill homes. Harvard alumni William Sturgis Bigelow, Edward Sylvester Morse, and Ernest Fenollosa spent several years in Japan and returned with art treasures that they gave to the Boston Museum of Fine Arts. In 1876, William Smith Clark, president of the University of Massachusetts, took a leave of absence to become the first president of Sapporo Agricultural College (now Hokkaido University). Two Boston residents, Joseph Grew and Edwin O. Reischauer, served as ambassadors to Japan.

Today, there are thirty-one Japan-America societies located in major cities throughout the United States. I serve on the executive committee and the board of the national association and was its chairman for two terms. During that time, I led a delegation to Japan to celebrate the seventy-fifth anniversary of the America-Japan Society of Tokyo.

When the twenty-fifth anniversary of the Boston-Kyoto sister city relationship was being celebrated, I was invited to give the keynote address at a symposium in Kyoto. After my presentation, the mayor invited me to a Japanese luncheon. He asked what sort of gift he could give me. I protested several times that I did not expect a gift. Realizing that I could not put him off, I finally said, "My wife and I have always admired your beautiful, decorative sake barrels." The gift from Kyoto now graces our front hallway in Brookline. I asked the mayor what I could give him in return. He, too, insisted that a gift was not necessary, but finally agreed that he would like to have a rock from Massachusetts to place in his garden. Marion and I scoured the beach at Martha's Vineyard and found a perfect specimen. It cost us $85 to send it to Kyoto. When the postmaster asked what was in the package and I told him, he gave me a quizzical look.

Over the years, many visitors from Japan have been entertained in our home or in my office. Several families have brought teenage youngsters, hoping that I could help them gain admission to preparatory schools, colleges, or universities. I have carried out this responsibility for several Japanese young people.

We have been fortunate in Boston to have excellent consuls general representing Japan. Consul General Iguchi became ambassador to Bangladesh. Minoru Tamba is ambassador to Saudi Arabia. Consuls General Hogen and Mochizuki moved on to high positions in the Ministry of Foreign Affairs in Tokyo, and Consul General Abe is representing Japan in the United Nations. Sadakazu Taniguchi, most recently ambassador to New Zealand, initiated a Japan Society–sponsored symposium that each year features distinguished speakers from Japan and the United States analyzing the relationship between our two countries. While he was consul general, Ambassador Taniguchi conferred upon me the Order of the Rising Sun on behalf of the late Emperor Showa.

In 1985, Prince Hiro, as he was known at the time, visited Boston. Together with Consul General Sadakazu Taniguchi, we arranged for him to tour the historical sites in the Greater Boston area as well as Fairhaven, Massachusetts, where the fourteen-year-old Manjiro Nakahama lived after being rescued in 1841 by whaling ship Captain Whitfield. We entertained Prince Hiro at the Somerset Club and at Anthony's Pier 4, known for their lobster specialties. Apparently the prince gave his parents, now the emperor and empress of Japan, a complete report, because when they visited Boston two years later they asked to be shown all the places Prince Hiro had seen. Fairhaven and Pier 4 are on the "must-see" list of almost every Japanese visitor wishing to replicate the Boston visit of the imperial family.

Shortly after Consul General Taniguchi had returned to Tokyo, I was visiting in Japan. Through his good offices, arrangements were made for me to play tennis with Prince Hiro on the imperial palace courts. Our partners were two young officers in the Ministry of Foreign Affairs, and Taniguchi served as referee-umpire. In the first set I was paired with Toshio Mochizuki, who years later became consul general in Boston. He and I lost the first set 6–3. The prince is an outstanding player, having ranked the varsity's number one when he was at Oxford doing graduate work. When I had the opportunity to play as his partner, we quickly dispatched our ministry opponents.

After the tennis sets, Prince Hiro invited us to join him in the nearby tea house for refreshments. He described a recent trip to the United States, the highlight of which seemed to be a visit to Princeton University. When he hauled out some scrapbooks, the reason was clear: there were several photographs of the prince and Brooke Shields. Jokingly, I asked him what his parents would have thought had he brought Miss Shields back to Japan. The prince giggled, but his retainers were shocked by the brashness of this foreigner from Boston.

When his father ascended to the throne, Prince Hiro became Crown Prince Naruhito. Because his younger brother was already married and had a child, there was concern in Japan about the crown prince's unmarried status. Newspapers carried rumors of various prospective brides, especially singling out Masako Owada, the daughter of the senior officer in the Ministry of Foreign Affairs, Hisashi Owada. We had known the Owada family for several years, dating back to the time he was a visiting professor at the Harvard Law School. Masako attended Belmont High School and Harvard before beginning what she expected would be a career in the Ministry of Foreign Affairs. While attending a conference in Tokyo, I was surprised and pleased to discover that Masako Owada had been assigned by the ministry as my aide during the conference. I teased her about the rumors of her involvement with the crown prince. "No way!" she replied laughing.

Two years later, Marion and I were invited to the wedding reception of the crown prince and Princess Masako. It was held in the huge reception hall of the imperial palace and attended by several hundred Japanese, many in formal dress. Refreshments were served, and the crown prince gave a brief speech, followed by a formal receiving line. We were informed that a special reception would be given for foreign guests at the Akasaka Palace immediately after the formal reception. The overseas guests—twenty of us in total—were shown to a bus to take us to Akasaka. In the group were Harvard classmates and teachers of the princess and Oxford friends of the crown prince. A neighbor couple from the Owadas' Belmont days and we rounded out the group. At Akasaka Palace, we were delighted to be received by the emperor and empress, by Mr. and Mrs. Owada, and, of course, the crown prince and princess. More refreshments were served, and the setting was quite informal as each member of the imperial family circulated about the room and held lengthy conversations with all of their guests. We did not bring a camera because we thought it would be a serious breach of etiquette. Happily, some of the younger guests did, and their majesties appeared to be delighted to have photographs taken with each of us. After the reception, the Owadas invited us to a beautiful Western-style dinner at a private restaurant for a warm, family-type celebration.

Shortly after we returned to Boston, we began receiving newspaper and magazine clippings from various friends in Japan. Apparently, the photograph sent to the media by the Imperial Household Agency was one showing Marion and me being received by the crown prince and princess. We were further surprised to receive the official wedding book, which included the same photograph.

FOR SEVERAL YEARS, Yohei Kono was the chairman of the Liberal Democratic Party—the party that dominated Japanese politics for many years in the post–World War II era. In the coalition government of Prime Minister Murayama, he served as deputy prime minister and minister of foreign affairs. In 1987, Ambassador Taniguchi introduced me to Mr. Kono, then a member of the House of Representatives of the National Diet. I learned that his daughter, Haruko, was interested in attending a prep school in New England prior to attending a U.S. university. Shortly after I returned to Boston, Mrs. Kono and Haruko arrived to look over schools. I took them to Northfield Mount Hermon, where we met with the headmaster, Rev. Richard Unsworth. Haruko was subsequently admitted and spent two successful years at Northfield before being admitted to George-town University.

In my initial meeting with Mr. Kono, I found out that he was president of the Inter-University Athletic Union of Japan and that he was keenly interested in track and long-distance running. He had been an outstanding runner for Waseda University, competing in the famous Ekiden relays. The Ekiden is a long-distance race (approximately 107 kilometers) in which teams of eight runners run legs ranging from 9.5 kilometers to 19.7 kilometers. Every January, the major universities compete in the Tokyo-to-Hakone Ekiden, and in November twenty-three Japanese colleges and universities compete in the national championship Nagoya-Ise Ekiden. Mr. Kono admitted that he had hoped for many years that runners from the Ivy League might participate as guests in one of the major ekidens. He volunteered to underwrite a trip by the long-distance coaches of Brown and Harvard—Dan Challener and Ed Sheehan—to observe the January 1990 Tokyo-to-Hakone Ekiden. Both returned with television tapes of the race and expressed great enthusiasm for Ivy League participation.

A month later, I traveled to Japan with the chief executive officer of the Augat Company, Marcel Joseph, to visit the major Japanese automobile manufacturers. While in Tokyo, I met with Mr. Kono, Ambassador Armacost, and Herb Lee and Bob Neville of the U.S. embassy. We discovered that it would not be possible to compete in the Tokyo-Hakone Ekiden until 1994 and that the November Nagoya-Ise Ekiden would interrupt the fall cross-country season for Ivy League schools, making it impossible for current undergraduate runners to participate. We agreed that Brown and Harvard would make the arrangements to send ten runners—all graduates of Ivy League universities within the past two years—and two coaches to the 1990 Nagoya-Ise race. Formal invitations were sent to the presidents and head coaches of Brown and Harvard. President Gregorian and Coach Rothenberg of Brown responded with enthusiasm; Harvard did not reply. Hence, Brown has been given the responsibility for organizing and coaching the Ivy League representatives each year since 1990.

Mr. Kono invited me to accompany the first Ivy League team, which included five runners from Brown, two from Harvard, two from Dartmouth, and one from Penn. The team was led by a six-time All-America runner from Brown, Greg Whiteley, who had run the mile in under four minutes. More than a million spectators lined the sixty-three-mile course and at least thirty million watched the race on television. Mr. Kono, representatives of the sponsor, the newspaper *Asahi Shimbun,* and I followed the race in a Mitsubishi automobile. Throughout the morning, rain and winds of almost typhoon force buffeted the runners. We rolled down the car window to cheer on the runners, but could not get it closed. By the time we reached the end of the race at the sacred shrine of Ise, we each had a lap full of water. So much for the vaunted quality of Japanese cars, we laughingly told Mr. Kono.

Two years later, Yohei Kono invited Marion and me to attend the women's championship ekiden in Osaka. Together with Dr. Nishijima, the former president of Kyoto University, I spoke at the prerace international symposium held in Osaka's magnificent concert hall. That same year Mr. Kono traveled to Boston to observe the Keio-Waseda championship football game in Harvard Stadium. The teams were prepared for the game by the coaches of Harvard and Yale. During the first half, I sat on the Waseda side with Mr. Kono, but spent the second half on the Keio side, having taught in the Keio-Harvard advanced management program in the early 1960s.

Shortly after Mr. Kono was appointed deputy prime minister and minister of foreign affairs, an article appeared in Japanese and U.S. newspapers, reporting on the financial assets of Japanese political leaders. Yohei Kono led the list with reported assets of $87.6 million.

In 1980, I led a delegation to China, again with a group of some twenty Massachusetts business leaders. We met with top Chinese officials in Beijing, Shanghai, and Guanghou. We visited factories, commenes, and schools and were graciously entertained by every official we met. Several members of our mission developed business relationships that involved an up-front investment with the expectation that it might take years to show any return. We were impressed by the fact that Japanese electronic and automobile companies had already made long-term investments. We were also impressed with the beauty of such places as Guilin. I had always thought that the craggy, cone-shaped mountains rising out of the rivers were a figment of the artists' imagination. They were for real.

When Governor Ed King succeeded Michael Dukakis, he renamed our council the Massachusetts Business Development Council and asked me to serve as chairman. Under the new economic affairs secretary, James Carlin, there was an emphasis on growth of local industries, but we continued to lead trade missions to East Asia and Europe.

When the council was dissolved after Governor King left office, I received invitations to travel to Japan at least three times per year. In October 1984, Governor Joseph Garrahy asked me to lead a delegation of Rhode Island businessmen and academic leaders to Japan. Representing Brown University were President Howard Swearer and Dr. Pierre Galletti, vice president and professor of medical science. The mission prepared itself well, taking brochures and a film, all in Japanese, and carefully-defined objectives to seek opportunities in biotechnology, underwater electronics, boat building, the fishing industry, and tourism. We met with Prime Minister Nakasone, Ambassador Mansfield, and business leaders in Tokyo, Osaka, and Kyoto. Ambassador Mansfield described our trade mission "the most successful he had observed in his years in Japan."

With membership on the arts council at the Massachusetts Institute of Technology, I became involved in raising funds for the media technology laboratory. Yaichi Ayukawa, chairman of the Techno-Venture Company (Japan's first venture-capital firm), was known as "Mr. MIT" in Japan. Through his connections, he raised money from Japanese corporations to establish a dozen or more endowed professorships and sparked MIT's corporate associates program, attracting several million dollars each year to support research activity. Yaichi was asked to chair the media lab's fund-raising effort in Japan, and I headed the U.S. effort. We succeeded in raising enough money to finance the building of the media technology center, now appropriately named for the late president of MIT, Jerry Weisner.

The media lab is involved in leading-edge research in the field of "intelligent agents," programs that may one day handle all our electronic demands and even make routine decisions for us. When visiting the labs, one might see a researcher wearing an experimental headgear that includes earphones, a video camera, and a tiny screen that shows live video and computer data—all connected to a computer in the vest that is linked by a wireless modem to the worldwide web. Or another researcher might walk by with an imbedded computer in his Nike shoe, which serves as a personal secretary for the wearer.

DURING THE PAST few years, I have spent a substantial portion of my time as honorary consul for Thailand. King Bhumibol Adulyadej, who officially appointed me in 1991, was born in Cambridge, Massachusetts. In 1996 he celebrated his fiftieth anniversary on the throne —the world's longest-serving monarch. His father, Prince Mahidol of Songkla, studied at the Harvard Medical School, and his mother earned a degree in nursing at Simmons College. They took modern medicine to Thailand. My responsibilities include issuing visas, entertaining visiting Thai dignitaries, and assisting Thai citizens who encounter difficulty. For example, two students from Boston universities died in tragic accidents, requiring me to work closely with doctors, lawyers, policemen, undertakers, and members of the families.

Perhaps the most interesting visitor from Thailand was Princess Maha Chakri—an intelligent, attractive, and extremely popular member of the royal family. While in Boston, she officiated in the dedication of a city square in Cambridge in honor of her father and participated in symposia held at the Harvard Medical School, the

School of Public Health, and Simmons College. Each morning, Marion and I arose at five o'clock to join the princess in a morning jog along the Charles River. One morning she asked to stop at Au Bon Pain for a cup of coffee. Dressed in plain jogging clothes, she did not look much like a princess, so she did not cause the same kind of stir as she did when she arrived at Logan Airport and the Ritz-Carlton Hotel. Thai citizens abased themselves on their hands and knees in her presence.

Our trips to Thailand have been memorable. Despite the unbelievably heavy traffic and smog, the splendor of the temples of Bangkok and the natural beauty of Chiang Mei are remarkable. We are always impressed with the spontaneous warmth, friendliness, and courtesy of the Thai people.

On April 22, 1997, at the Thai Embassy in Washington Ambassador Nitya Pibulsonggram, on behalf of the King of Thailand, conferred upon me the Royal Decoration—"Our most Noble Order of the Crown of Thailand."

SWIMMING IN POLITICAL WATERS

I have already mentioned some of my early associations with people in political life; while working at the Boston Company, I became involved in two other political campaigns—one for a Republican candidate, Illinois Senator Charles Percy, and one for a Democratic aspirant to the presidency, Sargent Shriver.

Chuck Percy was invited to be the keynote speaker at the Harvard Business School National Conference in the early 1950s. He was then the chief executive officer of Bell & Howell in Chicago. As a young assistant dean, I was impressed with Percy's polished presentation, delivered without a text or even an outline. He spoke from the front of the platform, perhaps to demonstrate that he was not relying upon a speech crafted by an assistant. The conference marked the beginning of a long-time friendship with Chuck Percy. It was not surprising that he moved into the political arena and was elected senator from Illinois. He soon became a leading light in the Republican Party and was mentioned frequently as a potential candidate for the presidency.

Along the way, Chuck caught the eye of Tom Watson Jr., chairman of IBM. Tom and I served together for many years on the board of our alma mater, Brown University. Although he later became a strong supporter of John Kennedy and was appointed by Lyndon Johnson as ambassador to the Soviet Union, Tom was involved in Republican Party king-making in the 1950s. Tom Watson enlisted my help in promoting Chuck Percy for the presidency. Maxwell Rabb, Watson, and I flew around the country in the IBM plane raising money and talking up Percy's candidacy. Tom had had a heart attack a year or two before our barnstorming tours, but he didn't hesitate to take over the controls of the IBM plane from time to time. He had distinguished himself as a World War II pilot, but Rabb and I were relieved that a copilot was up front with him.

Chuck Percy did not secure the nomination at the Republican convention, but we continued to see each other from time to time in Chicago or Washington. When Jimmy Carter was elected president in 1976, Chuck Percy recommended me as a candidate to be ambassador to Japan. Senators John Glenn, Ted Kennedy, and Jay Rockefeller also spoke to the president and wrote letters on my behalf. President Carter set up a screening committee to review the list of more than 250 names of persons recommended for the ambassadorship, Massachusetts Lieutenant Governor Tom O'Neill, son of House Speaker "Tip" O'Neill, being a member of the committee. In early 1977, Tom telephoned me to report that the list of candidates had been narrowed down to three and that I had survived the cut. A week later, Chuck Percy called and said that two names were being sent over to the president's desk and that my name was one of the two, "But don't get your hopes up," he added. A few days later, the press reported that Jimmy Carter would appoint Mike Mansfield as ambassador to Japan—clearly an outstanding choice. Many Americans are familiar with his record as majority leader of the Senate, but few are aware that he had taught Far Eastern history at the University of Montana. Former Harvard Professor Ed Reischauer and former Senator Mansfield were unquestionably the two greatest representatives to Japan since the end of World War II. During his eleven years as ambassador, Mansfield was revered by the Japanese people.

On visits to Japan, I frequently called upon Ambassador Mansfield in his embassy office around 7:30 or 8:00 o'clock in the morning. He always met me with his shirt sleeves rolled up and offered to make me a cup of coffee in his small, private kitchen. He became famous for his oft-stated remark that the relationship between Japan and the United States was "the world's most important—bar none." Americans living in Japan irreverently called Mansfield's office "the Bar None Ranch."

SARGENT SHRIVER traveled to Ohio University in the early years of the Kennedy administration to announce a $400,000 grant to enable us to train one of the first groups of Peace Corps volunteers. He seemed to be especially pleased that we had committed university resources to the development of the depressed Appalachian area. Subsequently, we were the first university to grant special admission and credit to returning Peace Corps veterans.

This was the beginning of a long friendship with Sargent Shriver and his family. As described in my notes about President Johnson, Shriver asked me to join his task force planning the Economic Opportunity Program and specifically the U.S. Job Corps. I was impressed with Shriver's ability to attract academic, business, labor, and athletic talent in planning the Vista Volunteers, Head Start, and Job Corps programs. When he left his office on Washington evenings, he carried two briefcases completely packed with homework. His energy, good humor, and intelligence inspired all those who worked with him.

Even though I had declined his and the president's invitation to head the Job Corps after the legislation was passed, our friendship with him and Eunice, his wife, has continued to this day. Almost every year he telephones a day before Eunice's birthday celebration (the date varies according to their schedule at Hyannis). Whenever possible, we have changed our plans and raced down to the Cape to join the fun-loving Shriver family and their guests. On one of those occasions, Barbara Walters was there. This was shortly after Rose Kennedy had published her book about her late husband, Joseph Kennedy. Walters kept pressing Mrs. Kennedy as to why she had not been more critical of her husband: "Why did you willingly stay in Brookline while Joe was in Washington as head of the SEC?" Mrs. Kennedy's reply: "All of the children were in orthodonture, and if we had gone to Washington, they wouldn't have had their famous Kennedy smiles."

Eunice jumped into the conversation: "But, Mom, why did you let him go alone to California and not take us with him?" "He was busy, my dear, and besides, he was bringing home the bacon."

In 1971, Shriver—along with several other Democratic Party hopefuls—decided to run for the presidency. I have registered as an independent most of my life, but I agreed to support him and raise funds for his candidacy. Shriver—conservative and practical on fiscal issues, liberal on social issues—would, I felt, appeal to many Boston businessmen whose outlook was quite similar. I was confident that some might be persuaded to assist him with contributions. Shriver had celebrity status, and about a couple of dozen Boston chief executives showed up at the cocktail reception I gave in my office suite at the Boston Company. Unfortunately, a few weeks later Shriver dropped out of the race.

MARION AND I were invited to the wedding of Maria Shriver and Arnold Schwarzenegger. Stadium-type stands had been erected to accommodate the curious throng of people who wished to ogle the long line of celebrities filing into the church. The ceremony began with a moving tribute given by Arnold to his parents and to the Shriver family. About ten minutes into the wedding vows, there was a tremendous roar from the throng outside, reminiscent of crowd roars after a winning touchdown had been scored. As all heads turned toward the rear of the church, in walked Andy Warhol on the arm of the black model Grace Jones, who was wearing a green, skin-tight, full-length gown.

When Rose Kennedy died at the age of 104, her funeral was a major event in Boston. Thousands of people lined the streets to watch the Kennedys and invited celebrities as they entered the church. Long before the services began, the huge grandstand erected in front of the church was filled with observers. The funeral service, conducted by Cardinal Bernard Law in the church that Rose Kennedy had attended as a child, was inspiring. Several of the Kennedys gave moving tributes to their mother and grandmother. I thought that those given by Eunice Kennedy Shriver and John Kennedy Jr. were especially impressive. Guests were invited to share in communion at the conclusion of the service, which was covered by local and national television. Two of our friends who had watched on television chided Marion and me, both non-Catholics, for taking communion.

In November 1995, Sarge Shriver celebrated his eightieth birthday. Marion and I were invited to the Shriver's beautiful home in Maryland along with several hundred others who had been involved in the Peace Corps or War on Poverty programs. The Shriver home is a veritable museum of photographs and memorabilia of the John Kennedy presidency, of Robert and Ted Kennedy, and of Eunice and Sargent Shriver.

During the cocktail reception, a torrential rain came down, accompanied by almost hurricane-force wind. Three trees were blown down, damaging several cars, including Arnold Schwarzenegger's. The dinner was delayed for fear that the large tent would collapse. Power went out but the standby generator system provided sufficient illumination as we waded into the tent for dinner. Maria and Arnold had prepared a special film for the occasion, but without sufficient power it could not be shown. Nevertheless, both Eunice and Sarge Shriver, unflappable, lively, and impeccable hosts, carried off the evening in grand style. As guests left around midnight, we were startled to step out into four or five inches of snow. Another memorable and delightful evening with the Shrivers!

CHAPTER 12

Serving on Corporate Boards

DURING THE PAST forty years, I have been privileged to participate on fifteen boards of directors of business corporations or financial institutions. On five—Digital, Colgate-Palmolive, Mead, McGraw-Hill, and the Boston Safe Deposit and Trust Company—I have served twenty years or more. I continue to enjoy and learn from the association with colleagues at each company. The media and the academic world too often criticize business leaders beyond a reasonable level of justification. I am enormously impressed with the integrity, the intelligence, and commitment of executives and board members. Without exception, each group with whom I serve takes seriously their responsibility to employees, customers, shareholders, and the community. I have not observed any lack of concern for the environment or for the public responsibility of corporations.

Without writing a several-hundred-page volume, it would be impossible to describe all of the fascinating, enlightening, and humorous experiences I have enjoyed on various boards. At two companies —Mead and McGraw-Hill—we as directors met for countless hours trying to fend off hostile takeover attempts. On three boards, I had the unpleasant experience of sharing with fellow directors the responsibility of asking the chief executive officer to step down. All of the companies have enabled directors to visit plant sites throughout the United States and overseas. With the Ludlow Corporation, we inspected jute plants in Calcutta, India. Colgate-Palmolive gave us an opportunity to observe Buddhist priests dedicating a new soap and toothpaste facility in Bangkok and to visit plant sites and laboratories in the Philippines, Australia, Belgium, and France. Sonesta International Hotels invited directors to inspect their luxury hotels in Egypt and cruise down the Nile in their *Nile Goddess* ship. Augat, Intermet, and Mead asked me to travel to Japan several times. GPG, a British holding company, required my traveling to London six times in one summer to oversee the disposition of several of its acquisitions.

Lacy Herrmann, a long-time friend from Brown and Harvard Business School days, created in several states tax-free trusts, equity, and money market funds managing more than $3.2 billion. I serve on the boards of three of the funds—Hawaii, Oregon, and Rhode Island. Each board meets four times a year, once or twice in the state involved, with additional meetings being held in locations convenient to all the funds. Lacy always arranges for us to meet in the finest hotels and resorts in California, Arizona, Hawaii, and Oregon. Each of the funds has a statewide distribution of shareholders, so "outreach" meetings are held in locations throughout the state. In Oregon, our board has visited every area of the state, and in Hawaii we have met with shareholders on every island except Molokai. The opportunity to meet at least twice a year with directors of the other tax-free funds—Colorado, Arizona, and Kentucky—is a stimulating experience. Lacy Herrmann has attracted to his various boards leading citizens in each of the states involved.

Tom Lee, one of the nation's most successful independent investors, teamed up with Merrill Lynch in 1986 to establish three acquisition funds making mezzanine investments in promising middle-size companies. Tom asked me to join Professor Joseph Bower and Stanley Feldberg as an independent general partner. In its ten years of operation, the funds have brought to the public several outstanding issues—Snapple, Playtex, and General Nutrition, among others. Snapple made news headlines recently when the purchaser, Quaker Oats, sold the company for a $1 billion loss.

Tom Lee is a remarkably thoughtful and generous person. He has made major gifts to the Boston Museum of Fine Arts and to the Guggenheim Museum in New York. He recently contributed $22 million to Harvard College, $19 million of which is completely unrestricted, a remarkable act of generosity.

TAKEOVERS AND TURNAROUNDS

There are interesting stories to relate about each company and investment group, but I will comment on only four:

Digital Equipment Corporation
Kenneth Olsen and Harlan Anderson, young graduates of MIT, in 1957 received a loan of $60,000 from the American Research and Development Company (ARD) to begin building systems modules. They established Digital with three employees and 8,500 square feet of production space in a converted woolen mill in Maynard, Massachusetts. General Georges Doriot, president of ARD and a colleague on the Harvard Business School faculty, invited me to join the board of directors in 1959, when sales totaled $94,000.

Four years later Digital introduced the PDP-1, the world's first small interactive computer. In 1965, the PDP-8 became the world's first mass-produced minicomputer. Digital opened sales and service offices in Europe and Canada in 1963 and Japanese headquarters in Tokyo in 1968. Step by step, Ken Olsen led the company through every stage of development from zero to $13 billion in sales. Usually an entrepreneurial founder is succeeded by a manufacturing specialist and in turn by a marketing expert, and then perhaps a financial wizard. Ken led the company through every phase of development until 1992. By 1974, Digital ranked 475th among the Fortune 500 companies. By 1980, sales had reached $2 billion, and 200,000 computers had been shipped. Three years later, the famous VAX computer system was announced, and Digital ranked 95th in *Fortune* magazine's top 100 industrial companies.

The 1980s were heady days for the company. A DECWORLD sales exposition drew 48,500 people, with the *Queen Elizabeth 2* and starship *Oceanic* serving as floating hotels and conference centers. In 1988, Digital's stock hit an all-time high at $199. Marion and my children are still cross at me for persuading them not to sell any of their holdings at the time. *Fortune* magazine described Kenneth Olsen as "arguably the most successful entrepreneur in the history of American business." Sales climbed to $13 billion; the company was the thirtieth largest in the United States and was doing business in sixty-four countries.

But as we entered the 1990s, the directors began to express concern that all was not well with Digital. Other companies, most notably Hewlett-Packard, were chipping away at us. While they were moving toward UNIX-based systems, Ken Olsen was describing UNIX as "snake oil." A fellow director, Bob Everett, who was also consulting for the company, reported unrest in the engineering area. Key people were leaving the company. We were being pushed into large acquisitions in Europe without adequate background information. The directors were concerned about the size of our workforce—135,000—making us the least productive company in the industry. We had more engineers in central engineering than Sun Microsystems had in total employees. Ken Olsen continued to resist our orders to reduce the size of the workforce, arguing that "these are highly trained people; we'll need all of them when the economy turns around."

However, we as directors had the impression that the company had become a bloated, internally focused organization. George Colony, president of the Forrester Research Group, was quoted in the *Boston Globe*: "At IBM the value was in the customer, so people focused outward. At DEC, the internal mattered so much. It was a very political culture that placed a high value on people who could play the political game, the budget game, the meeting game. They spent their lives playing with each other." A cruel observation, but one that became increasingly apparent as the company began losing market share.

In the summer 1992, the directors concluded that we had to take action. We met in executive session in the offices of the Raytheon Company, arranged by fellow director Tom Phillips. Reluctantly, the independent directors unanimously agreed to replace Ken Olsen. This is one of the most difficult decisions any board must make. It was especially difficult to ask a good friend of more than thirty-five years, the founder of the company and the "ultimate entrepreneur," to leave his company. It was Ken's choice not to remain on the board.

Bob Palmer, a senior manufacturing vice president, had made several presentations at board meetings. He had joined Digital with excellent experience in the semiconductor industry and a broad vision of the world of technology. He now assumed leadership of the company, and has overseen a remarkable turnaround. The workforce has been cut in half, several plants have been closed, dynamic new executives have been recruited, and Digital once again is growing and showing a profit. Digital's Alpha Server systems are the fastest-growing line of high-end UNIX servers from any supplier. It has established itself within the Internet buying community as a leader by ingeniously making its Alpha Vista/Alpha Server search engine available for free to Internet users. Bob Palmer has structured several strategic alliances and partnerships—with Microsoft and its Windows NT, with Oracle, Intel, Computer Associates, MCI, and Samsung. He scored a major coup by attracting Bruce Claflin from IBM to head up Digital's personal computer line. Digital is truly a global company. Sales to customers outside the United States amounted to 66 percent of the total operating revenue in 1996.

A director who deserves much credit for the turnaround is Philip Caldwell—chairman of the audit committee until his retirement. When he was chief executive of Ford Motor Company, Phil was responsible for the company's major recovery. The pressure he exerted through discerning questions asked at audit committee meetings and his private sessions with management contributed much to the pace and success of Digital's recovery.

In 1998, I will reach the retirement age and regretfully have to leave the board after thirty-nine exciting and rewarding years.

McGraw-Hill

My first involvement with McGraw-Hill came when I was helping Sargent Shriver plan the U.S. Job Corps. We asked publishers to consider developing curricular materials for the Job Corps centers and camps. In 1970, I was asked by Lord Walter Perry in England to assist in the creation of the Open University. Again, we needed curricular materials prepared and published by reputable commercial organizations. The typical college or university was not a fertile source of help, because each institution developed its own home grown course material. Bob Slaughter, senior vice president of McGraw-Hill, and I met several times with Lord Perry in McGraw-Hill's former headquarters building on Forty-second Street.

Perhaps at Bob's suggestion, I met in fall 1972 with Sheldon Fisher, then CEO of McGraw-Hill. In February 1973, I was elected to the board of directors, along with Bill McGill, president of Columbia University, and Jim Webb, formerly the head of NASA. At the time, all the other directors were members of management. Over the next twenty years—the length of my service—the composition of the board changed dramatically. Today, only two members are "insiders"—the rest are independent, outside representatives.

In the late 1970s, the president of American Express (AMEX), Roger Morley, was elected to the board. At all of our meetings he was seated next to me at the board table. At first I thought he was the most conscientious director I had ever met, because he took page after page of notes at every meeting. In January 1979, the reasons for Morley's careful homework became apparent. American Express surprised us with a takeover offer. I had gone through a similar experience at the Mead Corporation, when Occidental Petroleum made a hostile pass at Mead. I became well-acquainted with the defense strategies of Joe Flom, a well-known lawyer-specialist in that field, and at McGraw-Hill we quickly came to know Marty Lipton, equally famous and skilled as a defensive lawyer-coach.

As battle lines were drawn, McGraw-Hill was determined to preserve its independence. We argued that our editors, authors, and professional personnel required the nurturing environment Mc-Graw-Hill had created; they would be destroyed under the commercial pressures of American Express. Each director was subjected to heavy pressure from AMEX directors and parties of interest. I recall a lengthy telephone conversation with Lloyd Cutler, then an attorney for the White House. Our chairman, Harold McGraw, was determined not to let the company slip away, and he rallied the troops in a magnificent defensive effort. We sued American Express, arguing that its president, Roger Morley, had collected earnings projections and other confidential information, concealing his takeover plans from his fellow directors at McGraw-Hill. The flurry of suits and countersuits ended when American Express withdrew its bid in February 1979.

The aborted attempt was apparently the end of Roger Morley. He was subsequently fired, and the last I heard of him he was "somewhere in Europe."

In 1980, Harold McGraw appointed a three-director task force of independent directors—Peter Lawson-Johnson, Howard Tuthill, with me as chairman—to review the committee structure of the board, the meeting agenda, the process for identifying and recruiting new directors, director compensation, and other matters involving board participation. When Joe Dionne succeeded Harold as CEO, he created two advisory committees, which signaled McGraw-Hill's rapidly growing international outreach—one for Europe and the other for Asia. Each group was graced by distinguished business and academic leaders. Joe asked me to serve as chairman of the Asian advisory council and to assist in the selection of its seven members. We met twice annually: once in New York, the other time in Asia or Europe.

A member of our group was Amnuay Viravan, the chairman of the Bank of Bangkok. He subsequently became deputy prime minister of Thailand. In 1991, the king, who was born in Cambridge, Massachusetts, decided that Thailand needed an honorary consul general in New England. Because of our academic and high-tech environment, a desirable candidate needed to have a background in education and business. Amnuay Viravan proposed my name, and I have represented Thailand since 1991.

Joe Dionne took over as CEO when the publishing business was undergoing dramatic change. With sound strategies for growth, Joe has transformed the company into one of the world's foremost multimedia publishers. McGraw-Hill is using technology to deliver information in new and innovative ways. The financial services area, led by Standard and Poor's rating and information groups, has shown dramatic growth.

Both Marion and I have missed interaction with the directors, management, and their spouses since my retirement from the board in 1993.

Colgate-Palmolive

In 1974, I joined the board of Colgate-Palmolive Company, succeeding Harold Helm, who was chairman of the board of trustees of Princeton University and chairman of the Chemical Bank in New York. Harold was largely responsible for my being invited to join the board. Three years earlier, he had telephoned me to request that I set up an appointment with the Kendall Company president for David Foster, the chief executive of Colgate-Palmolive. I was then serving on the board of Kendall, a company with interests in textiles and pharmaceuticals.

There had been rumors that Kendall might be for sale because of a rift between the chairman and largest shareholder, John Kendall, and the chief executive officer, Willard Bright. Bright had ordered Kendall to move out of his office in company headquarters, prompting John to begin quietly seeking out a buyer for the company.

On two occasions, David Foster canceled appointments to visit the Kendall Company because of illness. Eventually officials of both companies got together and Colgate made an offer. Meanwhile, the Brunswick Corporation expressed interest through John Kendall. The Textron Company also made a proposal through its chief executive officer, William Miller, who years later became U.S. secretary of the treasury. Bill Miller and General Georges Doriot were directors of both Textron and Kendall. The only independent directors of Kendall who had no conflict of interest in the impending sale of the company were "Spike" Beitzel of IBM and myself. The two of us were given the responsibility of meeting with representatives of Colgate, Brunswick, and Textron. On the morning of the "auction," the president of Brunswick made an offer, but after consulting by telephone with his key directors, he withdrew from the bidding. Colgate-Palmolive's offer was eventually accepted by the directors of Kendall.

Before leaving the story of Kendall, I should describe a fascinating event that took place several years earlier. Harold Marshall, who was then chief executive officer, arrived at a board meeting with a broad grin on his face, announcing that the oil giant Esso had offered $50,000 for the right to buy a product name from Kendall and to rename itself Exxon. Exxon happened to be a rather obscure little drug product owned and copyrighted by Kendall. What none of the directors knew at the time was that Esso had budgeted more than $100 million to make the transition to a new name.

When the Colgate offer to Kendall was consummated, John Kendall and Will Bright were offered seats on the Colgate board. Bright lasted only a year or so as president of the new Colgate subsidiary and a member of the board. After his departure and Harold Helm's retirement, I was invited to join the Colgate board.

David Foster, Colgate's chairman, president, and chief executive officer, ran the company in a fairly autocratic manner. He was unchallenged by the board as he made several acquisitions following the Kendall Company purchase—the Helena Rubenstein cosmetic company, Maui Divers jewelry company, Princess House glassware, a golf course in Italy, and the Mission Hills golf course development in Palm Springs, among others.

At the Mission Hills golf course, the company sponsored the Colgate–Dinah Shore Open for the Ladies Professional Golf Association. Along with the other directors and their spouses, Marion and I were invited over a period of ten years to spend a week every April participating in the Pro-Am foursomes, the dinners, and the entertainment features of the week. We were able to play golf with such celebrities as Bob and Dolores Hope, Andy Williams, Jack Lemmon, President Ford, Robert Stack, Willie Mays, and, of course, with Dinah Shore and the women professionals. On Wednesday evenings, Dinah arranged to have her Hollywood friends put on an elaborate show for the Colgate guests.

One year, Frank Pace, a Colgate director, arranged for a private golf match among directors. Frank had been secretary of the army under President Truman, who sent him to Korea to summon General MacArthur for his firing by the president. Each of us had a lady pro and a fellow director as partners. We put $200 apiece in a pool for the winners. At the end of the eighteen-hole tournament, Frank Pace, Marlene Hagge, and I were the winners and looked forward to pocketing about $1,000 each. Then fellow director Tom Wilcox suggested, "Let's give it all to the lady pros for being so nice as to join us."

When David Foster resigned, Keith Crane was appointed chairman and chief executive officer. Keith, an Australian, had joined the company at about the age of nineteen and had compiled an outstanding record managing Colgate subsidiaries throughout the world. Before being tapped for the CEO post, Keith had managed the Kendall subsidiary. Because of our prior association with Kendall, John Kendall and I had closely observed Keith's performance and strongly supported his promotion.

During his tenure, Keith Crane did a remarkable job of turning the company around, selling off the golf courses and almost all of David Foster's acquisitions. The company was in excellent shape when he was succeeded by Reuben Mark. Year after year, Reuben has achieved higher and higher levels of sales and profitability. He has introduced reward and recognition systems that have engendered employee morale equaled by very few major corporations. The company has continued to grow in sales and in new product development, setting new records for profits year after year. In the past decade, Colgate's global sales have risen 140 percent, from $3.5 billion to more than $8.4 billion, with operating profits around 13 percent of sales.

Several important acquisitions have been made—the Mennen and Kolynos companies, for example—that have significantly strengthened our market share, especially in Latin America. Colgate-Palmolive sells its products in 206 world markets supplied by plants in 62 countries. It surprises many to learn that the company operates in more countries than Coca-Cola. Colgate leads all other oral-care brands in 167 countries of the world. It is first in toothpaste and toothbrush sales volume worldwide. Between 1991 and 1996, Colgate opened operations in 35 developing countries and hired or transferred 100 managers to fill slots in new global markets. During the next five years, the company will begin operations in 35 additional countries, and young managers are being trained for those positions. Only 20 percent of those managers will be U.S.-born. As a result of training and experience abroad, Colgate has a strong and deep pool of management talent. By the time a manager reaches a top position in the company, he or she will have served as a manager in several countries.

Mead

The Mead Corporation owned a large paper mill in Chillicothe, the location of a branch of Ohio University. Mead had generously contributed a building and airplanes to the university, and I became acquainted with Mead's president, George Pringle, and other executives. In 1965, I was asked to join the board of directors, the beginning of a happy and rewarding twenty-year relationship.

As a major producer of paper, Mead also had an interest in art, influenced primarily by my fellow director Arthur Harris. Mead conducted each year an "Art Across America" competition, rewarding and displaying the works of contemporary U.S. artists. As Mead's sponsorship spread to Europe, several members of the board were invited to Paris by then Ambassador Sargent Shriver to view an exhibition at the Louvre.

My first experience with an unfriendly takeover came when Occidental Petroleum tried to acquire Mead. A director's true mettle and stamina are tested when under that pressure. We were bombarded with telephone calls from the media and management as we raced to Dayton to attend meetings, sometimes twice a week. Mead eventually fended off the attack, but the price in executive effort, in lawyers' fees, and in lost time was enormous.

Once a year, the board met with the top management of Mead at Cabin Bluff, a log-cabin retreat located near Brunswick, Georgia. For three or four days we discussed company strategies, rose at dawn to hunt turkeys, and generally to relax while we strategized on the year ahead.

Jim McSweeney was a remarkable chief executive officer. As a Southerner, he had grown up in various responsibilities within the corporation. (Incidentally, he was a high school classmate of Dinah Shore). Mac, as we called him, had an unusual appreciation for corporate responsibility. He established a committee by that name and asked me to chair it. Included in its membership were directors, middle management members, nonsalaried employees, and even a union representative. We were given free rein to examine any aspect of the corporation's operations. I learned more about Mead by exposure to members of that committee than in any number of directors' meetings.

Jim McSweeney also asked me to chair a committee to review the responsibilities of the board of directors—its composition, size, diversity, retirement age, committee structure, compensation, and so forth. The committee made a major contribution to the strength and influence of the board. As a measure of his leadership, Mac appointed Barbara Jordan, the well-known black congresswoman, to our board. With the heavy preponderance of Southern shareholders, the appointment met resistance. Mac stuck to his guns, and Barbara turned out to be a brilliant, knowledgeable director. At our annual meetings at Cabin Bluff, we especially enjoyed her hearty singing of spirituals.

We also held meetings in Atlanta, the home of directors Arthur Harris and Ivan Allen Jr. Ivan was Atlanta's next-to-last white mayor. Although his ancestors were rich, proud Confederate slaveowners, Ivan Allen led the way to the integration of Atlanta. His leadership of the white business community helped to shape the South's most progressive city.

Mead established an entity called Mead Data Central, which developed an ink-jet printer capability, but more importantly pioneered in a legal information retrieval system called Lexis. This was followed by an electronic news-gathering service called Nexis. Mead bought the rights to publication of newspaper and magazine items throughout the world. The *New York Times,* for example, gave Nexis the right to include in its system all articles and news reports within twenty-four hours of publication. The cost to Mead was $10 million for rights in perpetuity. The *Times* realized later what it had given away and bought back its rights for hundreds of millions of dollars.

Because of my early involvement with Japan, I frequently traveled there with Nelson Mead to visit with Japanese partners who were joint-venturing with Mead. In the 1960s Mead had acquired several businesses outside the papermaking field. We bought the Lynchburg foundry in 1968 and built new foundries in Archer Creek and Radford, Virginia. When members of the board visited the foundries, we were struck by how out-of-date the facilities and processes appeared to be. From what I had read about Japanese foundries, I was convinced that we could learn much from them before upgrading our facilities.

I wrote to Dr. Shoichiro Toyoda, chairman of Toyota Motors, asking whether Nelson Mead, two of our foundry engineers, and I could visit one or two of the Toyota foundries. I was surprised by his prompt and gracious response. The visit to Japan began with an elaborate luncheon at the Okura Hotel in Tokyo, hosted by Dr. and Mrs. Toyoda. The visits to the foundries astonished and opened the eyes of the Mead engineers. They brought back to the company an urgent plea to improve substantially the quality of the Mead facilities and processes.

Toyota and Mead

When I returned to Boston in 1969, the Toyota Motor Corporation was the largest in Japan and the third largest automobile company in the world. When Dr. Toyoda's son, Akio, was preparing to enter Babson College, Dr. Toyoda wrote to me asking that we keep an eye on him. We entertained him in our home for several days before he found permanent lodging at the home of the Babson President Dr. Ralph Sorenson.

Akio received his MBA at Babson in 1981 and began his climb up the ladder at Toyota, starting with a humble position on the factory floor, progressing to selling Toyotas from door-to-door, and eventually working his way up to assistant manager of the Toyota Corolla Dealer Administration Division. When Akio married the attractive, highly intelligent, and personable Hiroko, Marion and I were invited to the wedding. Unfortunately, I had commitments that kept us from traveling to Japan. We have regretted ever since that we did not cancel everything and attend the wedding. It was reported to be one of the "most spectacular ever" in Japan.

A few months later, the Toyodas visited Boston. Both Dr. and Mrs. Toyoda are avid golfers. They were thrilled when I invited them to play with me at The Country Club in Brookline, which was about to host the U.S. Open. Off the first tee—a long par four—I hit what can be described as a "career drive." My second shot landed four feet from the hole and my putt holed for a birdie—the first and only time I have ever done that well on the number-one hole. Off the second tee, I had another sensational drive. Before we reached our balls on the fairway, it began to rain, then hail, followed by thunder and lightning. We rushed to the clubhouse to wait for the heavy torrent to subside. After an hour went by, the grounds were completely soaked. We never finished our round, and to this day the Toyodas think I am an unusually good golfer.

In 1982, the Mead Corporation decided to sell its money-losing foundries and concentrate its efforts once again on paper-making. George Mathews, a classmate at the Harvard Business School, expressed interest in acquiring the Mead foundries to complement his foundries in Columbus, Georgia, and Neunkirchen, Germany. In 1986 George invited me to join the board of directors of Intermet Corporation.

As Honda, Toyota, and Nissan built manufacturing plants in the United States, their market shares in this country rose rapidly. George Mathews, already a supplier of ductile iron castings to General Motors, Ford, and Chrysler, hoped to land the Japanese companies as customers. I advised George that a joint venture with Toyota or one of its major suppliers might be an appropriate beginning. We traveled together to Japan and met with Dr. Toyoda, who introduced us to the officers of Aisin Takaoka, a member of the Toyota group of companies. After several discussions and detailed negotiations, a joint venture was established with Intermet owning 60 percent and Aisin 40 percent. The new entity was named Intat Precision, Inc., and an advanced technology foundry was located in Rushville, Indiana, to supply castings to Japanese-owned U.S. automotive manufacturers.

In April 1988, George Mathews and I traveled again to Japan to participate in the elaborate contract-signing ceremonies in Nagoya, the headquarters of Aisin Takaoka. Stopping off in Tokyo, we joined Dr. Toyoda at a luncheon and shared breakfast with Ambassador Mike Mansfield—who was delighted that an American and Japanese company had agreed to work together. Through the good offices of a former consul general in Boston, Sadakazu Taniguchi, we had an audience in the imperial palace with the then crown prince, now Emperor Akihito. Tani also arranged for us to visit the famous egg-shaped Tokyo Dome to watch the Yomiuri Giants baseball team work out.

At the contract-signing ceremonies in Nagoya, the representatives of Aisin Takaoka were seated on one side of the room, facing the line of Intermet executives. The room was full of flower arrangements and U.S. and Japanese flags. Speeches, toasts, and the formal signing ceremony, which included the traditional painting of one eye of a large daruma doll, preceded an elaborate luncheon. Tours of the high-quality Aisin Takaoka and Aisin Seki foundries further cemented goodwill between the signing parties and augured great success for the joint venture. Unfortunately, the joint venture did not work out as well as planned. There were complaints of poor quality from the Rushville foundry, a turnover of executives, and finger-pointing for blame by both sides. Eventually, Aisin Takaoka bought out Intermet's share for more than Intermet had invested, even though Intat had never made a profit.

Another rewarding opportunity afforded by the Intermet board is the privilege of serving with Curtis Tarr. George Mathews, Curtis, and I were members of the class of 1950 at Harvard Business School. Curt was one of my roommates. He has had a distinguished career: Ph.D. from Stanford, president of Lawrence College, under secretary of state, head of selective service, vice president of Deere & Company, and vice chairman and director of Intermet. He is also a voracious reader, an author, and a deeply religious person who looks like a younger Billy Graham. I was touched by his comment one day: "I pray for you every day, Vern."

Shortly after Toyota announced the launching of its luxury car, the Lexus, I read that the company was being sued by the Mead Corporation for the use of the name. Mead owned and marketed the computerized information retrieval system for lawyers called Lexis. Although I had retired from the Mead board several years before, I knew well the chief executive officer, Burnell Roberts. When I telephoned him to express concern that Mead appeared to have forgotten how generous and hospitable the Toyota Company had been to Mead representatives, he explained, "It's gone too far. It's in the hands of the lawyers, and I can do nothing about it."

Through Dr. Toyoda, I arranged to meet on the West Coast with the head of the Lexus-U.S. operations, who turned out to be Dave Illingworth, an Ohio University alumnus who was a student during my presidency. I explained that I had failed to persuade the CEO at Mead to abandon the suit, and we discussed various ways in which the Toyota position could be strengthened. I mentioned that Mead had never brought suit against a maternity clothing company named Lexis and that for many years McGraw-Hill, on whose board I was serving, had a publication called *Dodge Reports*. There had never been any concern expressed by either Chrysler's Dodge subsidiary or McGraw-Hill. I don't know whether Toyota's high-priced Manhattan lawyers used this argument in their briefs, but Toyota won the case.

When the new Lexus was introduced, at an elaborate show in Monterey, California, Dr. Toyoda invited me with hundreds of dealers and dignitaries to attend the three-day extravaganza. The program included a speech by Mrs. Ronald Reagan, a jazz concert, a visit to the famous Monterey Aquarium, and golf outings at Pebble Beach and Spanish Bay. We were given an opportunity to drive a Lexus, a Mercedes, and a BMW for comparative purposes. Race-car drivers rocketed us at speeds up to one hundred miles an hour on the test track. Needless to say, we were impressed with the comfort, quietness, and luxury of the Lexus. I told Dave Illingworth that a ride in a Lexus was like floating on a cloud with wheels. A dealer from Boston offered to give me a Lexus if I, as president of the Japan Society of Boston, would be photographed with him as he presented the new car. By the time he returned to Boston, he had apparently forgotten that brilliant idea.

In 1994, Dr. Toyoda became the chairman of Keidanren, Japan's prestigious business council, the highest honor any Japanese business leader can receive. In that same year, he was awarded an honorary degree by Babson College. Akio attended the commencement exercises on behalf of his father. It was satisfying to see a maturing, confident young business leader, perhaps some day to be the chairman of the great Toyota Motor Corporation.

COMMON THREADS: UNIVERSITY PRESIDENTS AND CORPORATE LEADERS

All my adult life, I have been interested in education, business, and international activity. Fortunately, each of my jobs has permitted me to participate in all three areas. For twenty years—roughly one half of my working life—my professional responsibilities were in higher education; the latter half of my career has been in business and corporate affairs. Frequently, I am asked to compare the two: academia and business. A friend who has been both a university president and a corporate CEO remarked, perhaps with tongue in cheek: "A corporate leader's job is like playing checkers—a university president's is like chess."

It is fascinating to explore whether there are common threads in the administration of a business, a university, a cultural organization, or a government agency. Perhaps, if I describe some of these differences, we can more fully appreciate how difficult it is to measure the quality of an educational institution.

Below, as I enumerate some of the differences, it is in many ways much easier to judge the performance and quality of a business enterprise:

1. There are measures of business performance that are quantifiable and well understood by executives as well as the general public—sales growth, earnings per share, return on investment, return on net assets, market share, and so on. Furthermore, the public appraisal of the performance of a company and its managers can be determined every day by looking at stock market quotations. There is nothing comparable in academia. I doubt very much whether faculty members, students, parents, administrators, trustees, and the general public would agree on the criteria by which educational institutions should be judged. Even those standards of cost accounting, investment performance, or faculty teaching loads that have been established in university business offices or coordinating boards are controversial and lack standardization.

   Any judgments about the quality of a college or university tend to be highly subjective. Universities acquire their reputations over a period of many years. It usually takes a long time for an institution to enhance its reputation. The impressions of parents, students, and alumni tend to lag many years behind present-day reality.

2. The directors of a business corporation, as a group, are more involved in its activities than the trustees of a university. Business directors typically have at least a modest personal financial investment in the corporation; their responsibilities are clearly defined by regulatory agencies, and the concept of directors' liability and responsibility is clearly established.

3. Managers of business corporations are carefully trained for their responsibilities. As they move step-by-step up the corporate ladder, they are generally well-prepared for the next step. Through in-company and university-sponsored advanced-management programs, corporations spend considerable amounts of money on management development.

   A university president may have had experience as a provost, a dean, and a department chair, but responsibilities in previous administrative jobs are not full preparation for the pressures and obligations of the presidency. In recent years, foundations and educational associations have made efforts to identify and prepare potential educational leaders, but these efforts are optional and have been pitifully small as compared with industry.

4. Most corporations are consumer-oriented or they wouldn't stay in business. Universities still tend to be faculty-oriented. In most academic institutions, what the faculty wants is what gets done; what it does not want, eventually gets forced out of the system. A consumer of a business product usually can exercise some choices. Student "consumers" in our present higher-educational system, on the other hand, feel that they must go to college to be certified for employment in our society. Colleges have a monopoly upon certification. The curriculum in most colleges tends to be remarkably similar to curricular offerings at other institutions, and until recently the views of consumer-students have not been taken seriously.

5. The reward system in business—good salaries, stock options, and other incentives—attracts well-prepared administrators into business, and the decision maker is backed by expert help in the form of tax specialists, real estate specialists, accountants, lawyers, auditors, and other professionally trained experts. Reward systems in universities generally lack these incentives.

    People within a corporation, its customers, its suppliers, and the general public expect a middle-level manager to be well-qualified to provide significant information about a company. In colleges and universities, the decision-making responsibility and communication with the public tend to fall upon the university president himself.

6. It has been my experience that one can engage in rational discussion somewhat more readily with people in business cor-

porations—individuals who are committed to finding solutions, who share common corporate objectives, and who all have had significant management experience.

The university world does not have the kind of internal discipline that the corporation has, nor should it. Much of the president's time is spent in discussion with students, faculty, parents, townspeople, and others who do not share common objectives and often have quite different motivations. John Corson, a senior partner of the consulting firm of McKinsey and Co., has observed that members of the academic community, more than any other group, tend to translate personal motivations into philosophical beliefs. All too often, the university president is on defense, having to respond to inaccurate information that appears in the student newspaper or public press.

7. On the other hand, in academia there are qualities of life that business may never offer: the campus, with the brilliance and independence of faculty members, their sense of style, and their desire to contribute to their fields of knowledge, and the freshness, spontaneity, and enthusiasm of students. A person who has lived on a university campus does miss this dimension of excitement in the business world.

8. Perhaps most striking of all the differences between academia and business is the relatively meager resources devoted by universities to objective research and tough-minded thinking about the major problems of the institution. Nearly everybody who has intimate knowledge about higher education is highly involved in the action. Very few people are detached enough, and therefore objective enough, to have the positive perspective that only detached objectivity will give.

CHAPTER 13

A Look at the Moon with Neil Armstrong

AN AMERICAN NEVER FORGETS where he was when the Japanese attacked Pearl Harbor or when President Kennedy was assassinated. The same is true of Neil Armstrong's walk on the moon. I was in Columbus, Ohio, at the home of Dan Galbreath, son of the chairman of the board of Ohio University, John Galbreath.

We watched in fascination as Neil Armstrong took that "giant leap for mankind." I did not know Colonel Armstrong at that time, but a few years later when he was on the engineering faculty at the University of Cincinnati, he telephoned me in Boston. "I am planning a trip to London to try to secure funds for my research project," he explained. "I've heard you're good at raising money. Would you be willing to go with me?"

In London, we called upon several prospects. It was not difficult for Neil to gain entry into even the most private of British firms. The directors of Lloyds were delighted to be called upon by the first man to walk on the moon. They invited us to a small private dinner at one of London's most exclusive clubs. During cocktails one of the directors sidled up to me and asked if I could persuade Colonel Armstrong to talk about his historic flight. "Neil is terribly shy, you know, but I'll do my best," I promised.

It was not an easy task. Neil argued that he wasn't very good at after-dinner speeches. "They've promised you the money for your project," I said. "I think you have to say something about your moon walk, even if it's brief." After dinner, Neil rose and spoke for a solid hour. Fortunately, I had a pen and a pad of paper so I was able to take notes. He began by describing his childhood days on a farm in Ohio. He was fascinated with flying, almost as soon as he could walk; he earned his pilot's license before he learned to drive a car. During the Korean War, Neil flew seventy-eight combat missions before becoming a test pilot, flying the X-15 rocket plane at five times the speed of sound. It was on one of his X-15 flights, at 210,000 feet above the earth, that he experienced the feeling of space and decided to apply to NASA for the space program.

Neil described the months and months of intensive preparation for the flight to the moon. The grueling training routine was not without its perils. In 1966, Gemini 8, piloted by Neil, spun out of control, tumbling end over end until he brought it under control. Two members of the crew of Gemini 9 were killed in their aircraft prior to their scheduled launch. In 1967, three astronauts perished in a fire on the launching pad aboard Apollo 1.

Never in history had there been so much training and preparation for an event that would last less than three hours. At times the training was intense, ruthless and complex, stretching the skills of the astronauts and straining their patience almost beyond endurance. Armstrong and Buzz Aldrin, the two members of the three-man crew who were scheduled to land on the moon, one day practiced simulated landings of their lunar module for six hours: four of the five simulated landings had to be aborted. On another simulated descent to the moon, the landing vehicle crashed, causing Armstrong's colleagues to wonder whether they would be scratched from the actual landing.

On July 16, 1969, Neil Armstrong, Buzz Aldrin, and Michael Collins were rocketed from the Cape Kennedy launching pad, reaching the 25,000 mph speed necessary to reach the moon. Neil described the thrill of seeing the crystal-like blue earth—encircled by brilliant white plumes of clouds swirling around the globe—as they hurtled toward their destination.

Four days later, the command ship *Columbia* was prepared to release the lunar module *Eagle* with Armstrong and Aldrin aboard for their descent to the moon. *Eagle* was traveling a mile every second, headed toward their proposed landing site at the Sea of Tranquillity. Neil was worried that at that speed they might land miles beyond their target. At 5,000 feet above the moon, they were traveling at 100 feet per second, and at 3,000 feet at 70 feet per second (approximately 50 miles per hour). *Eagle* was still controlled by computer directions from Houston. At 1,000 feet, Neil observed a huge crater surrounded by boulders that could jeopardize their landing. At 500 feet he took over the controls from the computer so that he could pilot the craft over the boulders to a safe landing spot. When they reached 200 feet above the moon, they were too low to abort the flight, and if the engine failed they were going too fast for their ascent engine to start and take them back to *Columbia*.

At 100 feet from the moon there was another concern. They had only ninety seconds of fuel left; a twenty-second supply would be needed to return them to the command module. At 50 feet Neil wrestled with the controls when it appeared that the module was drifting backward and in danger of landing on the boulders. At last they landed in a blinding flurry of moon dust and reported to Houston: "The *Eagle* has landed."

The plan had been for Armstrong and Aldrin to sleep for four hours before stepping out on the moon, but they were concerned that the press would report that the landing was four hours late. So at 8:00 P.M. Midwestern time—prime U.S. television time—Neil stepped out of the lunar module, tested his toe on the sooty lunar surface to make sure that he would not sink above his head, and then stepped on to the lunar surface with the words millions of people heard on television: "That's one small step for a man—one giant leap for mankind."

Neil went on to describe the stark beauty of the lunar landscape, the gathering of rocks, and the gray/black soil—the color of graphite. He concluded his hour-long speech by describing his and Aldrin's ascent to the command module and their triumphant return to earth. When he was finished, he invited questions from his fascinated audience. One of the directors asked, "What impressed you the most about your trip to the moon?" "The fact that it was so easy," Neil replied. "We were prepared for almost every possible emergency, and the whole trip went off without a hitch."

WHEN I WAS INVITED to join the board of directors of McGraw-Hill, I met James Webb, who had retired as the administrator of NASA. Much of the credit for the success of NASA and the flights to space belongs to Jim Webb. With remarkable skill, he persuaded Congress to allocate the necessary funds and guided the program toward meeting John Kennedy's pledge to land a man on the moon within a decade. Having known John Glenn, Neil Armstrong, Alan Shepard, and Frank Borman, I was fascinated by the "inside stories" Jim Webb shared with me about the development of the space program.

Dean LeBaron, chairman of Batterymarch Financial Management in Boston, asked me in late November 1990 to accompany him in his jet plane to Russia to assist him in establishing an investment fund in the Soviet Union. While in Moscow, we were invited to fly to Baikonur, the Soviet launch site in Kazakhstan to observe the lift-off of a Japanese journalist, Toyohiro Akiyama, and two Soviet cosmonauts. The Russian generals in charge of the space program were especially hospitable, inviting us to inspect the entire base from which *Sputnik,* bearing Yuri Gagarin, and 329 other Soviet space thrusts had been launched. We were even permitted to visit the rocket launch pad, steaming with oxygen and kerosene fuel. We were surrounded by fire engines and Japanese cameramen. The cosmonauts made their way through the crowd and chatted with us informally before they climbed up to the capsule to be blasted off in the *Soyuz* TM-11 capsule carrying them to the MIR-2 space station.

We retreated about a mile to observe the launch, which was completed precisely at the time scheduled. The Soviet Space Commission officials then took us to buildings where rockets and boosters were being assembled and two other space shuttles (*Boron* I and II) were being prepared for launching. The openness and friendliness of the Soviets was surprising and impressive.

It was interesting to see the military and space capability of the Soviets. Our experience on this visit was in sharp contrast to what Marion and I observed when we accompanied our son David, who ran in the Moscow 10K race in Lenin Olympic Stadium in 1982. Upon arrival at the Moscow airport, we had to wait two hours for our luggage, and we invariably waited for sullen waiters and waitresses to serve us at mealtime. At the time we expressed concern to our traveling companions about the productivity and motivation of the Soviet people.

One depressing impression I carried away with me from the Space visit was the amount of alcohol consumed by our military hosts. Brandy was sipped at breakfast and vodka and wine flowed freely at luncheons and dinners. Even on the military plane that carried us to and from Baikonur, our hosts chugged down vodka until they had florid faces.

On Martha's Vineyard

WHEN WE MOVED to Ohio, we sold our share of the Bermuda vacation home that we owned with the dean of the Harvard Business School. We knew that from Athens we could not fly to Bermuda as easily as we had from Boston, nor would we be able to promote and rent our house when we did not occupy it. In August of our first summer in Athens, Don Hurley, a prominent lawyer in Boston and a director of the Boston Company, invited us to stay with his family at Martha's Vineyard. We enjoyed the island so much that we rented a vacation home the next two Augusts while we explored the possibility of buying a place there. We were fortunate to find a small cottage on an eight-acre site overlooking Stonewall Pond on the east and the Vineyard Sound on the west. Fortunately, 1960s prices were ridiculously low; today we could not afford the property.

Over the years we moved and expanded the house, purchased and refurbished an adjacent home, and built a smaller dwelling on the edge of Stonewall Pond. Marion has put her interior design and architectural skills to good use in creating three unusual summer homes. During the summer season we rent out two of the places and travel to the Vineyard as often as we can to occupy the third.

When the contractor was digging the foundation for one of the houses, he uncovered several Indian relics, ancient clam shells, and a Celt knife. Carbon tests by a New York museum indicated that the knife dated back to approximately 800 B.C. We were concerned when the *Vineyard Gazette* ran a front-page story describing the dig for fear that we would be overrun by amateur archaeologists.

Don Hurley and I often went fishing for blue fish and bass on his boat, the Miriam G, named after his wife. At one time he invited Harold Helm, chairman of the Chemical Bank, to join us. Neither of us knew each other at the time. I was dressed in dungaree shorts and a ragged shirt as I scampered about the boat, baiting hooks, cleaning fish, and swabbing the deck. When we returned to Don's dock, Harold Helm asked him, "Where did you find that young man? Is he a boathand from Edgartown?"

"No, he is the president of Ohio University."

Mid-August has become a reunion event for the larger Alden family. My brother Don competes in the senior bracket of the Chilmark 5K race along with his son, Don Jr., and his bride, Gail. My brother Burt, together with his son, Brenn, cheer the two thousand or so runners from the sidelines. My son Robert travels from California with his wife, Joan, and his two lively sons, Willie and Andy, to bike, boat, fish, ride horses, and explore the trails of the Vineyard. Son David consistently wins or places among the top three in the race, having held the overall record for several years. Daughter Anne competes in the race but does not expect to win. Poor Marion, with the help of Burt and Don's wife, Eunice, has to cook for the whole gang.

I hold the record for the runners over seventy in a time of 22:54 for the hilly, 3.1-mile course. A year ago, having been timed at 20 minutes and 8 seconds on a three-mile course in Florida, I had hoped to lower my record in Chilmark. I made the mistake of overtraining and tore the cartilage in my knee, keeping me out of the 1996 race.

MOST OF THE magazine and newspaper articles about the Vineyard mention the celebrities who vacation there: Art Buchwald, the William Styrons, Katharine Graham, Bob McNamara, David McCullough, Carly Simon, James Taylor, Spike Lee, Vernon Jordan, Jules Feiffer, Beverly Sills, Mike Wallace, Diane Sawyer, Mike Nichols, and of course President and Mrs. Clinton. It is possible to party every evening in Edgartown or Vineyard Haven, but in the rural portion of the island where we live, we can avoid the hectic social whirl.

Walter and Betsy Cronkite have a summer home on Martha's Vineyard and we have the privilege of visiting with them occasionally in our home or theirs. Walter is an avid sailor and accomplished yachtsman; an afternoon sail on his boat, the *Wyntje,* is a memorable experience. Despite his celebrity reputation, Walter Cronkite is a modest, delightful, and generous person. When our daughter Anne was assigned to do a film interview with some well-known person, she telephoned Walter. asking him to be her subject. He not only agreed, but was unusually helpful in giving professional advice.

At a cocktail party in our Vineyard house, Walter announced to our guests that he planned to die some day "in the arms of an eighteen-year-old gal on an eighty-foot boat." Betsy immediately snapped back, "Walter, you're going to die in the arms of an eighty-year-old woman on an eighteen-foot boat."

ON THE SUNDAY before Labor Day each year, Jacqueline Onassis would host a huge picnic on the beaches of her Martha's Vineyard estate. A few weeks before the event we would receive a telephone message with a soft, almost whispering voice: "This is Jacqueline. I'd be pleased if you could join us for our party on Sunday September——." All of the celebrities on Martha's Vineyard were there. The entire Kennedy clan would come by boat from Hyannisport and be bused from Vineyard Haven. The younger crowd played volleyball or swam in the surf, and the older crowd talked politics or traded Vineyard gossip. Jacqueline, dressed in an attractive swimsuit, made sure that her guests helped themselves to enough hot dogs or hamburgers.

Although I had met and been with John Kennedy several times before and after he was elected president, I had never met Jacqueline Kennedy Onassis until after the president died.

John Kennedy Jr. was a classmate at Brown with our son Jim. It was through John that we first met his mother. John frequently came to our Vineyard house to get together with Jim. A few weeks before John was to graduate from Brown, his mother asked if I would present John's diploma to him. Commencement exercises at Brown are customarily held on the College Green with the presentation of diplomas taking place at departmental convocations throughout the campus. On commencement day, the campus was alive with activity. Press from all over the world had traveled to Providence. Video cameramen positioned themselves at every department building, not knowing where John's diploma would be presented. Helicopters fluttered overhead, disturbing the solemnity of the Commencement proceedings. Through it all, the Kennedy family maintained their accustomed composure, and John received his diploma without incident.

On three occasions, John Kennedy, our son Jim, and two other companions spent two summer weeks in kayak adventures. One memorable trip involved kayaking from Finland to Sweden by way of the small islands in between. In the rough waters off Sweden, one of the voyagers panicked when his kayak overturned and had to be rescued by John and Jim. John's account of the trip was published in the *New York Times* magazine section.

When John and Jim decided to kayak north of Canada near the Arctic Circle, Mrs. Onassis had some concerns. While they were gone, she called us several times to ask whether we "had heard anything from the boys." We tried to assure her that Jim was an experienced sailor and navigator, and the young men had equipment that could reach the Coast Guard by satellite communication if they ran into any difficulty. As they made their way back toward civilization, they visited a tiny home on an almost-deserted island occupied by a native family. The young girl in the family immediately recognized John Kennedy from having watched television—hundreds of miles away from the "civilized world." John brought back to his mother a small mobile he had constructed from animal bones he had collected on the barren beaches of far-north Canada. She hung it above her dining room table at the Vineyard and appeared to treasure it more than any Calder mobile she might have acquired.

Jacqueline Kennedy Onassis was a wonderful mother. She protected Caroline and John from reporters and camera people who threatened their privacy almost every day. Both of them have turned out to be thoughtful, modest, attractive, and well-disciplined young adults. Jacqueline had many remarkable qualities, but I admire her most of all for her accomplishment as a mother.

SUNSETS ARE EXOTIC when viewed from the deck of the Outrigger Canoe Club in Honolulu, from the top-floor porch of the Kazmaier home at Ocean Reef in Florida, or overlooking the Pacific near Golden Gate Park in San Francisco. But Marion and I think we have special sunsets when viewed from the widow's deck of our Martha's Vineyard home. Throughout the year, whenever we are on the island, we climb to our perch and watch the sun as it dips beneath the Gay Head hills and the Elizabeth Islands. A golden glow settles over Quitsa and Menemsha Ponds, and clouds on the horizon highlight the majestic and subtle shades of color—magenta, russet, lavender, pink, light-blue, peach, and coral. Minutes after the setting sun drops from view, the entire sky comes alive with color. The afterglow behind us is reflected on the broad expanse of the Atlantic Ocean and captured in microcosm on Stonewall Pond.

Sunrises are equally fantastic. From our Japanese-style bedroom, we lift our heads from the pillow to watch an orange and pink sky preluding a brilliant sunrise. Suddenly a huge, red ball rises over the Atlantic, looking like the model for the Japanese flag. The mist on the pond is quietly drifting away. A cormorant pokes his head above the water, and the stately blue heron has positioned himself at the end of the dock.

Full moons, when viewed from our family room, cast a wide, golden glow over the Pond and extend out over the ocean. As the moon rises, the glow widens, and Stonewall Pond becomes a magic, golden carpet under a canopy of deep-blue sky.

Stonewall Beach is available only to property owners adjacent to the pond. To reach the beach from our home, we can canoe or swim across the Pond or walk the path next to the home of Trudy Taylor, mother of singer James Taylor. A short trail through beach grass and over rocks pushed up by the strong Atlantic tides takes us to the wide sandy beach. We sit and watch the waves lift and curl and fall and slowly slide away. When we are ready to test the chilly water, we dive into the churning surf and ride the waves in.

When the sea is raging, huge, white curlers crash over the rocks and the spindrift forms an evanescent lacey pattern. Whitecaps ruffle the Pond as the tide surges over the marshland surrounding our dock. Secure behind our solid window, we watch gulls careening in the high winds and hope that our visiting blue heron has found safe cover.

From our first days on Martha's Vineyard, we have been involved in programs to preserve the environment of the island. I was a founding member of the Vineyard Open Land Foundation. Often we walk the trails that have been made available to future generations through the generosity of individuals who have left property to conservation groups.

Aware that Marion and I have lived into the later part of our lives, we have made arrangements for the place where we might spend our afterlife. Both Marion's and my parents are buried in Chicago, which unfortunately we have few occasions to visit. Our Martha's Vineyard homes, for which we have already made provision for our children, will always be a place where they will return. We have a plot in the cemetery on Abel's Hill, fortunately far enough away from the grave of John Belushi that our plot will not be trampled by tourists.

EPILOGUE

Life Has Been Good to Me

I KNOW OF NO studies to support my observation, but I have discovered that a surprisingly large number of college presidents, deans, and professors had fathers who were ministers. I have no idea how most sons and daughters of university presidents have fared in the world. One might conjecture that because they spend so much time traveling, giving speeches, raising money, and counseling other parents' children, their offspring would turn out to be misfits, druggies, or lost souls.

Happily, this is not the case with our family, and I credit Marion for that. Despite her many commitments as a president's wife, she did a spectacular job of raising our children. Early on, she provided art materials and easels, encouraging in them the artistic abilities inherited from her. All four children are skilled at drawing, cartooning, painting, and building constructions. They amuse us and each other with their creative drawings.

At spring vacation time in Ohio, Marion packed our station wagon with the children and their friends and headed off to Washington, D.C. for a week of visiting art galleries, the Space Museum, the U.S. Mint, FBI headquarters, and so forth. When Anne began riding horses and performing in shows, Marion hooked up the horse-van to our station wagon and drove up and down the steep hills of southeast Ohio and West Virginia.

Birthday parties were special. Each of the children invited friends to the third floor of our Ohio home, decorated with artwork they had created. Especially popular was the cardboard popcorn-vending machine that Jimmy constructed. He had a special little friend who was always invited to his birthday party—Maya Lin, the daughter of Professors Henry and Julia Lin (he a well-known ceramicist, and she a poet of note). Maya, of course, is famous today for having created the Vietnam Veterans' Memorial in Washington, the Civil Rights Memorial in Montgomery, Alabama, the "Groundswell" sculpture at the Wexner Center for the Arts in Columbus, Ohio, and other public commissions.

Every August, we drove to Martha's Vineyard for a month of fishing, swimming, and sailing at our summer home. As we rolled along the Pennsylvania Turnpike, our vintage station wagon was filled with joyous singing, laughter, and storytelling. One summer on the day before our return to Athens, we caught twenty-seven bluefish. We searched the island in vain for dry ice so that we could take the fish back with us for the winter. We had to improvise by filling styrofoam boxes with ordinary ice and stopping behind Howard Johnson restaurants every two hundred miles or so to replenish the melting ice. We made it all the way back to Athens with brief stops only for ice and for coffee and hot chili to keep us awake.

No matter how busy were our schedules, Marion and I always gave top priority to attending events when the children performed —track meets, horse shows, crew races, and football games. One evening I came close to missing the southeastern Ohio championship track meet held under the lights in Chillicothe. I had a dinner speaking engagement in Cincinnati. The audience was treated to one of my shortest speeches before I rushed to the airport, boarded the university plane, and landed in Chillicothe just in time to watch Rob set a new conference record in the two-mile event. The track team, the coach, and I celebrated on the late-night bus ride back to Athens.

When we moved back to Boston, Rob was accepted at three well-known preparatory schools, but we discovered that the record times for the mile and two-mile in the private school league were slower than his Athens High School mark. He enrolled in Brookline High School's advanced college preparatory section so that he could compete with the state's top distance runners. He continued to star in cross-country and track while achieving top grades in his academic work, qualifying him for early acceptance at Harvard.

At Harvard, Rob was a geology major, spending his summer months on geological digs in the U.S. West or working with Robert Ballard on deep-sea projects at the Wood's Hole Oceanographic Institute. Well into his junior year, Rob met Harvard classmate Joan Freeman, a pre-med major who won a prestigious film festival award for a short movie she had produced. Upon graduation, Rob and Joan were married at the Cleveland home of her parents.

Rob pursued an MBA at the Harvard Business School while Joan worked for NOVA at Station WGBH. Upon graduation they moved to Washington where Rob worked in the consulting firm Strategic Planning Associates. Joan lived in New York, working for CBS News—the "Walter Cronkite Universe." Frustrated after a couple of years of a commuting marriage, Rob and Joan decided to try full-time filmmaking. Working out of an apartment in New York, their first film was financed by Roger Corman and entitled *Streetwalkin,* depicting the life of an innocent young girl lured into prostitution upon arriving in New York with her little brother. Their second, *Satisfaction,* featured Julia Roberts in her first commercial film. The lead was Justine Bateman, who was cofeatured with the Irish actor Liam Neeson, in his first leading role in the United States. Both films can still be seen from time to time on late night television as well as video. When the weekly commute between Hollywood and New York became difficult, Rob and Joan moved to Santa Monica, where they now live with two bright little sons, Willie and Andy. Taking time off from filmmaking to raise the children, Rob and Joan have stayed close to home, rewriting film scripts and writing children's books.

Beginning with coaching from Gill Whalen in Athens, Anne developed into an excellent rider, performing in horse shows throughout southeastern Ohio and West Virginia. When we moved to Boston, we brought her horse with us, hoping to find a suburban home with a barn and acreage. We chose a large, old Victorian home overlooking the Brookline reservoir without suitable accommodation for horses. Anne and Marion had to commute several miles after school every day to Medway, where Anne continued her training under Jenny Neher. Soon she became talented enough to require a top-flight jumping horse. When we acquired Beetle, we also bought a small house in Dover with horse barns and sufficient acreage for workouts. Jenny was invited to live in the house in exchange for training lessons. Under her tutelage, Anne became one of New England's most talented riders, performing in events throughout the Northeast, Florida, and Canada. One day when Anne was away, Jim tacked up her ribbons and arranged her trophies in her bedroom. The blue-and-red ribbons covered all four walls of her room.

While in preparatory school at Winsor, Anne took Greek and French, and spent one summer studying in Paris. Upon graduation and entering Brown University, Anne gave up her riding career and sold Beetle. She has kept her German-made saddle in the event she takes up serious riding again. While at Brown she majored in the classics. As a reward for her outstanding performance in a classics course, Anne and Marion embarked on a cruise of the Greek Islands with a Brown tour group and her favorite professor, John Workman.

Upon graduation, Anne joined Bain and Company, the consulting firm, as a senior research assistant. Her background work on companies was so thorough and creative, senior consultants frequently took her on trips to make presentations to clients. She was accepted for admission by the University of Virginia Graduate School of Business, but she chose instead to accept an offer to work for *Chronicle*, a nightly magazine television show featured on Channel 5 in Boston. She soon became associate producer for *New England Sunday* and *Good Day,* a live, morning talk show. By 1986 she was elevated to producer of *Consumer Journals,* generating ideas for consumer news segments, conducting research and interviews, and writing on-air stories.

On the side, Anne produced greeting cards, featuring cartoons and humorous messages for birthdays, party invitations, and travel greetings. This activity developed into the creation of Anne Alden Designs—located in California—where she did freelance illustrations and designs for magazines, corporations, and nonprofit organizations while completing a master's degree in clinical psychology. She is now studying for her Ph.D. in San Francisco while working part-time as a therapist.

Jim is a rugged sailor, skier, and oarsman. At Buckingham, Brown & Nichols School he starred in football and crew, competing in the famed Henley Regatta in England. While an undergraduate at Brown, he was chosen captain of crew by his teammates. Trained early by his older brother, Jim has become an avid sailor, competing every year in the Bermuda Race. At Martha's Vineyard he was offered a tiny black puppy he named Jessie. Throughout Jim's career at Brown, Jessie was a constant companion, waiting faithfully outside the classroom and following Jim wherever he went. Jessie was an unusually smart dog. Jim taught him several complicated tricks, which inevitably surprised friends and earned Jessie appearances on television programs. For many years, Jim celebrated Jessie's birthday by staging a sailing regatta at Martha's Vineyard or Newport, featuring racing and entertainment for the dozens of invited friends.

When he graduated from Brown, Jim thought he wanted to be an architect. I suggested that he seek advice from my friend I. M. Pei, who told him to first acquire field experience from the ground up in a construction firm. He went to work for Gilbane Building Company as an associate field engineer with responsibility for overseeing some seventy-five trades people in site preparation and construction of such major projects as the Faneuil Hall Market in Boston.

In 1984, Jim became a commercial real estate broker. His success in locating properties for Japanese companies led him to establish his own business, East Asia Trading Partners, working with investors throughout the Pacific Rim. To shore up his technical knowledge, he acquired a master of science in real estate at MIT and completed a special marketing seminar at the Wharton School. In 1995, he was asked by the Government of Thailand to become its trade representative in New England. Traveling frequently to Thailand, Jim works closely with Thai and U.S. companies and investors.

In 1994, Jim married Sabra Delany, a graduate of William Smith College with an MBA from Boston College. Jim has participated as a best man or groomsman in more than twenty weddings of his friends; so, of course, he had to have a number of groomsmen at his wedding—eight. Jim and Sabra exchanged vows in Manchester Village, Vermont, near the Delany ski home on Stratton Mountain. With Sabra's appointment as marketing director of the Thai trade office, Jim and she work together on trade promotion for Thailand. Adept on her Digital Hi-Note computer, she also manages the financial operations of the office. They live in a Boston condominium decorated with oriental art and Jim's paintings. Jim and Sabra sail as often as they can on their forty-seven-foot sailboat *Chimera*.

Our Athens-born son, David, has collected animals since he was a small child. He has owned frogs, iguanas, turtles, snakes, a de-scented pet skunk, and goldfish. Guests were shocked when he came into the living room with a boa constrictor wrapped around his shoulders. He now owns a business that creates dinosaur sculpture for museums and traveling exhibits.

While a student at the Dexter elementary school, David joined a group of classmates, led by a Dexter teacher, touring the United States from the East Coast through the South, out to Hawaii, and returning through the Northern states. At Dexter, all students are required to participate in football, basketball, hockey, and baseball. He was not a stand-out in any of those sports, but when the first field day was held, he outran all of his classmates in the track competition. Following in the footsteps of his brother Rob, he starred on the cross-country and track teams at Brookline High School. In his junior year, he transferred to Northfield Mount Hermon, known for its outstanding distance-running coach Pat Mooney. During preseason training for cross-country, David expressed concerns that the team was so strong that he was afraid that he might not be one of the top runners. I traveled to Northfield to watch the intrasquad race before the start of the season. I was astonished to see David approaching the finish line several hundred yards ahead of his teammates. He led the Northfield–Mount Hermon squads to New England championships in both cross-country and track. In the process, he broke the cross-country record of alumnus Frank Shorter, the Olympic marathon gold-medal winner, and appeared in the "Faces in the Crowd" column of *Sports Illustrated*.

In his senior year, David was invited to Moscow to compete in the 10,000-meter race. He placed fifth among several hundred competitors. The Soviet press was so astonished that a high school runner had beaten so many of their good runners, they corralled him into a tiny, smoke-filled press room immediately after the race, not even permitting him to warm down. They pressed him on his training methods, his coach, and his equipment. Without water or a warm down or fresh air, David developed hypothermia and had to wear four layers of warm jackets when he stood on the victory platform in Lenin Olympic Stadium and saw his name flashed on the giant, lighted scoreboard. When he finally had an opportunity for a warm-down run along the Moscow River, he invited me to join him. Since then, I have been running two or three miles every day.

When David arrived at Brown, the cross-country and track teams were just being rebuilt under new coach Bob Rothenberg. As a freshman, David came in first for Brown against Yale. As other outstanding runners were recruited—Chris Schille, Greg Whiteley, Adam Berlew, Fergel Mullen, and Peter Loomis—Brown became a major contender in the Ivy League. In David's senior year, the cross-country team placed eighth nationally in the NCAA championship.

After graduation, David competed in the Stockholm marathon with a time of 2:23 and placed fifth in the Hokkaido marathon in Japan. Marion and I bought all-day passes on the subway and in a dress rehearsal timed ourselves so that we could reappear on the running route at least eight times to watch the leading runners go by.

The first road race in the United States was held at Northfield–Mount Hermon School. Every year a so-called Pie Race is held for students, faculty, and alumni, competing over a five-mile course through the woods and over the hills on campus. The one-hundredth anniversary of the race featured the return of Frank Shorter to his alma mater. Frank, though beyond his peak years, was heavily favored to win. David surprised everybody by finishing more than a hundred yards ahead of him.

David made an initial investment in the Marathon sporting goods store, but found that day-after-day work in his store was not challenging. He sold out his interest and established Saurian Studios to create and sell authentic reproductions of prehistoric dinosaurs. David frequently visits dinosaur digs in Utah, Mexico, and Alberta, Canada, and he has become an expert on all forms of prehistoric life. He writes columns for *Dinosaur Times*, and he recently lectured to a gathering of paleontologists in Tempe, Arizona, presenting a highly technical paper entitled, "Life Restoration of Acrocanthosaurus Atokensis." Saurian Studios has rapidly become the highest-quality producer of products for museums and paleontologists.

In 1995, David and Becky Gambrill, a graduate of Goucher College, were married in Ogunquit, Maine, with Becky's father officiating. The wedding took place in a lovely, old seaside church where Becky's grandmother had been married. David and Becky have a home in Weston, which houses his basement workshop, his top-floor display center, and his office. Becky works as a tour organizer and summer school teacher in the historic Golden Ball Tavern Museum and is an excellent photographer and gardener. She does all of the photography work for Saurian Studios' attractive catalogues.

How can I find sufficient and appropriate words to describe my commitment and gratitude to Marion? Last year—1996—we celebrated our forty-fifth wedding anniversary. We have had a lifetime of happiness and fulfillment together. She has been my greatest supporter and my most informed critic. Marion has not lost her youthful appearance and sparkle. She is the greatest dancer I have ever met and is unbelievable at remembering names and relationships.

A member of the Odd Lot investment group for some twenty years, she follows the stock market with avid interest, much more than I do. She enjoys her choice seat at the Boston Symphony Orchestra on Friday afternoons, is a member of the Arts Council at MIT and the Arts Advisory Council at the Harvard Graduate School of Education, a board member of the American Repertory Theatre, a director of the Kennedy Museum at Ohio University, and a former vice president and director of Boston Children's Services.

As the founder and president of Creative Concepts, Ltd., an interior-design firm, Marion continues to pursue her interest in all areas of design. Without an architect's degree, she has an eye for structure and design as sharp as many practicing architects. My father instilled in me ambition and competitive drive, but Marion provides focus and meaning in my life.

INDEX

Antigua, 131; burial site of, 200–201; Eisenhower and, 70; faculty families and, 46; FBI agent and, 22; first Athens visit of, 4; football star on, 15; front-row seating and, 24; garden named for, 155; Harvard deanship and, 2; Hokkaido marathon and, 209; at imperial reception, 158–59; Japanese friends of, 154–55; Kemmerle and, 35; Kennedy Lecturers and, 73, 74; Lederers and, 135; library collection named for, 18; McGraw-Hill staff and, 176; Maha Chakri and, 164; Methodism of, 34; in Moscow, 194; mothering by, 202–3; nomenclature "campaign" and, 13; O'Bleness and, 66, 67; at Osaka ekiden, 161; in Pro-Am foursomes, 178; rioters and, 119; Rohrs and, 41; SDS and, 110; second Athens visit of, 6; Shrivers and, 167–68; L. Stevens and, 71, 72; stock holdings of, 172; summer homes of, 196; testimonials to, 86–87, 210; Toyoda wedding and, 182; trophy awarded by, 145; Trustees Academy and, 65; wedding anniversaries of, 5, 210; Westmoreland and, 92; at White House, 88

Alden, Robert (son), 145, 204–5, 206, 208; at Martha's Vineyard, 196; schooling of, 2, 15

Alden, Sabra Delany (daughter-in-law), 207

Alden, Willie (grandson), 196, 205

Alden Library. See Vernon Roger Alden Library (Ohio University)

Aldrin, Buzz, 191, 192, 193

Alexander, Andy, 58

Alexander, Emily, 100

All-America athletes, 42–43, 161

All-Star Games, 5

Allegheny Ludlum Steel Corporation, 60

Allen, Ivan, Jr., 181

Allison, Dwight, 149, 150, 151

"Alma Mater, Ohio" (song), 8

Alpert, Warren, 68

Alpha Server systems, 173

Alumni: in auto business, 185; on board of trustees, 103; in communication field, 58; donations by, 65, 66–68; graduate work of, 37; in medicine, 55; plaque dedicated by, 131; visits to, 128

Alumni Fun (TV program), 66

America-Japan Society of Tokyo, 156

American Airlines Celebrity Golf Tournament, 141, 142

American Association of University Professors, 32

American Broadcasting Company, 58

American Council on Higher Education, 50

American Express Company, 151, 174–75

American Federation of Labor–Congress of Industrial Organizations, 110, 112

American Federation of State, County, and Municipal Employees, 110, 111, 118–19, 129

American League, 5

American Legion, 35. See also Junior American Legion

American Nazi Party, 35

American Repertory Theatre, 210

American Research and Development Company, 18, 171

American Revolution, 6, 131

American Telephone and Telegraph Company, 38

American Western University. See Ohio University

Anastas, Jim, 100

Anderson, Amos, 5

Anderson, Harlan, 171

Anne Alden Designs (firm), 206

Anthony's Pier 4 (restaurant), 157

Antigua, 131

Apollo 1 (spacecraft), 191

Appalachian Highway, 30

Appalachian Program, 83

Appalachian region: coal mining in, 69; economic efforts in, 111, 166; Job Corps and, 79, 81; LBJ tour of, 85; student opportunities in, 101

Appalachian Regional Commission, 30

Appel, Marguerite, 91

Appleton, Pete, 25

Aptheker, Herbert, 35

Area Development Act, 83

Area Redevelopment Administration, 85, 98

Arizona, 170

Armacost, Michael H., 160

Armco Steel Corporation, 132, 150

Armstrong, Neil, 190–93

Army Supply Corps, 18

Arnelle, Jesse, 40, 63

"Art Across America" (competition), 180

Asahi Shimbun (newspaper), 161

Asia, 176

Associated Press, 43

Association for Research Libraries, 18

Astronauts, 191–93

AT&T (firm), 38

Athens (Greece), 9

Athens (Ohio): bluefish transported to, 203; campus closing and, 114; church search in, 34; development of, 99–100, 127; economy of, 98; *Good News* program and, 59; hospitality facilities of, 95; liquor issue and, 96; police of, 67–68; Post Office building and, 53–54; racial attitudes in, 61; snowfall in, 117–18; speaker selection and, 36; transportation to, 11, 30–31, 74, 97–98, 99; union movement and, 110, 113

Athens Civil Rights Action Committee, 62

Athens Country Club, 66

Athens County, 31

Athens High School, 204

Athens Messenger (newspaper), 67, 86, 100, 126–27

Athens National Bank, 66

Athens State Mental Hospital, 53, 95

Athletes, 79, 141

Athletics, 40–45, 196. *See also* Baseball; Track athletics; *etc.*

Atlanta, 181

Atomic Energy Commission, 51

Au Bon Pain (shop), 164

Auerbach, Red, 141

Augat Company, 160, 170

Ayukawa, Yaichi, 155, 162–63

Babson College, 182, 186

Baikonur (USSR), 193–94

Bain, Bill, 139–40

Bain and Company, 205–6

Baker, John C.: absences of, 54; on architecture, 15; graduate programs and, 104; Gubitz and, 102; Hecht and, 55; legacy of, 8, 126; in New Vernon, 5; on O'Bleness, 66; Ohio University Fund and, 64; recruitment by, 1, 3–4; state officials and, 28; on tenure, 46; White and, 11–12

Baker Center (Ohio University), 10, 84

Baker Fund (Ohio University), 72

Ball, George, 92

Ballard, Robert, 204

Baltimore Orioles (baseball team), 141

Banca Ambrosiano, 133

Bangkok, 170

Bangladesh, 157

Bangor Punta Corporation, 143–44

Bank of Bangkok, 176

Bank robbers, 21–22

Banton, Elmore, 42

Barnes, Jim, 63

Baseball: boyhood interest in, 22–23, 24; at Brown University, 25–26; at Ohio University, 41, 43; professional, 5, 141, 142–43

Baseball cards, 20–21

Baseball Hall of Fame (Cooperstown), 43

Basic Instinct (film), 61

Basketball. *See* Bobcats (basketball team)

Bateman, Justine, 204

Chicago Art Institute, 19
Chicago Bears (football team), 44
Chicago Cubs (baseball team), 22, 23, 41
Chicago White Sox (baseball team), 25
Chicago World's Fair (1932), 21
Children's Museum (Boston), 144, 155
Chillicothe branch campus, 180, 203–4
Chilmark 5K race, 196–97
Chimera (sailboat), 207
China, 91, 152, 161–62
Chronicle (TV program), 206
Chrysler Corporation, 183, 185
Chubb Library (Ohio University), 17
Church activities, 23, 34–35
Cincinnati Post-Times, 29
Civil rights, 61–63
Civil Rights Memorial (Montgomery),
    203
Civil service, 110, 111, 112
Civilian Conservation Corps, 78
Claflin, Bruce, 173
Claremont College, 38, 130
Clark, Kenneth, 8
Clark, William Smith, 156
Classical High School (Providence), 19,
    24, 26
Cleveland Indians (baseball team), 25
Clifford, Carl, 100
Clinton, Bill, 197
Clinton, Hillary Rodham, 140, 197
Clinton administration, 140
Coast Guard, 199
Cockcroft-Walton accelerator, 50–51
Coe, Bob, 58
Colasurd, Donald, 114
Colgate Games, 141
Colgate–Dinah Shore Open (tourna-
    ment), 178
Colgate-Palmolive Company, 144, 169,
    176–79; Bangkok facility of, 170;
    Boston Symphony and, 146; Mays
    and, 141, 143
College of the Holy Cross, 25
Collins, Michael, 192
Colony, George, 173
Colorado, 170

Columbia (spacecraft), 192
Columbia Broadcasting System. *See* CBS
    Inc.
Columbia University, 26, 72, 154, 174
Columbus Dispatch (newspaper), 93
Commager, Henry Steele, 72
Communism, 33, 35, 91, 93
Computer Associates (firm), 173
Computer industry, 172–73
Conant, James, 82
Connor, Halden, 97
Construction projects, 14–15, 56–57, 70,
    127
Consumer Journals (TV program), 206
Continental Congress, 7, 11, 103
Continental Oil Company, 132
Converse, Bill, 56
Coppola, Francis Ford, 134
Corman, Roger, 204
Cornell University, 18, 107, 109
Cornuelle, Herb, 150
Corporations. *See* Business corporations
Corson, John, 189
Cosmonauts, 193–94
Council for Advancement and Support
    of Teaching, 50
Courtney, Tom, 132, 133, 147, 148
Covenant Congregational Church
    (Waltham, Mass.), 34
Cowens, Dave, 141
Crane, Keith, 178–79
Creative Concepts, Ltd., 210
Cronkite, Betsy, 197
Cronkite, Walter, 58, 197, 204
Cubs (baseball team), 22, 23, 41
Culbert, Taylor, 48
Cunningham, James, 26–27
Cutler, Lloyd, 175
Cutler, Manasseh, 6, 7, 16
Cutler Hall (Ohio University), 13

Danforth Report, 60
Danner, Richard, 90
Darby Dan Farm, 41–42
Dartmouth College, 7, 161
David, Donald, 4, 18, 71

Mellon Foundation, 38
Mennen (firm), 179
Mercedes automobile, 185
Merrill Lynch and Company, 171
Merry, Robert, 3
Methodism, 34
Mets (baseball team), 142
Mexico, 1
Miami University, 45, 103, 106
Microsoft Corporation, 173
Mid-American Conference, 43, 45
Midshipman's School (New York), 26, 154
Miller, William, 177
Millett, Catherine, 103
Millett, John, 103, 104, 105, 106
Milliken, Russell, 90, 91, 94
Mine workers, 110–11
MIR-2 (space station), 194
Miriam G (boat), 196
Mission Hills golf course, 178
Mitchell, Darnell, 42
Mochizuki, Toshio, 157
Moeller, Walter, 83
Moline Daily Dispatch, 22–23
Moline High School, 23
Moline Plows (baseball team), 22
Monks, Robert, 150, 151
Monterey Aquarium, 185
Moon landing, 8, 190–93
Mooney, Pat, 208
Moore, Garry, 98, 100
Morfit, Mason, 39, 100
Morgan, Frank, 42
Morita, Akio, 68, 155
Morley, Roger, 174–75
Morris, Frank, 152
Morris, Jean Cagney, 58–59
Morrison, Jack, 58–59
Morrison, Mary Anne, 59
Morse, Edward Sylvester, 156
Morton, Robert, 52, 128
Moscow, 194, 208
Moyers, Bill, 84
Moynihan, Pat, 79
Mullen, Fergel, 209

Mundus Artium (periodical), 49
Murata, Junichi, 68
Murayama, Tomiichi, 159
Murphy, Grayson, 133, 147, 148
Museum of Fine Arts (Boston), 2, 144, 155, 156, 171
Museum of Science (Boston), 144
Muskie, Ed, 138
Muskingum County, 102
Mussolini, Benito, 134
Mustang automobile, 132
My Lai Massacre (1968), 93

Nagoya (Japan), 184
Nagoya-Ise Ekiden, 160
Nakahama, Manjiro, 157
Nakahara, Nobuyuki, 155
Nakasone, Yasuhiro, 162
Namath, Joe, 141
Naruhito (Hiro), Crown Prince, 157–59
Nash, Willma (Billie), 11, 12
National Aeronautics and Space Administration, 98, 174, 191, 193
National Archives Center for Legislative Archives, 76
National Broadcasting Company, 121
National Collegiate Athletic Association, 42, 69, 209
National Guard, 121, 122
National League, 5
National Science Foundation, 51
National Student Association, 109
Naval ROTC, 25
Navy V-12 program, 19, 20–21, 25, 26, 154
Nazism, 33, 35
NBC-TV, 121
NCAA, 42, 69, 209
Neher, Jenny, 205
Neighborhood Youth Corps, 100
Nelsonville (Ohio), 122
Neville, Bob, 160
New Bedford (Mass.), 140
New England Sunday (TV program), 206
New Frontier program, 8
New Left, 108

Republican Party: Appalachian develop-
ment legislation and, 30; F. John-
son and, 94; 1968 presidential race
and, 93; Percy and, 164, 165; War on
Poverty and, 79
Reston, James, 58
Revolutionary War, 6, 131
Rhode Island, 162, 170
Rhode Island School of Design, 19
Rhode Island University, 25
Rhodes, James, 28–30; board of regents
and, 103; in Japan, 114; LBJ and, 84,
86; National Guard and, 121; presi-
dential visits and, 31
Rhodes, Mrs. James, 31, 86
Rhodes administration, 104
Rhodes Scholars, 140
Richard III, King of England, 49
Richard O. Linke Scholarship program,
66
Rigaku (firm), 153
Rinfret, Pierre, 138
Rinfret-Boston Economic Advisory Ser-
vices, 132, 138
Roberts, Bill, 99
Roberts, Burnell, 185
Roberts, Julia, 204
Robinson, Wade, 79
Rockefeller, Jay, 165
Rockefeller family, 135
Rockwell, George Lincoln, 35–36
Rogers, Will, 137
Rohr, Bill, 41–42, 45
Rohr, Mary Ellen, 41
Rollins, J. Leslie, 38, 39, 40, 138–39
Roman Catholic Church, 134
Romney, George, 93
Roosevelt, Franklin, 4
Roosevelt, Franklin, Jr., 31, 85
Rotenberg, Jon, 39
Rothenberg, Bob, 160, 208
Route 33 (Ohio), 11, 30
Route 128 (Mass.), 4
Royal Decoration (Thailand), 164
Royal Dutch Shell Group, 132
Royal McBee Corporation, 53

Rudman, Ed, 132, 135, 151
Rural Action for Better Consumer De-
velopment program, 100
Rusk, Dean, 92, 93, 98, 101
Russell, Henry (Tim), 139, 151
Ryan, Cornelius, 58

Salem State College, 130
Salgo, Nicholas, 143–44
Salomon, Dick, 68
Samsung Electronics Company, 173
San Francisco State University, 107
Sandburg, Carl, 74
Sapporo Agricultural College, 156
Sarah Lawrence College, 3, 72
Saratoga (aircraft carrier), 19, 26, 154
Sargent, Frank, 145
Satellite tracking system, 51, 52
Satisfaction (film), 204
Saudi Arabia, 157
Saurian Studios, 209, 210
Savage, Robert, 55, 57
Savings and Loan scandals (1980s), 146
Sawyer, Diane, 197
Saxbe, William, 111–12, 113, 114–15
Schille, Chris, 209
Schmidt, Mike, 43
Schmidt, Norman, 49
Schott, Michael, 39
Schram, Ward, 100
Schulte, Rainer, 49
Schwarzenegger, Arnold, 167, 168
Scott Paper Company, 60
SDS, 107, 108, 110
Secret Service, 84
Securities and Exchange Commission,
147, 148, 149, 167
Seigfred, Earl, 58
Sella, George, 44
Selma March (1965), 63
Sevier, John, 39
Sharpe, Henry, 68
Shearson Loeb Rhoades, Inc., 151
Sheehan, Ed, 160
Sheltering Arms Hospital (Athens), 68
Shepard, Alan, 193

Tupper Hall (Ohio University), 40
Tuthill, Howard, 175

Udall, Stewart, 13
Union Carbide Corporation, 60
Unionization, 109–17, 118–19, 129
United Nations, 157
United Press/International Poll, 43
University for Presidents, 2
University of California–Berkeley, 107, 108, 109
University of California–Los Angeles, 58
University of Can Tho, 91
University of Chicago, 37
University of Cincinnati, 190
University of Colorado, 154
University of Hawaii, 3
University of Hue, 91
University of Iowa, 41
University of Kansas, 43
University of Kentucky, 69
University of Maryland, 39
University of Massachusetts, 144, 156
University of Miami, 39
University of Michigan, 14, 37, 42, 85
University of Missouri, 66
University of Montana, 166
University of North Carolina–Chapel Hill, 33–34
University of North Carolina–Greensboro, 81
University of Notre Dame, 98, 135
University of Oxford, 158, 159
University of Saigon, 91
University of Virginia, 206
University of Wisconsin, 90
UNIX (computer operating system), 172, 173
Unsworth, Richard, 159
Upward Bound program, 100, 101
U.S. Agency for International Development, 11, 37, 89–90, 91
U.S. Area Redevelopment Administration, 85, 98
U.S. Army Supply Corps, 18

U.S. Atomic Energy Commission, 51
U.S. Civilian Conservation Corps, 78
U.S. Coast Guard, 199
U.S. Congress, 155, 193
U.S. Congress. Senate, 113, 137, 138, 166
U.S. Corps of Engineers, 31
U.S. Department of Defense, 79
U.S. Department of Labor, 79
U.S. Department of State, 25
U.S. Department of the Interior, 102
U.S. Department of the Treasury, 155
U.S. Embassy (Tokyo), 154, 160
U.S. Federal Aviation Administration, 98
U.S. Federal Aviation Development Administration, 100–101
U.S. Federal Bureau of Investigation, 21, 137, 203
U.S. Federal Housing and Home Finance Agency, 99
U.S. General Services Administration, 54
U.S. Information Agency, 93–94
U.S.-Japan Friendship Commission, 155
U.S. Job Corps: camps of, 80; McElroy and, 79–80; McGraw-Hill and, 174; proposed chair of, 77, 78, 124; public image of, 81–82
U.S. Marines, 93
U.S. Military Academy, 92
U.S. Mint, 203
U.S. National Aeronautics and Space Administration, 98, 174, 191, 193
U.S. National Archives Center for Legislative Archives, 76
U.S. National Science Foundation, 51
U.S. Naval ROTC, 25
U.S. Navy V-12 program, 19, 20–21, 25, 26, 154
U.S. Occupation Force (Japan), 154
U.S. Office of Economic Opportunity, 101
U.S. Open (tournament), 183
U.S. Peace Corps: former members of, 100, 168; training grant for, 89, 166; volunteers for, 108, 109
U.S. Post Office, 53–54
U.S. Secret Service, 84

Woods, Geoff, 91
Wood's Hole Oceanographic Institute,
    204
Workman, John, 205
World Series, 22–23
World War I, 14
World War II, 18, 58, 70, 131, 165. *See also*
    Pearl Harbor attack (1941)
World's Fair (1932), 21
Wren, Bob, 43, 44
Wright, Frank Lloyd, 71
Wriston, Henry, 4, 19, 25, 26–27, 68
Wyntje (boat), 197

X-15 (rocket plane), 191

Xerox Corporation, 80, 125

Yale University, 7, 26, 117, 161, 208
Yanity, Joe, 100
Yankees (baseball team), 25
Yomiuri Giants (baseball team), 184
Young, Stephen, 83
Young, Wayne, 43
Young Presidents' Organization, 2, 135

Zammataro, Frank, 39
Zanesville branch campus, 102
Zimmer, Don, 25
Zukowski, Jerry, 147